The Happy Hacker

A Guide to (Mostly) Harmless Computer Hacking

by
Carolyn P. Meinel

American Eagle Publications, Inc.
Post Office Box 1507
Show Low, Arizona 85902
—1998—

Technical Editors:
Macintosh: John D. Robinson
Windows: Roger A. Prata and Daniel Gilkerson
Unix: Damian Bates and Mark Schmitz
Legal editor: Troy Larsen, Computer Forensics, http://www.forensics.com

CONTENTS

ACKNOWLEDGMENTS

This book was made possible by the work of hundreds of hackers who contributed their knowledge to the Happy Hacker email list. For archives of their contributions, see http://www.happyhacker.org.

I want to especially point out those who have served as moderators of this list, who played the essential role of keeping it from drowning in flames, nonsense and crime. They have included Matt Hinze, Jon McClintock, Strider, Roger Prata, Strider, Ruben D. Canlas, Jr., and R.J. Gosselin, Sr.

We also relied on those who volunteered their services to keep us on the Internet, despite incessant attacks by those computer criminals who don't want you to learn what is in this book. Our knights in shining armor have included Tobin Fricke, Patrick Rutledge, Carl Muhlenweg, Damian Bates, Adam Christopher, Mark Schmitz, and Gerard Cochrane, Jr.

We also thank the army of volunteers who have put my Guides to (mostly) Harmless Hacking on Web sites around the world, even translating them into other languages. It is thanks to their help that many talented hackers joined our mail list and contributed their knowledge.

Special thanks go to the technical editors of this book: John D. Robinson, Roger A. Prata, Daniel Gilkerson, Damian Bates and Mark Schmitz; and to Mark Ludwig, who owns this book's publisher, American Eagle Publications. Ludwig distinguished himself by being courageous enough to put out a book that editors at three major publishers had at one time begged me to give to them. But in each case upper management had a fainting spell. A hacker how-to book? Eek!

If you wonder why Ludwig wasn't afraid of *Happy Hacker*, run out and buy his *Giant Black Book of Computer Viruses*. I think we should be thankful that überhacker Ludwig has a kind heart, or we'd all be in a lot more trouble than we are. Yes! Honest! The owner of this publishing company is also an überhacker.

The most special thanks of all go to our sworn enemies, who have done more than we ever could, to prove to the world that us Happy Hackers really are against computer crime. Otherwise why would gangs commit felonies trying to shut us down? In particular we thank the Gray Areas Liberation Front (GALF) and johnny xchaotic, who have been kind enough to take public credit for their destructive attacks on ISPs kind enough to provide accounts for Happy Hacker and me.

The Happy Hacker

Introduction
So You Want to Be a Hacker?

Are you a newbie at hacking? If all you know today is how to get on the Internet, within just hours you can perform feats of hacking that will amaze your friends. Better yet, if you already know how to use a Unix shell account, within hours you can propel yourself into the upper ranks of hacking. How? Read this book.

Welcome to *Happy Hacker*. Here you can discover the wisdom, wisecracks, cheap tricks and daring exploits of the thousands of hackers—good guy hackers—who have collaborated in our Happy Hacker project. For the first time in print we bring you hundreds of cool, and mostly harmless hacks, complete with screen shots and detailed descriptions of how you can make these tricks work. Whether your favorite computer is a Macintosh, runs Windows, or is a Unix box, you'll find the right stuff here.

But, But—Hackers Are All Criminals, Right?

"You mean you can hack without breaking the law?"

That was the voice of a high school freshman. He had me on the phone because his father had just taken away his computer. He had been arrested—and convicted —of a computer crime. He hoped I could talk his father into letting him get back into hacking.

A year later that boy, his parents and I were having a great time, along with some 1500 other hacking enthusiasts, at the Las Vegas Def Con V convention. By then his folks had realized that while some hackers are bad guys, most of us are harmless hobbyists. Some of us are much more: white hat cowboys of the frontiers of cyberspace. Hackers play a big role in keeping the Internet from collapsing from spam (those "make money fast" emails), computer criminals and information warriors. In fact, most computer security experts first learn their trade from the world of hackers.

"I would like to know how to blow up someone's TV over the net. If you do tell I thank you very much and I am forever in debt to you"—wannbe hacker writing to me.

OK, I admit that someone will be reading this book in the hope of becoming the most vicious dude on the Internet. (Quick clue: you can't blow up a TV over the Internet.) But a career as a highly paid computer professional is much more fun than hard time in prison. So if your parents or friends give you grief for owning this book, just advise them to—*hey, wipe those words out of your mind!*—advise them that you are not one of those people who enjoy having a miserable life. Tell them you have a clue.

Besides, if you want to become a computer criminal, there are plenty of people you can meet on the Internet, or maybe even in your neighborhood, who will be happy to mess up your life. You don't need to read *Happy Hacker* for that.

Why Hack?

Hacking can be both a healthy recreation and a free education that can lead to a high paying job. Many systems administrators, computer scientists and computer security experts first learned the ins and outs of computers and networks from their hacker friends.

Most important, ultimately the Internet is safeguarded not by law enforcement agencies, not by giant corporations, but by a worldwide network of, yes, us good guy, white-hat hackers.

You, too, can become one of us.

And hacking can be surprisingly easy.

Regardless of why you want to be a hacker, it is definitely a way to have fun, impress your friends, and get dates. If you are a female hacker, you become totally irresistible to men. Take my word for it!

What Will this Book Teach Me?

Happy Hacker can be your gateway into the world of hacking. After reading just the first chapter in Section 1, *How to Turn Your Windows 95 Computer into a Haxor Box*, you will be able to pull off stunts that are legal, phun, won't make anyone mad, and will impress the heck out of your friends. Chapter 2 says it all: *How to Break into Windows 95 Computers*. Then you can learn *How to Use Windows to Hack the Internet*. Chapter 4 is *Mac Hacking*. Become the hero on your High School campus with *How to Become a Hero in Computer Lab*! Tired of IRC warriors taking over and ICMPing your favorite channels? Help is on the way. Want to play jokes with forged email? See how you can make Eudora Pro perform amazing tricks of email forgery. *How to Dig up Hacker Information on the Web* shows how to find good stuff without wasting your time searching those Web pages full of flaming skulls, obscene language and exploit programs that don't work or maliciously trash your computer. We point you to where serious hacker info hides.

In Section 2 you can get really serious about hacking. You will encounter the excitement of the Unix operating system, which all truly good hackers use. You will learn how to get a Unix shell account from an Internet Service Provider that will put amazing hacker tools at your fingertips. You will then discover port surfing (he, he, wait until you find out what that is!), and industrial strength email and news group forging techniques. You will learn how to install and run the Linux form of Unix on your Windows computer. You will learn how to map the Internet and probe what kinds of computers are linked to each other.

Section 3 is the war portion of this book. You, too, may become one of the good guys fighting to save the Internet from spammers, computer criminals and information warfare attacks. You will discover how to break into computers—and how to keep people from breaking into them.

You will discover the gateway to an amazing underground where you can stay on top of almost every discovery of computer security flaws as they happen. You can learn how to either exploit them—or defend your computer against them!

You will see how hacker wars are fought, and how to keep the bad guys at bay through purely defensive, legal means.

Section 4 covers hacker culture. It tells the history of hacking as it has never been told before, shows you how to meet other hackers, and plan a career strategy that can catapult you to the pinnacle of the hacker world. We finish with the hacker humor test—have you become elite enough to catch the laughs?

What Do I Need in Order to Hack?

You may wonder whether hackers need expensive computer equipment and a shelf full of technical manuals. The answer is NO! *Hacking can be surprisingly easy.* In fact, if you know how to search the Web, you can find almost any computer information you need for free.

In fact, hacking is so easy that if you have an online service and know how to send and read email, you can start hacking immediately. This book shows you where you can download free programs for Windows and Unix that actually work and won't land you in jail. We'll show you lots of easy hacker tricks you can use them for.

Suppose you want to become an elite hacker? All you will really need is an inexpensive "shell account" with an Internet Service Provider.

You can even make it into the ranks of the Überhackers without loading up on expensive computer equipment by installing a Unix type operating system on your Mac or Windows computer. For example, Linux, which runs on PCs, is so powerful that many Internet Service Providers use that operating system to run their online services. Yet you can buy it on a CD-ROM for approximately $30 or download it for free—we tell you where.

About Happy Hacker

There are lots of books that glamorize hackers. To read these books you would think that it takes many years of brilliant work to become one. Of course we hackers love to perpetuate this myth because it makes us look so incredibly kewl.

But how many books are out there that tell the beginner step by step how to actually do this hacking stuph? None! Seriously, have you ever read *Secrets of a Superhacker* by The Knightmare (Loompanics, 1994) or *Forbidden Secrets of the Legion of Doom Hackers* by Salacious Crumb (St. Mahoun Books, 1994)? They are full of vague and out of date stuph. Give us a break. But, heck, we've told you what they are, buy them if you like.

If you get on one of the hacker news groups on the Internet or chat channels on IRC and ask people how to hack, some of them insult and make fun of you. In fact, most of them get really ugly.

We see many hackers making a big deal of themselves and being mysterious and refusing to help others learn how to hack. Why? Because they don't want you to know the truth, which is that most of what they are doing is really very simple!

We thought about this. We, too, could enjoy the pleasure of insulting people who ask us how to hack. Or we could actually teach thousands of people how to hack. Muhahaha.

We started out with the Happy Hacker email list. Despite one hacker war after another waged against us by the guys who want to shut us down, we have continued to grow and have fun. Pooh on those bad guy hackers who hate us! If you want to join the fun and get our ezine full of the latest hacker fun and games, email *hacker@happyhacker.org* with message "subscribe hh".

This book owes much of its knowledge to the people who contributed to the Happy Hacker Digest ezines. If we were to include all their knowledge in this book, it would look like an unabridged dictionary and weigh enough to give you a sore back. If you want to read all this unabridged hacking information and find out who the hundreds of good guys are who helped us put together the treasure trove of hacking information at our Web site, check out our archives at *http://www.happyhacker.org*.

Just in case we are down when you check us out (hacker wars, probably), email *hacker@techbroker.com* with message "subscribe hh" or check out *http://tech-broker.com*. Computer criminals can inconvenience us, but they'll never shut us totally down. That's because we're hackers!

How to Use Happy Hacker

If you know how to use a personal computer and are on the Internet, you already know enough to start. You don't even need to read every single chapter to become a hacker.

You can count on anything in Section 1 being so easy that you can jump in about anywhere and just follow the instructions. For Section 2, if you know how to use a Unix shell account, you can jump right in.

If your plan is to become "elite," you will do better if you read all the chapters, especially those in Section 3. Check out the many Web sites and newsgroups to which we will point you, and find a mentor among the many talented hackers who post to our Happy Hacker email list.

If your goal is to become an Überhacker, the kind of person who discovers major problems with computer security and the way the Internet works, and who figures out how to fix these problems, *Happy Hacker* will be only the first in a mountain of material that you will need to study. However, we offer a study strategy that can aid you in your quest to reach the pinnacle of hacking.

How to Not Get Busted

The big problem with hacking is that if you step over the line, you can go to jail. We will do our best to warn you when we describe hacks that could get you into trouble with the law. But, although this book has been reviewed by Troy Larson, a lawyer who specializes in computer forensics, this book does not provide everything, or even very much, of what is known about cyberlaw. In addition, every state and every country has its own laws. And these laws keep on changing. So you have to use common sense about computer crime.

The best protection against getting busted is the Golden Rule. If you are about to do something that you would not like to have done to you, forget it. Do hacks that make the world a better place, or that are at least fun and harmless, and you should keep out of trouble. Besides, it's more fun to be a white hat on the frontier of cyberspace.

So if you get an idea from this book that helps you do something malicious or destructive, it's your problem if you end up being the next hacker behind bars. The law won't care if the guy whose computer you trash was being a dork. It won't care that the giant corporation whose database you filched shafted your best buddy once. The law won't care how funny your hack of that Republican Party web site was. They will only care that you broke the law.

To some people it may sound like phun to become a national sensation in the latest hysteria over Evil Genius hackers. But after the trial, when some reader of this book ends up being the reluctant "girlfriend" of a convict named Spike, how happy will his news clippings make him?

Conventions Used in the Book

You will notice that we sometimes spell words funny, like "kewl" and "phun." These are hacker slang terms. Since we often communicate with each other via email, most of our slang consists of ordinary words with extraordinary spellings. For example, a hacker might spell "elite" as "3l1t3," with 3's substituting for e's and 1's for i's. He or she may even spell "elite" as "31337. We sometimes use these slang spellings to help you learn how to write email like some hackers do.

Of course, the cute spelling stuph we use will go out of date fast. So we do not guarantee that if you use this slang, people will read your email and think, "Ohhh, you must be an Evil Genius! I'm sooo impressed!"

Take it from us, guys who need to keep on inventing new slang to prove they are "k-rad 3l1t3" are often losers and lamers. So if you don't want to use any of the hacker slang of this book, that's okay by us. Most Überhackers don't use slang, either.

Because some readers may have hacker mayhem in mind (noooo!), in all hacking sessions I show you in this book, the Internet addresses of the computers have been fubared.

 Newbie note: The verb "to fubar" means to obscure email addresses and Internet host addresses by changing them. Tradition holds that it is best to do so by substituting "foobar" or "fubar" for part of the address. "Fubar" stands for "fined up beyond all recognition," a term that originated in World War II.

Who Are You?

We've made some assumptions about who you are and why you are reading *Happy Hacker*:

- You own a PC or Macintosh personal computer
- You are on-line with the Internet
- You have a sense of humor and adventure and want to express it by hacking
- Maybe you want to become one of the heroes of cyberspace fighting criminals and spammers
- Or—you want to impress your friends by making them think you are an Evil Genius
- You aren't some wannabe bad haxor d00d

Does this picture fit you? If so, start your computer. Are you ready to hack?

Section 1, Chapter 1
How to Turn Your Windows 95 Computer into a Haxor Box

I was kinda bored at school, so after impressing my friends ... with some Email spoofing, I printed out every chapter of the GTMHH on the laser printer there...I just thought you might want to know that the GTMHH is infiltrating yet more young impressionable minds... AHAHAHAHAHAHA-HAH!

You may be interested to know that my school has shut down its Internet connection indefinitely. The cause? No, we weren't infected by some sUpEr 31337 haxor's virus. In fact it was the administrators, themselves, that shut it down! They were a bit concerned that the most use it was getting was for students who were eager to print out all of the GtMHH.

These folks are talking about the early versions of this book that are plastered over so many hacker Web sites. Welcome to the excitement!

Want to start your hacking career with something fun, easy, legal, and that will make your friends' hair stand on end? You can do it with Windows 95.

Win95. Some hackers call it Lose95. Or Winblows. Or Windoze. They make fun of us for using it. Too bad for them. Us real hackers like to mess with many operating systems. Since Windows 95 is (at this writing) the most widely used operating system in the world, let's learn how to make it sit up and bark like a dog!

Besides, Windows NT computers are coming into widespread use as Internet servers. If you want to learn how to hack NT, using your home computer running Windows 95 is a good place to start.

In this chapter you will learn how to:
- Make your own Windows 95 start up, logoff and background screens
- Create animated start-up screens—make your friends' eyeballs pop!

- How to change start-up screens when you are on a LAN
- Customize desktop icons
- How to get your boring Windows graphics back

Let's say you are hosting a wild party in your home. You decide to prove to your buddies that you are one of those dread haxor d00dz. So you fire up your computer and what should come up on your screen but the puffy white clouds logo for "Windows 95." Lame, huh? Your computer looks just like everyone else's box. Like some boring corporate workstation operated by a guy with an IQ in the 80's.

If you already are a serious hacker, you could boot up Linux or FreeBSD or some other kind of Unix on your personal computer. But let's say you've invited over friends who wouldn't know a Linux login screen from a DOS prompt. They wouldn't be impressed. But you can social engineer them into thinking you are fabulously elite just by customizing your Win95 start up screen.

 Newbie note: "Social engineering" is controlling how people think and feel. A computer criminal uses social engineering to talk people into giving away passwords. But we teach harmless social engineering—hey, you can always admit to your friends later you were just kidding about being an el1t3 haxor. Or you could finish this book and actually become a serious hacker!

Let's say you want to boot up to a black screen with orange and yellow flames and the slogan " K-Rad Doomsters of the Apocalypse." This turns out to be easy. Heck, that's what my start-up screen looks like.

But here's the problem: Every time you boot up, Microsoft wants you to advertise their operating system. They want this so badly that they have gone to court to try

Figure 1: Meinel's startup screen.

Evil Genius tip: One of the rewarding things about hacking is to find hidden files that try to keep you from modifying them—and then to mess with them anyhow. That's what we're doing today.

Win95 startup graphics are hidden in two files, C:\LOGO.SYS and C:\IO.SYS. To see these hidden files, open File Manager, click "view", then click "by file type," then check the box for "show hidden/system files." Then, back on "view," click "all file details."

Next, on the left window click on c:\ (or whatever is your boot drive). On the right window you will see a complete listing of all directories and files in the root directory of your boot drive. To the right of the files LOGO.SYS and io.sys you will see the letters "rhs." These mean these files are "read-only, hidden, system."

LOGO.SYS is labeled as a system file—when it really is just a graphics file with and animation program added.

IO.SYS really is a crucial systems file. But hidden inside it is a copy of the start up graphic in LOGO.SYS. So if you delete LOGO.SYS, you still get the same bootup screen. This is how Microsoft tries to trick you into thinking logo.sys doesn't hold the bootup graphic. But we're hackers, muhahaha!

to force computer retailers to keep the Micro$oft bootup screen on the systems these vendors sell.

M$ doesn't want you messing with their start-up screen, either. So they tried to hide the software that runs it. Here's how to totally thwart their plans—plans so important that if you were a big company they'd sue over this.

The easiest way to thwart these Windoze 95 start-up and shut-down screens is to go to *http://www.windows95.com/apps/* and download some of their programs for designing your own. But we're hackers, so we like to do things ourselves.

The first thing you may want to do is save the original logo files. The safest way to bring back your original Win95 logos is to save them. Bring up File Manager. Click "file," then "copy." In the "from" box put "c:\logo.sys." In the "to" box put "c:\logo.bak." Do this with C:\LOGOW.SYS and LOGOS.SYS also. OK, now you are safe.

Now you are ready to make your own evil haxor start up and shut down screens. You may use either super easy or elite techniques. To begin, we start the Paint program.

Note: some versions of Win 95 don't have a logo.sys file. If you are missing it, try the instructions below—they still might work.

Super Easy Way to Make Your Startup Screen

1) Within the paint program, click "File"
2) Click "Open"
3) After "File name" type in *c:\windows\logos.sys*. This brings up the graphic you get when your computer is ready to shut down saying "It's now safe to turn off your computer." This graphic has exactly the right format to be used for your start up

Newbie note: Can't find File Manager or Paint? They usually are in the accessories folder. To get them, click "Start," then "Programs," then "Accessories."

But just in case you're like me and keep on moving things around, here's the fail-safe Win95 program finding routine:

    1) Click "Start" on the lower left corner of your screen.

    2) Click "Find"

    3) Click "Files or folders"

    4) In the "named" box type in "Paint" (or whatever you are trying to find).

    5) In the "Look in" box type in "C:"

    6) Check the box that says "include subfolders"

    7) Click "find now"

    8) An icon of a paint bucket turns up in a window. Double click.

This starts the paint program.

graphic. So you can play with it any way you want (so long as you don't do anything on the Attributes screen under the Images menu) and use it for your start up graphic.

4) Now we play with this picture. Just experiment with the controls of Paint and try out fun stuff.

5) When you decide you really like your picture (fill it with frightening hacker stuph, right?), save it as *c:\logo.sys*. This will overwrite the Windows start-up logo file. From now on, any time you want to change your start up logo, you will be able to both read and write the file LOGO.SYS.

Super Easy Way to Change the Shutdown Screens

If you want to change the two shut down screens, they are even easier to modify using Paint. The first shut down screen is named c:\windows\logow.sys. The final "It's now safe to turn off your computer" screen graphic is named c:\windows\logos.sys. After "file name" in Paint, type in *c:\windows\logos.sys* (or *logow.sys*). Now mess with in until you like it.

Make Your Own Windows Wallpaper

It is even easier to make wallpaper graphics. You can pick up really outrageous wallpaper by surfing the Web until you find something you really like. When you get there, hit the "print screen" key. This puts everything on the screen into the Clipboard. Then bring up Paint and paste it in. From there you may edit it to just get the part you want.

YOU CAN GET PUNCHED IN THE NOSE WARNING: If you want to use someone else's graphics, it is a good idea to ask permission instead of just taking them. You may also be violating copyright laws.

When you are ready to save your new wallpaper, name it something like c:\windows\evilhaxor.bmp (substituting your filename for "evilhaxor"—unless you like

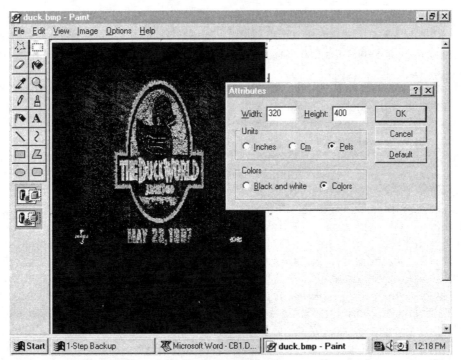

Figure 2: Paint with a squished graphic ready to be saved as LOGOW.SYS. This image came from the hacked web page for the movie Jurassic World.

to name your wallpaper "evilhaxor.") Your new graphics file must be in .bmp format and end with ".bmp." (or in .dib format and end with ".dib") Paint will put your graphic into .bmp format automatically. Next, set Windows to display your new wallpaper: 1) Click "start," then "settings," "control panel," "display," then "background." 2) You are now ready to choose your wallpaper. You have your pick of any .bmp or .dib file on your computer. Click "browse" and in the "file name" box, type in the name of your hacker wallpaper. Then, if you have just one image you want to display, click "center." If you have a small graphic you want repeated all over the screen, click "tile." Then click "OK."

Elite Way to Make Your Own Startup and Shutdown Graphics

The trouble with making your hacker start up and shut down screens by editing one of the existing Win95 logo files is that they only allow you to use their original colors. If you really want to go wild with any colors you want, open Paint again. 1) Click "Image," 2) Click "Attributes." 3) This brings up a box in which you can set "Width" to 320 and "Height" to 400. Make sure under "Units" that "Pels" is selected.

Remember to save the file as *c:\logo.sys* for your start up logo, or *c:\windows\logow.sys* and or *c:\windows\logos.sys* for your shut down screens. Make sure you save them as 256 color graphics.

What if you have a better graphics program than Paint? For the start up and shut down logos you still must set width to 320, height to 400, and set the units as Pels. In addition, you must make sure to save these as uncompressed bitmap (bmp) files. Paint does all this automatically.

If you want some really fabulous stuff for your start up and shut down screens, you can steal even more graphics from your favorite hacker pages on the Web. But it's more difficult than setting up cool wallpaper.

Here's how to make your start up and shut down graphics actually look good.

For some dadgummed reason, the start up and shut down screen programs take those 320x400 pels bitmaps, which are taller than wider, and turn them into graphics shaped like your monitor screen, wider than taller. The result? That start up graphic of Madonna now looks like Rosanne.

Here's how to fix this: 1) Click "image," then "stretch/skew." 2) Click the "horizontal" box and enter 49. As Figure 2 shows, it will shrink horizontally and look horrible in Paint, but great on your start up or shut down screens. 3) Click the "vertical" box and enter 83. 4) When you save it, set attributes to 320x400 Pels. Name it *c:\logo.sys*, *c:\windows\logow.sys*, or *c:\windows\logos.sys* depending on which screen you want, and save it as a 256 color graphic. 5) If this doesn't work, here's the easy way to save it so Windows will use it for the proper screen. Cut your graphic from Paint. Open the appropriate logo file. Paste your graphic on top. Make sure to save it as a 256 color graphic.

You can do the same things with other graphics programs, so long as you save your images as .bmp files with the right file names in the right directory, size them 320x400 Pels and 256 colors. Or paste them into the existing logo files.

How to Make an Animated Start up Screen

The Win95 start up screen has an animated bar at the bottom. But once you replace it with your own graphic, that animation is gone. However, you can make your own animated start up screen using the shareware program BMP Wizard. One download site for this goodie is: *http://www.windows95.com/apps.*

Evil genius tip: Want to directly edit the original Windows IO.SYS or LOGO.SYS files? Here's how to get into them. And, guess what, this is a great thing to learn in case you ever need to break into a Windows computer—something we'll look at in detail in the next chapter.

Click "Start" then "Programs" then "MS-DOS." At the MS_DOS prompt enter the commands: ATTRIB -R -H -S C:\IO.SYS ATTRIB -R -H -S C:\LOGO.SYS. Now they are totally at your mercy, muhahaha! However, IO.SYS holds a system program that is essential for the operation of your computer. Mess with it and be prepared to be hit with a huge mess.

But don't be surprised when Paint can't open IO.SYS. It is more than a mere graphics file. Try it out on some animation programs and see what you get.

Oh, yes—as always, save a backup of IO.SYS or you might be sorry!

Another option is to download LogoMania, which automatically resizes any bitmap to the correct size for your logon and logoff screens and can add animation, too. You can find it at *ftp://ftp.zdnet.com/pcmag/1997/0325/logoma.zip*. Or you may download a shareware animation program, Microangelo, from *http://www.im-pactsoft.com* Another one is WinHack, at *http://www.winsite.com.*

How to Change the Startup Screen if You Are on a LAN

Is your Win95 box on a local area network (LAN)? It isn't as easy to change your logos, as the network may override your changes. But there is a way to thwart the network. If you aren't afraid of your boss seeing "K-Rad Doomsters of the Apocalypse" here's how to customize your bootup graphics: 1) Find the program "regedit.exe." 2) It isn't there? You sysadmin must not trust you. Get it from your home Win95 box and take it to work on a disk (it's only 118 KB). 3) Run regedit. Click "Local Computer," then "Network," then "Logon" and then "Logon banner." It will bring up the current logon graphic. 4) Alter it.

Customize Desktop Icons

Would you like to change desktop icon titles? We'll use the recycle bin as an example because it's way easy! 1) Click "Start," then "Run." 2) Type in "C:\windows\regedit" (this assumes C: is your boot drive. It also assumes nobody has removed regedit.exe from your computer). Hit enter to run the regedit program. 3) You will see a list of names on the left pane of the regedit program. Click to highlight HKEY_CLASSES_ROOT. 4) On the task bar above, click "Edit," then "Find." 5) In the find box type in "Recycle Bin" and hit enter. 6) On the right pane you will see two headings: "Name" and "Data." Under the "Name" heading right-click on "default." 7) This brings up a screen labeled "Edit string." Type in your new name for the Recycle Bin. (I named mine "Hidden Haxor Secrets.") 8) Close the Registry Editor and reboot your system. Voila! You now have a desk top icon for "Hidden Haxor Secrets." 9) Oh, no, snoopy sister Suzie is coming to visit! If you don't want to put up with lots of lame questions, to get rid of this graphic, just redo this procedure by searching HKEY_CLASSES_ROOT for "Hidden Haxor Secrets" (or whatever you renamed the Recycle Bin), and rename it something like "Boring Junk."

Want to get rid of those little curved arrows on all your desktop shortcuts? Roger Prata, Windows technical editor of this book, shows us how as another example of a way to tweak the Registry so as to change your desktop icons.

1) Click on start, then run. Type "regedit" in the run box.

2) Double click on HKEY_CLASSES_ROOT. Under it scroll about halfway down until you get a folder that says "Lnkfile." Click once to highlight that folder.

3) On the right pane of the registry editor, look for a line that says "IS_Shortcut" and delete it.

4) Then scroll down further unitl you reach the Piffile folder. On the right side look for IS_Shortcut and delete it.

Warning: whenever you mess with the regedit program you are taking some risks. But if you are like me, you just can't resist, right? Of course there are icon editor programs, but we're hackers and that means doing things without the help of those lame proggies, right?

Of course you can do lots more with icons if you use programs such as Microangelo.

How to Get Those Boring Windows Graphics Back

Oh, no, snoopy sister Suzie is coming to visit and she wants to use your computer to read her email! You'll never hear the end of it if she sees that K-Rad Doomsters of the Apocalypse start up screen!

Or maybe you boss discovers what you did to circumvent your LAN. Oh, oh.

Here's how to get your Win95 graphics back. Just change the name of c:logo.sys (or logow.sys etc.) to something innocuous that sister Suzie or your boss won't notice while snooping with File Manager. Something like fu.bak. Better yet, see that evil genius note above and make it a hidden file. Then if you want it back, all you need do is change back its name.

Then rename the original logo files—you did save them, right?—to logo.sys etc.

Oh, no, what if you didn't save those Win95 logo graphics? What if somehow you screw up beyond all recognition the original files? You still may be OK. Just delete your new version of logo.sys and guess what happens? You get the original Windows start up graphic!

How the heck does that happen?

Those Microsoft guys figured we'd be doing things like this and hid a copy of their boring bootup screen in a file named io.sys. So if you rename or delete their original logo.sys, and there is no file by that name left, on bootup your computer displays their Windows 95 screen, pulled up from io.sys.

Warning! There are several variants of Windows 95 out there. We can't guarantee that this will work on every system. Also, have you heard of Murphy's Law: if anything can go wrong it will?

What if you wind up in a mess like this fellow? "Can someone please help me . . I successfully changed my Winblowz start-up and shut-down screens to be really kewl. Unfortunately . . . if (my parents) saw my cool Haxor start-up screens as they are now they'd probably kill me!!!

"I tried doing all of the io.sys bit . . . but am having no luck."

If you absolutely, certainly must be able to get back your Windows graphics, if your parents or boss would seriously kill you if you mess up, and you still do this stuph, remember, it was your idea to try this stuff. But here is your absolute desperate final solution. Just reinstall Win95 and every time it asks you if it should overwrite old files, say yes.

Okay, it's time to move on to more serious hacker fun in the next chapter, *How to Break into Windows 95 Computers*. In the meantime, if there are any 31337 hackers out there who are feeling insulted because this stuff is too easy to be called hacking, tough cookies. I'll bet my box looks more kewl than yours does. K-Rad Doomsters of the Apocalypse, yesss!

Section 1, Chapter 2
How to Break into
Windows 95 Computers

Windows 95 hacking? Lame! That's what some elite super-duper hackers will tell you.

Phooey on them. Besides the fact that there are more Win95 boxes than any other computer in the world, with Win95 you can learn some basic principles that later will help you with the most commonly installed workstation operating system in the world: Windows NT. NT is also is coming into wide use as a local area network (LAN), Internet, intranet, and Web server. So if you want to call yourself a serious hacker, you'd better get a firm grasp on Win NT.

 Newbie note: Even though Windows NT 4.0 looks a lot like Windows 95, it is actually a very different operating system. So don't assume that everything you learn in Win 95 is just a baby version of Win NT. NT is also much harder to break into. But the Registry, the part of NT that you use to break into it, is in some ways similar to the Win95 Registry.

In this chapter you will learn:
- Several ways to hack your Windows 95 login password
- How to mess with the msdos.sys file—and live!
- How to hack your Pentium CMOS password
- How to fool those babysitter program passwords
- How to hack a Windows Registry

Now you can have your buddies over to see you hack on your Windows 95 box. Heck, get them to bring their own, too. You're going to have some surprises for them. After seeing that "Doomsters of the Apocalypse" bootup screen they are already trembling at the thought of what, oh what have you got hidden behind that "Hidden Haxor Secrets" icon?

So what do you do next?

How about clicking on "Start," clicking "Settings," then "Control Panel" then "Passwords." Tell your friends your password and get them to enter a secret new one. Then shut down your computer and tell them you are about to show them how fast you can break their password and get back into your own box!

Warning: try this out in advance, because depending on how your computer is set up, there are several different techniques you may have to use. The first few techniques we're showing work on home Win 95 installations. But, especially in corporate local area networks (LANs), several of these techniques don't work. But I promise, you can break any password protection system if your Win95 computer has an a: drive, even if it is tied into a LAN.

Easy Win 95 Breakin #1:

1) Boot up your computer.

2) When the "system configuration" screen comes up, press "F5." If your system doesn't show this screen, just keep on pressing F5.

If your Win 95 has the right settings, this boots you into "safe mode." Everything looks weird, but you don't have to give your password and you still can run any of your programs.

Too easy! Okay, if you want to do something that makes you look more like a scary hacker, here's another way to evade that new password.

Easy Win 95 Breakin #2:

1) Boot up.

2) When you get to the "System Configuration" screen, press the F8 key. This gives you the Microsoft Windows 95 Startup Menu.

3) Choose the "MS-DOS Prompt" option. This puts you into MS-DOS. At the prompt, give the command "rename c:\windows*.pwl c:\windows*.zzz."

 Newbie note: MS-DOS stands for Microsoft Disk Operating System, an ancient operating system dating from 1981. It is a command-line operating system, meaning that you get a prompt (probably c:\) after which you type in a command and press the enter key. MS-DOS is often abbreviated DOS. It is a little bit similar to Unix, and in fact oldtimers claim its first version incorporated some Unix code.

4) Reboot. You will still get the password dialog screen. But now it will accept any password. You can fake out your friends by entering any darn password you want. It will ask you to reenter it to confirm your new password.

5) Your friends are smart enough to suspect you just created a new password, huh? You can put back the old one your friends picked. Use any tool you like—File Manager, Windows Explorer or MS-DOS— to rename *.zzz back to *.pwl.

6) Reboot and let your friends use their secret password. It still works! They'll think you actually cracked that password!

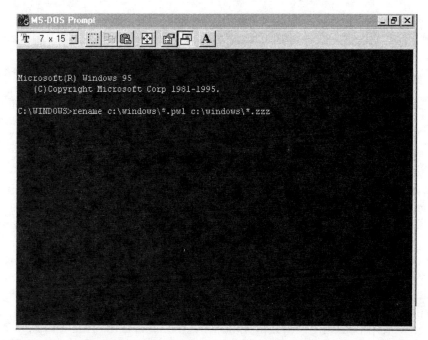

Figure 1: Disabling passwords from the DOS prompt.

Think about it. If someone were to be sneaking around another person's Win 95 computer, using this technique, the only way the victim could determine there had been an intruder is to check for recently changed files and discover that the *.pwl files have been messed with.

Evil genius tip: Keys that can do something during the bootup process are F4, F5, F6, F8, Shift+F5, Control+F5 and Shift+F8. Play with them!

How to Mess with the MSDOS.SYS file—and Live!

What if you discover that the function keys on your Win 95 box don't respond during bootup? You can still break in.

Or, if your computer does allow use of the boot keys, you may wish to disable them in order to be a teeny bit more secure.

Besides, it's phun to show your friends how to use the boot keys and then secretly disable these so when they try to mess with your computer they will discover you've locked them out.

The easiest—but slowest—way to either activate or disable the boot keys is to pick the proper settings while installing Win 95. But we're hackers, so we can pull a fast trick to do the same thing. We are going to learn how to edit the Win 95 msdos.sys file, which controls the boot sequence.

1) We are about to play with fire! Back up your computer completely, especially the system files. Make sure you have a Windows 95 boot disk. If you are doing this

on someone else's computer, let's just hope either you have permission to destroy the operating system, or else you are so good you couldn't possibly make a serious mistake.

 Newbie note: You don't have a boot disk? Shame, shame, shame! Everyone ought to have a boot disk for their computer just in case you or your buddies do something really horrible. If you don't already have a Win 95 boot disk, here's how to make one. You'll need an empty floppy disk drive and your Win 95 installation disk(s). Click on Start, then Settings, then Control Panel, then Add/Remove Programs, then Startup Disk. From here just follow the instructions

2) Find the file msdos.sys. It is in the root directory (usually C:\). Since this is a hidden system file, the easiest way to find it is to click on My Computer, right click the icon for your boot drive (usually C:), left click Explore, then scroll down the right side frame until you find the file msdos.sys.

3) Make msdos.sys writeable so you can mess with it. To do this, right-click on msdos.sys, then left-click "Properties." This brings up a screen on which you uncheck the "Read Only" and "Hidden" boxes.

4) Bring msdos.sys up in Word Pad. You must use Word Pad and not Notepad or any other word processing program! One way to do this is to bring up File Manager. Use it to find msdos.sys again (it's in the root directory, c:\msdos.sys) and click on it. Then click "associate" under the "file" menu. Then click on "Word Pad." Then double click on msdos.sys.

5) Word Pad is now up with msdos.sys loaded into it. You will see something that looks like this:

```
[Paths]
WinDir=C:\WINDOWS
WinBootDir=C:\WINDOWS
HostWinBootDrv=C

[Options]
BootGUI=1
Network=1
;
;The following lines are required for compatibility
with other programs.
;Do not remove them (MSDOS.SYS needs to be 1024
bytes).
;xxxxxxxxxxxxxxxxxxxxxxxxxxxxxxxxxxxxxxxxxxxxxxxxxx
;xxxxxxxxxxxxxxxxxxxxxxxxxxxxxxxxxxxxxxxxxxxxxxxxxx
.
.
```

To disable the function keys during bootup, directly below [Options] you should insert the command "BootKeys=0."

Or, another way to disable the boot keys is to insert the command BootDelay=0. You can really mess up your snoopy hacker wannabe friends by putting in both statements and hope they don't know about BootDelay. Then save msdos.sys.

6) Since msdos.sys is absolutely essential to your computer, you'd better write protect it like it was before you edited it. Click on "My Computer", then "Explore", then click the icon for your boot drive. Then scroll down the right side until you find the file msdos.sys. Right-click on it, then on the dropdown menu left click "properties." This brings back that screen with the "read only" and "hidden" boxes. Check "read only." You don't need to make it hidden again because that's just in there to make people think system files are hidden in the cabbage patch.

7) You are running a virus scanner, right? You never know what your phriends might do to your computer while your back is turned. When you next boot up, your virus scanner will see that msdos.sys has changed. It will assume the worst and want to make your msdos.sys file look just like it did before. You have to stop it from doing this. How you stop it depends on your antivirus program.

Hard Way to Edit your (or someone else's) MSDOS.SYS File.

Why learn the hard way to edit the msdos.sys file? Guess what, this technique can come in handy for serious Windows hacking. So now is as good a time as any to uncover this secret.

1) Put a Win 95 boot disk in the a: drive. Boot up. This gives you a DOS prompt. It looks like "A:/".

Evil genius tip: Learn how to do DOS and you are master of the Windows NT universe. But, but, the Super Duper hacker sputters, Win NT is running the NTFS file system! How can a Win 95 box allow me to run rampant! Ah, but a free program you may download from http://www.ntinternals.com allows Win 95 and DOS to recognize and mount NTFS drives for transparent access.

2) Make msdos.sys writeable. Give the command "attrib -h -r -s c:\msdos.sys"

3) Give the command "edit msdos.sys" This brings this file up into a DOS word processor.

4) Use this Edit program to alter msdos.sys. Save it. Exit the edit program.

5) At the DOS prompt, give the command "attrib +r +h +s c:\msdos.sys" to return the msdos.sys file to the status of hidden, read-only system file.

Boot Disk Magic

So now your computer's boot keys are disabled. Does this mean no one can break in? Maybe your friends can't break in any more, but you can. Guaranteed.

As you may have guessed from the *Hard Way to Edit Your MSDOS.SYS* instructions, your next option for Win 95 break-ins is to use a boot disk.

1) Shut down your computer.

2) Put the boot disk into the A: drive.

3) Boot up.

4) At the A:\ prompt, give the command: "rename c:\windows*.pwl c:\windows*.zzz".

5) Take out the boot disk and boot up again. You can enter anything or nothing at the password prompt and get in.

6) Cover your tracks by renaming the password files back to what they were.

How to Hack Your Pentium CMOS Password

Wow, this is too easy! Now what do you do if you want to keep your prankster friends out of your Win 95 box? Well, there is one more thing you can do. This is a common trick on LANs where the network administrator doesn't want people monkeying around with each others' computers. The answer—but not a very good answer—is to use a CMOS password.

Basic settings on your computer such as how many and what kinds of disk drives you have and which ones are used for booting are held in a CMOS chip on the mother board. A tiny battery keeps this chip always running so that whenever you turn your computer off, it still remembers its instructions. On a home computer, during bootup it will usually first look in the A: drive for the boot disk. If that is empty, it next will look at the C: drive.

There are a lot of different ways to change the CMOS settings. A common way is to press the delete key at the very beginning of the bootup sequence. Others use ctrl-esc, ctrl-s or ctrl-alt-esc. Check your hardware documentation if none of these works. (Read the documentation first? Horrors!)

Then, when the CMOS settings screen comes up, if you have previously instructed the CMOS settings to ask for a password, you have to give it your password before you can change anything. Because different computers may have different CMOS menus, you will have to check around to see how one sets passwords.

If you don't want someone to boot from the A: drive and mess with your password file, you can set it so it only boots from the C: drive. You can even set it so that it only boots from a remote drive on a LAN. (However, remember that if you tell it not to boot from a floppy drive, and you get into a big mess—can you say "hard disk crash"? —and want to use a boot disk, you'll have to be able to change it back.)

If you are trying to break into a Win 95 box that won't boot from a floppy drive, the first thing to try is to reset the CMOS to boot from the floppy. But what if the CMOS is password protected?

First, try some common CMOS passwords. Many CMOS memories come with a default password installed. Some defaults are:

```
lkwpeter
j262 )
award_sw
biostar
```

If these don't work, yes, we still have more hacker tricks. But before trying these out, be sure to write down all your CMOS settings. And be prepared to make a total wreck of your computer. Hacking CMOS can be even more destructive than hacking system files.

1) Get a phillips screwdriver and soldering iron (solder sucker optional).
2) Open up your victim.
3) Remove the battery.
4) Solder the battery back in.

What? You don't want to take the risk of turning up at a computer repair shop with the guts of your box looking like a hacker tried to break in? Here's an alternate step three. Many motherboards have a 3-pin jumper that can be used to reset the CMOS to its default settings. Look for a jumper close to the battery or, when all else fails, read your manual.

For example, on some computers you will find a three pin device with pins one and two jumpered. If you move the jumper to pins two and three and leave it there for over five seconds, it will reset the CMOS.

Warning—this will not work on all computers! If this jumper switch destroys your box, hey, that's the price of being a hacker, dude! RTFM! (That means "read the fine manual.")

5) Your victim computer now hopefully has gone back to the CMOS default settings. Now put everything back the way they were, with the exception of setting the CMOS to first check a floppy drive (usually A:) when booting up.

YOU CAN GET FIRED WARNING: If you do this wrong, and this is a computer you use at work, and you have to go crying to the systems administrator to get your box working again, you had better have a convincing story. Don't tell the sysadmin or your boss "*The Happy Hacker* book made me do it!"

6) proceed with the A: drive boot disk break-in instructions.

So did you decide to read this far before taking a solder gun to your motherboard? Heck, at least this chapter doesn't tell your to run fdisk or format c: (No! No! Don't give the command "format c:"!)

If you didn't read this far first, you will seriously kill me when you read this. There's an easy solution to the CMOS password problem. It's a program called KillCMOS which you can download from *http://www.koasp.com*. There are also a number of CMOS password crackers available on hacker Web sites. But using other people's programs to do things seemingly by magic isn't the hacker way, right?

How to Fool those Babysitter Program Passwords

Have you ever wanted to learn how to evade those obnoxious programs your employer or parents use to keep you from visiting the National Organization of Women or Electronic Freedom Foundation Web sites? Liberation is at hand!

This book does not intend to help guys in trench coats on the back alleys of the Internet feed pornography to little kids. But the sad fact is that these net censorship programs have no way of evaluating everything on the Web. So what they do is only allow access to a relatively small number of Web sites. Oftentimes the people who sell these programs also have a hidden political agenda. They will block sites purely to trick parents into only letting their kids see one narrow political view.

As the mother of four, I understand how worried parents can get over what their kids encounter on the Internet. But these Web censor programs are a poor substitute for parents spending time with their kids so that they learn how to use computers responsibly and become really dynamite hackers! Um, I mean, become responsible cyberspace citizens. Besides, these programs can be hacked way too easily.

The first tactic to use with a Web censor program is hit control-alt-delete. This brings up the task list. If the censorship program is on the list, turn it off by highlighting it and clicking "End Task." Then click "Cancel" and you are home free.

The next possibility is that your nemesis program may be launched into action during bootup from c:\windows\startm~1\programs\startup. Holding down the shift key during bootup may disable the startup folder. Or you can look for files with the extension .lnk. What the heck, kill them all! However, this may really mess up your computer. It is always safer to rename suspect files so you can put them back.

Another tactic is to delete or rename any file with the extension .pwl. Besides getting rid of your Windows logon password file, this may zap some other stuff. Also delete or rename c:/windows/system/password.cpl. Of course you may kill some stuff you didn't want killed, but you're a hacker, right?

If this doesn't work, another tactic is to edit the autoexec.bat file to delete any mention of the web censor program. Other files that may start up babysitter programs include system.ini and win.ini. To edit them, use the same techniques as you used above to edit msdos.sys. You will be looking for lines that say load= and run=. Delete those lines, and next time you boot up those programs won't be there.

Another way that can get rid of some passwords is to run a program called pwledit. If Windows Explorer can't find it, you can install it from the Windows 95 installation disk(s). You will find it in the path /admin/apptools/pwledit. This program will allow you to remove some passwords. It does not work on some screen savers or on the Internet Explorer security settings password.

What about the case where there aren't any babysitter programs on your computer, but you worry that someone will snoop on where you have been surfing? You've got to get rid of those incriminating records showing that you've been reading Dilbert!

Warning: the following techniques will only work if you don't have some sort of snooper program on your computer or network that will tattle on you.

It's easy to fix with Netscape 2.x. Open netscape.ini with either Notepad or Word Pad. It probably will be in the directory c:\netscape\netscape.ini. Near the bottom you will find your URL history. Delete those lines.

Netscape Communicator also makes it easy to delete the recent browsing history. Simply use Windows Explorer to find a file named pref.js. Open it in Wordpad. You will see something like:

```
// Netscape User Preferences
// This is a generated file! Do not edit.

user_pref("browser.bookmark_columns_win","v1   1   1:10000   2:2997
4:1999 3:1999");
user_pref("browser.bookmark_window_rect", "44,44,480,321");
user_pref("browser.cache.disk_cache_size", 5000);
user_pref("browser.cache.memory_cache_size", 600);
user_pref("browser.download_directory", "C:\\TEXT\\");
```

```
user_pref("browser.startup.homepage", "http://techbroker.com");
user_pref("browser.startup.homepage_override", false);
user_pref("browser.startup.page", 0);
user_pref("browser.url_history.URL_1", "amazon.com");
user_pref("browser.url_history.URL_10","http://www.netmeg.net/jar
gon/terms");
user_pref("browser.url_history.URL_11",
"http://www.cs.nmsu.edu/~jcordes");
user_pref("browser.url_history.URL_12",
"Hell:http://www.tacd.com/zines/bofh");
user_pref("browser.url_history.URL_13", "http://bofh.mysite.org
```

etc.

Evil genius tip: check out some of those URLs.

To get rid of your browsing history, simply delete any line that begins with "user_pref("browser.url_history.URL." Then save as a "Text File."

There is a second place where Netscape Communicator hides browsing history. Use Windows Explorer to find the file netscape.hst. Sorry, I haven't found an ideal editor to use on it. But just ignore the odd characters and focus on the URLs, which at least in Word Pad will appear in plain text. Delete the ones you don't like.

A third place that may hide browser histories is the /windows/temp directory. It temporarily caches files. If your computer loses power or crashes while your browser is running, it may leave something behind. Be sure to clean out those files.

Evil genius tip: You could make it look like you have been surfing all sorts of nonexistent places. Drive snoopers nuts trying to figure you out!

The browsing histories of Netscape Navigator and Internet Explorer are much harder to delete because they are hidden in the Registry.

Newbie note: The Registry! It is the Valhalla of those who wish to crack Windows. Whoever controls the registry of a network server controls the network—totally. Whoever controls the registry of a Win 95 or Win NT box controls that computer—totally. The ability to edit the registry is comparable to having root access to a Unix machine.

How to edit the Registry

This is even harder than editing the msdos.sys file! First back up all your files. Have a boot disk handy. If you mess up the Registry badly enough you may have to reinstall your operating system. So you'd better have a copy of the Windows 95 installation disk(s) on hand, too.

YOU CAN GET FIRED WARNING: If you edit the Registry of a computer at work, if you get caught you had better have a good explanation for the sysadmin

and your boss. Figure out how to edit the registry of a LAN server at work and you may be in real trouble.

YOU CAN GO TO JAIL WARNING: Mess with the Registry of someone else's computer and you may be violating the law. Get permission before you mess with Registries of computers you don't own.

1) Close any programs you are currently running just in case we totally trash our computers, right. Then click "Run," type in "regedit" and click "OK."
2) Regedit brings up several folders:

```
HKEY_CLASSES_ROOT
HKEY_CURRENT_USER
HKEY_LOCAL_MACHINE
HKEY_USERS
HKEY_CURRENT_CONFIG
HKEY_DYN_DATA
```

What we are looking at is in some ways like a password file, but it's much more than this. It holds all sorts of settings—how your desktop looks, what short cuts you are using, what files you are allowed to access. If you are used to Unix, you are going to have to make major revisions in how you view file permissions and passwords. But, hey, this is a beginner's lesson so we'll gloss over this part.

 Evil genius tip: You can run regedit from DOS from a boot disk. Verrrry handy in certain situations. . . . The names of the files that form the Registry are user.dat and system.dat. Mess with them at your own risk.

3) Get into one of these HKEY thingies. Let's check out HKEY_CUR-RENT_USER by clicking the plus sign to the left of it. Play around awhile. See how regedit gives you menu choices to pick new settings. You'll soon realize that Microsoft is baby-sitting you. All you see is pictures with no clue of what these files look like in DOS. It's called "security by obscurity." This isn't how hackers edit the Registry.

If you want to get rid of the Internet Explorer browsing history, click "software" then "Microsoft" then "Internet Explorer," then "Typed URLs." Your browsing history will come up in the right hand pane. Delete it.

4a) Now we get to act like real hackers. We are going to put part of the Registry where we can see—and change—anything. For Netscape Navigator, go up to the Registry heading on the Regedit menu bar. Click HKEY_CURRENT_USER . This will give you a screen with a left hand side and a right hand side window.

5a) Click the "Software" topic. This will give you "Netscape" on the left hand side. On the right hand side you will see the URL history. Just delete them and you're home free.

4b) For Internet Explorer, first click the HKEY_CLASSES_ROOT line to high-light it. Then go up to the Registry heading on the Regedit menu bar. Click it, then choose "Export Registry File." Give it any name you want, but be sure it ends with ".reg".

5b) Open your exported version of HKEY_CLASSES_ROOT in Word Pad. It is important to use Word Pad instead of Note Pad or any other word processing program. One way to get it into Word Pad is to right click on your exported file from Explorer. Warning: in Explorer, if you left click on a file with the .reg extension, it will automatically import it back into the Registry. If you had been messing with it, you could trash your computer big time. Don't ask me how I found this out.

6) Read. Enjoy! Everything you ever wanted to know about Windows security that Microsoft was afraid to tell you is floating around here. We see things that look like:

```
[HKEY_CLASSES_ROOT\htmlctl.PasswordCtl\CurVer]
"htmlctl.PasswordCtl.1"
[HKEY_CLASSES_ROOT\htmlctl.PasswordCtl.1]
"PasswordCtl Object"
[HKEY_CLASSES_ROOT\htmlctl.PasswordCtl.1\CLSID]
"{EE230860-5A5F-11CF-8B11-00AA00C00903}"
```

The stuff inside the brackets in this last line is an encrypted password controlling access to a program or features of a program such as the net censorship feature of Internet Explorer. What it does is encrypt the password when you enter it, then compare it with the encrypted version on file.

7) It isn't real obvious which password goes to what program. What the heck, delete them all! Of course this also means your stored passwords for logging on to your ISP, for example, may disappear.

8) (Optional) Want to erase your surfing records? For Internet Explorer you'll have to edit HKEY_CURRENT_USER, HKEY_LOCAL_MACHINE and HKEY_USERS. You can also delete the files c:\windows\cookies\mm2048.dat and c:\windows\cookies\mm256.dat. These also store URL data.

9) Import your .reg files back into the Registry. Either click on your .reg files in Explorer or else use the "Import" feature next to the "Export" you just used in Regedit. This only works if you remembered to name them with the .reg extension.

10) Oh, no, Internet Explorer makes this loud obnoxious noise the first time you run it and puts up a bright red "X" with the message "Content Advisor configuration information is missing. Someone may have tried to tamper with it."

To get rid of this warning , click on "View," then "Options" then "Security" then "Disable Ratings." It will ask you for a password, but just hit enter and the net babysitter feature is entirely shut down, tamper warnings and all.

Of course if your parents are smart they will check Explorer from time to time to see that the ratings feature is still enabled. But you can fix that by renaming the backups of the two files that make up the registry: system.da0 and user.da0. Use the instructions above on how to make a hidden read-only system file into something you can write. Then rename them system.dat and user.dat. Reboot your system. Then all the passwords are back and the netbabysitter feature works again. This is really fool proof because the registry files are always being updated by Windows. So it won't look the least bit suspicious if they have a recent time stamp on them.

What this means, parents, is the ONLY way to keep your kids out of trouble on the net is to teach them right from wrong. Windows is way too vulnerable to simple hacks.

How to Evade Babysitter Programs—and Everything Else—on a LAN

Are you on a LAN? Want to trash most of the policies that can be invoked on a workstation running Windows 95? Make these changes in the Registry. Warning: results may vary and you may get into all sorts of trouble whether you do this successfully or unsuccessfully. In [HKEY_LOCAL_MACHINE\Network\Logon] make these settings:

```
"MustBeValidated"=dword:00000000
"username"="ByteMe" (OK, this one is optional:)
"UserProfiles"=dword:00000000
```

In [HKEY_CURRENT_USER\Software\Microsoft\Windows\CurrentVersion \Policies] set:

```
"DisablePwdCaching"=dword:00000000
"HideSharePwds"=dword:00000000
```

In [HKEY_CURRENT_USER\Software\Microsoft\Windows\CurrentVersion \Policies\Explorer] set:

```
"NoDrives"=dword:00000000
"NoClose"=dword:00000000
"NoDesktop"=dword:00000000
"NoFind"=dword:00000000
"NoNetHood"=dword:00000000
"NoRun"=dword:00000000
"NoSaveSettings"=dword:00000000
"NoRun"=dword:00000000
"NoSaveSettings"=dword:00000000
"NoSetFolders"=dword:00000000
"NoSetTaskbar"=dword:00000000
"NoAddPrinter"=dword:00000000
"NoDeletePrinter"=dword:00000000
"NoPrinterTabs"=dword:00000000
```

Under [HKEY_CURRENT_USER\Software\Microsoft\Windows\CurrentVe rsion\Policies\Network] set:

```
"NoNetSetup"=dword:00000000
"NoNetSetupIDPage"=dword:00000000
"NoNetSetupSecurityPage"=dword:00000000
"NoEntireNetwork"=dword:00000000
"NoFileSharingControl"=dword:00000000
"NoPrintSharingControl"=dword:00000000
"NoWorkgroupContents"=dword:00000000
```

Under [HKEY_CURRENT_USER\Software\Microsoft\Windows\CurrentVe rsion\Policies\System] set:

```
"NoAdminPage"=dword:00000000
"NoConfigPage"=dword:00000000
"NoDevMgrPage"=dword:00000000
"NoDispAppearancePage"=dword:00000000
"NoDispBackgroundPage"=dword:00000000
"NoDispCPL"=dword:00000000
"NoDispScrSavPage"=dword:00000000
"NoDispSettingsPage"=dword:00000000
"NoFileSysPage"=dword:00000000
"NoProfilePage"=dword:00000000
"NoPwdPage"=dword:00000000
"NoSecCPL"=dword:00000000
"NoVirtMemPage"=dword:00000000
"DisableRegistryTools"=dword:00000000
```

In [HKEY_CURRENT_USER\Software\Microsoft\Windows\CurrentVersion \Policies\WinOldApp] set:

```
"Disabled"=dword:00000000
"NoRealMode"=dword:00000000
```

What to Do When Playing with the Registry Makes a Mess

Now suppose some guy has just made a really big mess of the computer. Let's say he's left incriminating records of Hustler visits all over the registry. The Win 95 desk top looks like a gang of teen hackers have defaced it and he dreads his boss/parents/spouse seeing what an obnoxious netizen he has been. And he can't figure out how to fix it. He comes to you for help. What now?

If you decide he deserves the mess he got into, you can have fun getting him out.

Erase the registry and its backups. These are in four files: system.dat, user.dat, and their backups, system.da0 and user.da0. (Don't tell him about simply using a boot disk and renaming the backup files from .da0 to .dat.) His operating system will immediately and spectacularly commit suicide. (This was a really exciting test, folks, but I luuuv that adrenaline!) If you suddenly feel sorry for him, the Recycle bin still works after trashing his Registry files, so you can restore them and his computer will be back to the mess he just made of it. Then you can chicken out and rename the registry backup files.

But if you really have guts, just kill all those files and shut it down.

Then use your Win 95 boot disk to bring his computer back to life. Reinstall Windows 95. The desk top will look different, but your friend will be grateful just to be alive. Then show him the Internet Explorer censorship program and every other babysitter program has been turned off. Your friend will think you are a genius.

Then if his parents/boss/wife catch him surfing a Nazi explosives instruction site or bianca's Smut Shack, don't blame it on *Happy Hacker*. Blame it on Microsoft security—or on parents being too busy to teach their kids right from wrong.

Perhaps you are wondering, in order to get around that babysitter stuff, why does this chapter make you suffer through all this regedit stuff instead of just telling you to delete those four files and reinstall Win 95? It's because if you are even halfway serious about hacking, you need to learn how to edit the registry of a Win NT computer instead of chopping it up with an axe. You just got a little taste of what is like, on the safety of your home computer.

You also may have gotten a taste of how easy it is to make a huge mess when playing with the registry. If you messed up on this lesson, you know first hand how disastrous a clumsy hacker can be when messing in someone else's computer systems. Even the best hacker makes mistakes.

So what is the bottom line on Windows 95 security? Is there any way to set up a Win 95 box so no one can break into it? Sorry, Win 95 is totally vulnerable. Even remotely on a LAN. Shoot, I didn't even tell you how trivial it is to grab and decrypt Win95 passwords when they are sent over a LAN.

In fact, if you have physical access to any computer, whether a SPARC running Solaris, a Vax under VMS, or lowly Win95, the only way to keep you from breaking into its data is to encrypt the files with a strong encryption algorithm.

Now be kind to Windows boxes, and don't frighten anyone too badly with your little hacks, okay?

Section 1, Chapter 3
How to Use Windows to Hack the Internet

If you want to jump right into serious Internet and network hacking, you can do a lot with just Windows 95, today. Also, for many people, Windows 95 is much easier to use than Unix type operating systems.

In this chapter we will learn how to:
- Do serious hacking with just an AOL or other online account.
- Use undocumented Windows 95 DOS commands to track down and port surf Internet host computers.
- Download hacker tools such as port scanners and password crackers designed for use with Windows 95.

This chapter also will give you some insights into how to hack Windows NT. How important is it to learn how to hack this operating system?

NT is making fast inroads on the Internet against Unix. For example, one expert projects that the Unix-based Web server market share will fall from 65% in 1995 to only 25% by the year 2000. The Windows NT share is projected to grow to 32%. This weak future for Unix Web servers is reinforced by an IDC report that market share of all Unix systems is now falling at a compound annual rate of -17% for the foreseeable future, while Windows NT is growing in market share by 20% per year.[1]

So if you want to keep up your hacking skills, you're going to have to get wise to Windows. One of these days we're going to be sniggering at all those Unix-only hackers.

Besides, even poor, pitiful Win95 can now take advantage of lots of free hacker tools that give it much of the power of Unix.

---

1 Mark Winther, "The Global Market for Public and Private Internet Server Software," IDC #11202, April 1996, pages 10, 11.

Hacking Using AOL— or any On-line Service

Since this is a beginners' lesson, we'll go straight to the Big Question: "All I've got is AOL and a Win95 box. Can I still learn how to hack the Internet?"

Yes, yes, yes!

The secret to hacking from AOL/Win 95—or from any on-line service that gives you access to the World Wide Web—is hidden in Win 95's MS-DOS (DOS 7.0). It offers several Internet tools, none of which are documented in either the standard Windows or DOS help features. But you can learn these hidden features today.

So let's jump right into hacking from Windows.

To succeed with all the haxor tricks you will learn in this lesson, you may need to fix your Win95 box so it can walk and chew gum at the same time. It needs to be able to run several Internet and network applications simultaneously so you can even use an ordinary AOL session to do lots of scary stuff. So let's make sure your box is ready for serious hacking. If you have problems doing what we suggest then:

1) Click "Start," then "Control Panel" then "Internet" then "Connection".

2) At the top of this screen is a box labeled "Dialing" and "Connect to the Internet as needed." If this box is checked, uncheck it. If this messes things up, then try checking it again.

What is the reason for making this change? This "Connect As Needed" feature makes your Win95 Internet utilities look for a program to dial an ISP and set up a PPP connection. Programs that call up different dialers (e.g. Compuserve's versus Microsoft's) can run into conflicts when another dialer has control of the modem. Disabling the "Connect as Needed" can avoid the dialer conflict while your program will see the already existing PPP connection and use it.

First connect to AOL or whatever supposedly lame online service you may use to get on the Internet. Then minimize your on-line service software and prepare to hack!

Next bring up your built-in Internet and network utilities by opening a DOS 7.0 window. Do this by clicking Start, then Programs, then MS-DOS.

For best hacking you will find it easiest to use DOS in a window with a task bar which allows you to cut and paste commands and easily switch between Windows and DOS programs. If DOS comes up hogging the full screen, hold down the Alt key while hitting enter, and it will go into a window. Then if you are missing the task bar, click the system menu on the left side of the DOS window caption and select Toolbar.

Now you have the option of eight TCP/IP utilities to play with: telnet, arp, ftp, nbtstat, netstat, ping, route, and tracert.

Of these utilities, telnet is the biggie. You can also access the telnet program directly from Windows. However, while hacking you may need to combine using telnet with the other utilities that can only be called from the DOS 7.0 window.

Newbie note: TCP/IP stands for Transmission Control Protocol/Internet Protocol. It is the most commonly used communications protocol on the Internet. When you get the kind of online connection that allows you to see pretty pictures on the Web, you are using TCP/IP.

For our first hacking experiment, let's show your friends how you can get into almost any strange computer on the Internet and give commands—and get results—without using a password to get in. This can scare the heck out them. Honest, I just tried this trick I'm about to show you on a neighbor. He got so worried that he quickly excused himself, ran home and phoned my husband to beg him to keep me from hacking his work computer!

The first step to terrify your neighbors and impress your friends is a "whois."

1) You have that PPP session running, right? Just get your online service that you use to see the Web going, and that can be your PPP session.

2) Go to the DOS prompt C:\WINDOWS and give the command "telnet." This brings up a telnet screen.

3) Click on Connect, then click Remote System. This brings up a box that asks you for "Host Name."

4) Type "whois.internic.net" into this box. Below that it asks for "Port" and has the default value of "telnet." Leave in "telnet" for the port selection. Below that is a box for "TermType." I recommend picking VT100 because, well, just because I like it best.

5) Click on Connect and you will soon get a prompt that looks like this:

```
[vt100] InterNIC
```

Then ask your friend or neighbor his or her email address. Then at this InterNIC prompt, type in the last two parts of your friend's email address. For example, if the address is "luser@aol.com," type in "aol.com."

I'm picking AOL for this lesson because it widely used, and hard to hack. Almost any other on-line service will be easier.

For AOL we get the answer:

```
[vt100] InterNIC  whois aol.com
Connecting to the rs Database . . . . . .
Connected to the rs Database
America Online (AOL-DOM)
12100 Sunrise Valley Drive
Reston, Virginia 22091
USA
Domain Name: AOL.COM
Administrative Contact:
O'Donnell, David B (DBO3) PMDAtropos@AOL.COM
703/453-4255 (FAX) 703/453-4102
Technical Contact, Zone Contact:
America Online (AOL-NOC) trouble@aol.net
703-453-5862
Billing Contact:
Barrett, Joe (JB4302) BarrettJG@AOL.COM
703-453-4160 (FAX) 703-453-4001

Record last updated on 13-Mar-97.
Record created on 22-Jun-95.

Domain servers in listed order:
```

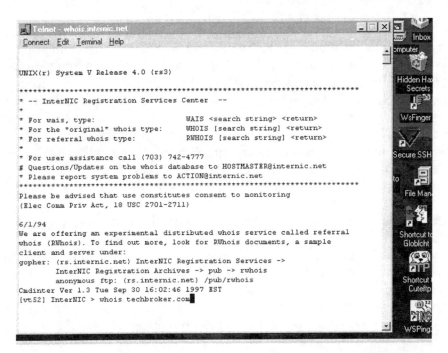

Figure 1: The InterNIC whois server login screen. I have just inserted the command "whois techbroker.com."

```
DNS-01.AOL.COM 152.163.999.42
DNS-02.AOL.COM 152.163.999.56
DNS-AOL.fu.NET 999.83.210.28
```

These last three lines give the names of some computers that work for America Online (AOL). If we want to play with AOL, these are a good place to start.

 Newbie note: We just got info on three "domain servers" for AOL. "Aol.com" is the domain name for AOL, and the domain servers are the computers that hold information that tells the rest of the Internet how to send messages to AOL computers and email addresses. Note that the 999's in this example are here to fubar the computer names. No numbers larger than 255 will appear in a real numerical IP address.

 Evil genius tip: Using your Win 95 and an Internet connection, you can run a whois query from many other computers, as well. Telnet to your target computer's port 43 and if it lets you get on it, give your query. Example: telnet to nic.ddn.mil, port 43. Once connected type "whois DNS-01.AOL.COM," or whatever name you want to check out. However, this only works on computers that are running a public whois service on port 43.

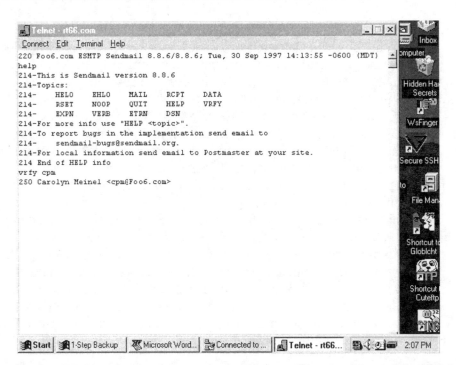

Figure 2: Surfing port 25 on a victim computer. Hey, it's talking to us without asking us first to login! Lines that are the computer's communications all have numbers in front of them. My commands don't have numbers. I just got this computer to verify that user name cpm belongs to me.

Honest, show this trick to your neighbors and they will really be terrified. They just saw you accessing a US military computer! But it's OK, nic.ddn.mil is open to the public on many of its ports. Check out its Web site www.nic.ddn.mil and its ftp site, too—they are a mother lode of information that is good for hacking.

Next we port surf AOL. With the Win95 telnet program you can hand scan Internet host ports almost as well as from a Unix telnet program. But there are several tricks you need to learn in order to make this work.

Newbie note: What the heck is port surfing? There are thousands of possible ways to connect to Internet host computers. Each of these ways—each of which is actually a different computer program—is called a "port" and has a number and often a name, too. For example, port 25 sends your email out into the Internet. Port 80 is where your browser docks to read Web pages.

For best port surfing results, on the telnet program click "terminal," then "preferences," then "local echo." You only want "local echo" while surfing ports so you can see what commands you have entered. Also, for some reason, if a port talks back to you (verrrry super for impressing friends), it may not show up on the screen unless you have that "local echo" option checked. Don't ask me why, it makes no sense, but it works on my computer. Yours might be different.

However, in some situations everything you type in will be doubled. For example, if you type in "hello" the telnet screen may show you "heh lelllo o". This doesn't mean you mistyped, it just means your typing is getting echoed back at various intervals. In such situations, turn local echo off. But, we absolutely must have local echo checked for today's hacking experiment to work.

So back to our port surfing experiment. Next I try a little port surfing on DNS-01.AOL.COM. Here's how you port surf with Win95 telnet. On the connect box in telnet, as usual put the name of your victim computer in the "host name" box. Below this is the "port" box. You will see "telnet". Erase it. Put in any number you like from 1 up into the thousands. One of the ports most likely to talk back to you—and even let you give commands—is 25.

But I can't find any ports open on this AOL box. So it's a safe bet this computer is behind the AOL firewall. So we fall back on more serious hacker tricks.

Next we minimize the telnet program and go back to the DOS window. At the DOS prompt we give the command "tracert 152.163.999.42." Or we could give the command "tracert DNS- 01.AOL.COM." Either way we'll get the same result. This command will trace the route that a message takes, hopping from one computer to another, as it travels from my computer to this AOL domain server computer. Here's what we get:

```
C:\WINDOWS>tracert 152.163.999.42
Tracing route to dns-01.aol.com [152.163.999.42]
over a maximum of 30 hops:
 1 * * * Request timed out.
 2 150 ms 144 ms 138 ms 204.134.999.201
 3 375 ms 299 ms 196 ms glory-cyberport.fumexico.westnet.
net [204.134.999.33]
 4 271 ms * 201 ms enss365.fumexico.org [129.121.1.3]
 5 229 ms 216 ms 213 ms h4-0.cnss116.albuquer.t3.fu.net
[192.999.74.45]
 6 223 ms 236 ms 229 ms f2.t112-0.albuquer.t3.fu.net
[145.222.112.221]
 7 248 ms 269 ms 257 ms h14.t64-0.Houston.t3.fu.net
[145.223.65.9]
 8 178 ms 212 ms 196 ms h14.t80-1.St-Louis.t3.fu.net [145.223.65.14]
 9 316 ms * 298 ms h12.t60-0.Reston.t3.fu.net [145.223.61.9]
10 315 ms 333 ms 331 ms 207.25.134.189
11 * * * Request timed out.
12 * * * Request timed out.
13 207.25.134.189 reports: Destination net unreachable.
```

What the heck is all this stuff? The number to the left is the number of computers the route has been traced through. The "150 ms" stuff is how long, in thousandths of a second, it takes to send a message to and from that computer. Since a message can take a different length of time every time you send it, tracert times the trip three times. The "*" means the trip was taking too long so tracert said "forget it." After the timing info comes the name of the computer the message reached, first in a form that is easy for a human to remember, then in a form—numbers— that a computer prefers. "Destination net unreachable" may mean tracert hit a firewall.

Let's try the second AOL domain server.

```
C:\WINDOWS>tracert 152.163.999.56
Tracing route to dns-02.aol.com [152.163.999.56]
over a maximum of 30 hops:

 1 * * * Request timed out.
 2 142 ms 140 ms 137 ms 204.134.999.201
 3 246 ms 194 ms 241 ms glory- cyberport.fumexico.westnet.net
[204.134.999.33]
 4 154 ms 185 ms 247 ms enss365.fumexico.org [129.121.1.3]
 5 475 ms 278 ms 325 ms h4- 0.cnss116.albuquer.t3.fu.net
[192.999.74. 45]
 6 181 ms 187 ms 290 ms f2.t112- 0.albuquer.t3.fu.net
[145.222.112.22 1]
 7 162 ms 217 ms 199 ms h14.t64- 0.Houston.t3.fu.net [145.223.65.9]
 8 210 ms 212 ms 248 ms h14.t80-1.St- Louis.t3.fu.net [145.223.65.14]
 9 207 ms * 208 ms h12.t60- 0.Reston.t3.fu.net [145.223.61.9]
 10 338 ms 518 ms 381 ms 207.25.134.189 11 * * * Request timed out.
 12 * * * Request timed out.
 13 207.25.134.189 reports: Destination net unreachable.
```

Note that both tracerts wound up at the same computer named h12.t60-0.Reston.t3.fu.net. Since AOL is headquartered in Reston, Virginia, it's a good bet this is a computer that directly feeds stuff into AOL.

Here's a little more sleuthing. We notice that h12.t60- 0.Reston.t3.fu.net, h14.t80-1.St-Louis.t3.fu.net, h14.t64-0.Houston.t3.fu.net and Albuquer.t3.fu.net all have numerical names beginning with 140, and names that end with "fu.net." So it's a good guess that they all belong to the same company. Also, that "t3" in each name suggests these computers are routers on a T3 communications backbone for the Internet.

Next let's check out that final AOL domain server:

```
C:\WINDOWS>tracert 999.83.210.28
Tracing route to dns-aol.fu.net [999.83.210.28] over a maximum of
30 hops:
 1 * * * Request timed out.
 2 138 ms 145 ms 135 ms 204.134.999.201
 3 212 ms 191 ms 181 ms glory- cyberport.fumexico.westnet.net
[204.134.999.33]
 4 166 ms 228 ms 189 ms enss365.fumexico.org [129.121.1.3]
 5 148 ms 138 ms 177 ms h4- 0.cnss116.albuquer.t3.fu.net
[192.999.74.45]
 6 284 ms 296 ms 178 ms f2.t112- 0.albuquer.t3.fu.net
[145.222.112.221]
 7 298 ms 279 ms 277 ms h14.t64- 0.Houston.t3.fu.net [145.223.65.9]
 8 238 ms 234 ms 263 ms h14.t104- 0.Atlanta.t3.fu.net [145.223.65.18]
 9 301 ms 257 ms 250 ms dns-aol.fu.net [999.83.210.28]
Trace complete.
```

Hurrah, we finally got all the way through to something we can be pretty certain is an AOL box, and because we don't get a "host unreachable" message, it looks like it's outside the firewall! But see how tracert took a different path this time, going through Atlanta instead of St. Louis and Reston. But we are still looking at fu.net addresses with T3s, so this last nameserver is using the same network as the others.

Now what can we do next to get luser@aol.com really wondering if you could actually break into his account? We're going to do some port surfing on this last AOL domain name server!

Maximize the telnet window. Click on Connect, then Remote System. Then enter the name of that last AOL domain server, dns-aol.fu.net. Below it, for Port choose Daytime. It will send back to you the day of the week, date and time of day in its time zone.

Aha! We now know that dns-aol.fu.net is exposed to the world, with at least one open port, heh, heh. It is definitely a prospect for further port surfing. And now your friend is wondering, how did you get something out of that computer?

 Newbie note: If everyone who reads this telnets to the daytime ports of AOL gateway computers, the sysadmins will say "Whoa, I'm under heavy attack by hackers!!! There must be some evil exploit for the daytime service! I'm going to close this port pronto!" Then you'll all email me complaining the hack doesn't work. Please, try this hack out on different computers and don't all beat up on AOL.

Let's check out that Reston computer. In telnet we select Remote Host again and enter the name h12.t60-0.Reston.t3.fu.net. We try some port surfing without success. This is a seriously locked down box! What do we do next?

First we uncheck that "local echo" feature, then telnet back to whois.internic. We ask about this fu.net outfit that offers links to AOL:

```
[vt100] InterNIC  whois fu.net
Connecting to the rs Database . . . . . .
Connected to the rs Database
FU CO+RE Systems, Inc. (FU-DOM)
 100 Clearbrook Road
 Elmsford, NY 10523

Domain Name: FU.NET

 Administrative Contact:
 Hershman, Ittai (IH4) ittai@FU.NET
 (914) 789-5337
 Technical Contact:
 FU Network Operations Center (FU-NOC)
noc@fu.net
 1-800-456-6300
 Zone Contact:
 FU Hostmaster (FU-ORG) hostmaster@FU.NET
 (800)999-6300 fax: (914)999-5310
 Record last updated on 03-Jan-97.
 Record created on 27-Sep-90.
 Domain servers in listed order:

NS.fu.NET 192.999.99.100
NIS.fu.NET 147.225.99.2
```

If you wanted to be a really evil hacker you could call that 800 number and try to social engineer a password out of somebody who works for this network. But that wouldn't be nice and there is nothing legal you can do with fu.net passwords. And Happy Hacker is a book on legal hacking, right?

Anyhow, you get the idea of how you can hack around gathering info that leads to the computer that handles anyone's email.

More Cheap Win95 Hacks: Ping

What else can you do with your online connection and Win 95? How about finding out whether a computer is alive and well on a network, and how long it takes to get messages between you and that computer prompt. Give the command:

```
C:\windows>ping hostname
```

where "hostname" is the address of some Internet computer.

For example:

```
C:\WINDOWS>ping fumexicobar.com
Pinging fumexicobar.com [999.59.999.165] with 32 bytes of data:
Reply from 999.59.999.165: bytes=32 time=233ms TTL=60
Reply from 999.59.999.165: bytes=32 time=190ms TTL=60
Reply from 999.59.999.165: bytes=32 time=176ms TTL=60
Reply from 999.59.999.165: bytes=32 time=144ms TTL=60
```

"Bytes=" tells you the size of the ping datagram your Win95 box generated to send to fumexicobar.com. A computer on that ISP's network echoed back the same datagram to your box. The time it took for that echo to get back ranged from 233 milliseconds ot 144 milliseconds.

The nice guy thing to use ping for is to tell whether a computer is up and running on a network, and if so, how long does it take to talk back and forth with it. But there are also bad things to do with pings. It turns out Win95 is about the baddest box there is for playing with ping.

In the chapter *Hacker Wars on IRC* you will see that flood ping can be used as a major—and illegal—denial of service weapon.

The worst of all is killer ping, also known as the ping of death. It's a good way to lose your job and end up in jail. If you happened to know the address of one of Saddam Hussein's military computers, however, you might want to give the command:

```
c:\windows\ping -l 65510 saddam_hussein's.computer
```

Note that -l is minus the letter "l", not the number one.

Don't really do this to a real computer without the owner's permission! Some, but not all, computers will crash and either remain hung or reboot when they get this ping. Others will continue working cheerily along, and then suddenly go under hours later.

YOU CAN GO TO JAIL WARNING: Even if killer ping is only a one line Win95 hack, if you use it to crash a computer without the owner's permission, you are breaking the law.

Okay, okay, you really have to try out killer ping? You can always find out whether it will work on your own computer. First try an ordinary ping on yourself. (You don't need to be online to do this.) Your own computer is always called localhost or 127.0.0.1, so enter either of these after the ping command like this:

```
C:\WINDOWS ping -f localhost
Pinging anteros [127.0.0.1] with 32 bytes of data:
Reply from 127.0.0.1: bytes=32 time=1ms TTL=32
Reply from 127.0.0.1: bytes=32 timems TTL=32
Reply from 127.0.0.1: bytes=32 timems TTL=32
Reply from 127.0.0.1: bytes=32 timems TTL=32
```

Evil Genius Tip: "Anteros" is the name I gave my computer when I configured it for Network Neighborhood. Here's how to name your computer, regardless of whether you are on a LAN:
> 1) Click "start," then "settings," then "control panel," then "network."
> 2) On the "network" window click the "identification" tab. In the box "computer name" give your computer its name.

You can really give your friends a laugh—or a scare—by choosing a creative, cough, cough, name for your computer.

Now let's try out that killer ping on your own computer. First, just in case, make sure you aren't running anything that you would hate to have crashed.

```
C:\WINDOWS>ping -l 65510 localhost
Pinging anteros [127.0.0.1] with 65510 bytes of data:
Request timed out.
Request timed out.
Request timed out.
Request timed out.
```

Why did it time out? That extra added -l 65510 creates a giant datagram. To be exact, a datagram 65510 bytes long. Your computer, being a Win95, probably did what mine did and told that ping to go to heck. But some computers, when asked to send back a datagram that big, get horribly confused and simply crash.

What is really cool about killer ping is that it is extremely difficult to create on any of those Super Duper hacker computers, but is just that simple one line command on Win95. Hah!

If you want all the gory details on the killer ping exploit (also known as the 'ping of death'), including how to protect computers from it, check out *http://www.soph-ist.demon.co.uk/ping*.

Fortunately most systems administrators have patched things nowadays so that killer ping won't work. But just in case your ISP or LAN at work or school isn't protected, don't test it without your sysadmin's approval!

Other TCP/IP and local area network commands hidden in DOS include:

- **ARP** IP-to-physical address translation tables
- **FTP** File transfer protocol. This one is really lame. Don't use it. Get a shareware Ftp program from one of the download sites listed below.
- **NBTSTAT** Displays current network info—super to use on your own ISP
- **NETSTAT** Similar to Nbstat
- **NET** A tool for Windows for Workgroups, Netware, Win95 and WinNT networks
- **ROUTE** Manages router tables—router hacking is considered extra elite.

Since these are semi-secret commands, you can't get any details on how to use them from the DOS help menu. But there are help files hidden away for these commands.

- For arp, nbtstat, ping and route, to get help just type in the command and hit enter.
- For netstat you have to give the command "netstat ?" to get help.
- For net, ask "net ?"
- Telnet has a help option on the tool bar.
- For ftp, type "?" at the "ftp>" prompt after you've started it.

Here's an example of the route command:

```
C:\WINDOWS>route -f print
Active Routes:
 Network Address Netmask Gateway Address
Interface Metric
 127.0.0.0 255.0.0.0 127.0.0.1 127.0.0.1 1
 999.59.176.0 255.255.255.0 999.59.176.187 999.59.176.187 1
 999.59.176.187 255.255.255.255 127.0.0.1 127.0.0.1 1
 999.59.176.255 255.255.255.255 999.59.176.187 999.59.176.187 1
 224.0.0.0 224.0.0.0 999.59.176.187 999.59.176.187 1
 255.255.255.255 255.255.255.255 999.59.176.187 999.59.176.187 1
```

For serious fun, "route add" is used to add routes to the table, and "route delete" will delete routes from the table. Of course you need to know where these router databases are located to change them. The route command help file conveniently explains, "All symbolic names used for destination or gateway are looked up in the network and host name database files NETWORKS and HOSTS, respectively."

YOU CAN GET PUNCHED IN THE NOSE, FIRED AND BUSTED WARNING:
If you can figure out how use these commands on a LAN where your are not the sysadmin, think twice. The sysadmin will strenuously dissapprove if you change the router tables.

Hacker Programs that Run on Win95

Do you want to do serious hacking that requires commands other than these we just covered? But you don't want to use Unix? Shame on you! But, heck, even though

I usually have one or two Unix shell accounts plus Walnut Creek Slackware Linux on my home computer, I still like to hack from Windows. This is because I'm ornery. So you can be ornery, too.

You can download a free WinNT password cracker, L0phtcrack! To download, go to *http://l0pht.com*. (Note that is the number "0", not the letter "O" in l0pht.) There are versions of this program that run on Win95 and even DOS.

YOU CAN GO TO JAIL WARNING: If you use L0phtcrack to break into someone else's system, you are just asking to get busted.

How would you like to trick your friends into thinking their NT box has crashed when it really hasn't? This prank program can be downloaded from *http://www.osr.com*.

YOU CAN GET PUNCHED IN THE NOSE WARNING: People sometimes get really mad when they think their computer has crashed and it turns out to be your idea of a joke.

Next cool hack: try automated port surfing from Windows! Since there are thousands of possible ports that may be open on any computer, it could take days to fully explore even just one computer by hand. A good answer to this problem is the "NetCop" automated port scanner, which can be found at *http://www.netcop.com/*. Another dynamite port scanner is "What's Up," available at *http://www.ip-switch.com*. This program does a lot more than simply scan ports—it maps entire subnets.

If you want to do really serious hacking, you should learn to program in C and Perl. C compilers for Windows are common. You can download a Windows Perl interpreter from the Perl Home Page, *http://www.perl.com*.

So far we have hardly begun to explore all the wonderful Windows hacking tools out there. It would take megabytes to write even one sentence about each and every one of them. But you're a hacker, so you'll enjoy exploring dozens more of these nifty programs yourself. Following is a list of sites where you can download lots of free and more or less harmless programs that can help you in your hacker career:

- *ftp://ftp.cdrom.com*
- *ftp://ftp.coast.net*
- *http://www.supernet.net/cwsapps/cwsa.html*
- *http://www.tucows.com*
- *http://www.windows95.com/apps/*

Warning: there are lots of bad Win95 freebie programs floating around. What do I mean by "bad"? How about programs containing viruses and trojan horses that will thoroughly trash your computer. Even a well-meaning programmer may write a program that runs fine on his box but will install a .dll file on yours that wrecks your system. So whenever you install a new freebie hacker program, make sure you have completely backed up your system first. Heck, I even save CMOS settings!

But even so, only once have I had a problem from any Win95 program I have downloaded. The majority of them are fun and safe. Please, before you read any further in this book, try out a bunch of these programs. Why put off your hacking fun?

Section 1, Chapter 4
Mac Hacking

"Can I hack with a Mac?"
The answer is yes. With a vengeance!

Even better, unlike your compadres who hack from Win95, it is easy to be proud to be a Mac user. The Macintosh boasts one of the most secure network operating systems known. Because of this, despite the fact that only about 2% of all personal computers are Macs, about one in every five of the world's webservers run on Macs, and over half of all Web sites are developed on Macs.

In this chapter you will learn:
- Why Macs are so hard to crack
- What Mac tools you need to hack other computers, and where to get them

The Appleshare Server, used to run Mac LANs, is also famous. Überhackers swear it is almost impossible to break into an Appleshare LAN unless one installs it with a backdoor.

 Newbie note: A backdoor is a type of program that hackers use to get into a computer system without going through the normal security procedures.

Just how secure are Macs? In February 1997, the Swedish company Infinit Information AB (http://infinit.se/) announced a contest to break into their Web server. It was a Power Mac 8500/150 with 64 megs of RAM, 2 gig HD on a 10 baseT Ethernet LAN. The server software was WebSTAR 2.0 with minimum plug-ins. Operating system was Mac OS 7.6 running Apple Script. No firewalls. No router filter. Just an unprotected Mac Web server.

To make a break-in worth the effort, they offered a prize of 10,000 Krona (roughly $1,350 US). After nearly three weeks, no one had come close to breaking in. So Infinit added another 740 Krona ($100) to the pot. "I feel pretty safe about the server," said Joakim Jardenberg, the Infinit employee who ran the contest. Infinit did, however, put an April 10 deadline on the contest.

Infinit probably felt pretty safe because only a few months before, Quarterdeck, the maker of the WebSTAR server software, had offered $10,000 US to anyone who could crack into it. WebSTAR won.

When the Infinit contest was first announced, elite hacker Bronc Buster advised us that a Mac Web server "has NO telnet process/program to attach to, and FTPs are not possible. Because of this lack of a 'shell' to get into, so you may change their web site . . . it leaves very little possibility . . . In addition to this, if you COULD somehow attach, you would need to be running a Mac, with AppleTalk of course, and be using a Mac TCP/IP stack. The only 'hole' . . . (is) the cgi-bin directory, which on a Mac server is not a hole at all . . . If someone does hack it, I'll eat a bug."

So did Bronc eat a bug? No way. The Mac won.

This got some Super Duper hackers bent out of shape. Angry that they couldn't prove how super they were in this contest, shortly after it ended they launched a wave of denial of service (DOS) attacks on Mac servers. But as you will discover elsewhere in this book, denial of service attacks are easy, lame, and may be the biggest threat to the Internet.

What do we learn from this contest? Macs are tough to break into and vandalize. Yet, as another elite hacker, StriderX, says, "The easiest way to hack a Mac is FROM a Mac."

So if you hack from your Mac, you can be proud to know that you are working from what is almost certainly the most hacker-proof box in the world. Yet you can use your Mac to mess around with all those Windows, Unix, VMS etc. boxes out there. You will be even better able to hack Macs than all those Unix weenies out there. Heck, working with your own Mac you may someday be able to win one of those contests to break into a Mac Web server. Yes, you Apple types are superbly positioned to become the best hackers on the planet.

Essential Mac Hacking Tools

So what are the beginner basics for Mac hacking on the Internet? First, you need to accumulate some essential tools. The biggest problem with Macs is that they don't have all the built-in hacking tools that Unix and Windows systems boast. But this problem is easy to fix. A good place to start is with the Mac Internet FAQ at *http://www.pacificcoast.net/macfaq1.html.*

Wait, you say, if I download all those free proggies, I'll fill up my hard drive three times over! OK, we'll be merciful to your hard drive. Here are the basics you'll need for Mac hacking:

1) An on-line service that will allow to you to see pretty pictures when you browse the Web — this proves that it gives you a PPP connection. Free PPP is great for this, but even AOL's Mac software will do. Get Free PPP and lots of other great Mac freebies at *http://www.elsinc.com.*

2) Once you have a PPP session going, use NCSA Telnet or Nifty Telnet for port surfing and lots of other fun. You can get telnet programs free at *http://www.share-*

ware.com, http://www.download.com, http://www.filez.com, or *http://www.data-beast.com/*.

4) Load up on the basic Internet probe tools: ping, traceroute, whois, nslookup, and port scanners. Get them free from *http://www.shareware.com, http://www.download.com*, or *http://www.filez.com*.

5) Are you serious? Really serious about hacking? Partition your hard disk, or add a second one, and install a Unix type operating system such as MkLinux from *http://www.mklinux.apple.com/*, or MacBSD from *http://www.macbsd.com/*. For those of you who have a Power PC CPU and want Unix and Mac OS running concurrently, try Mach 10 by Tenon Corp., *http://www.tenon.com/*.

6) Blow your socks off. Blow your friends' socks off. Buy the Whacked Mac CD-ROM, which carries serious hacker exploit programs, from *http://l0pht.com/warez.html* (that's the number "0", not the letter "O"). We don't normally recommend hacker exploit programs because they often contain nasty surprises. But the L0pht has an excellent reputation.

7) StriderX tells us "Get MacPerl (a Mac version of the Perl programming language). Its socket abilities are outstanding. It can do absolutely anything but Internet Control Message Protocol (ICMP) attacks, and that's coming soon, if I can help it. It's unbelievably fast, and if you can learn it, it'll do anything. My password cracker tries 2,220 passwords/minute, on an 040/33 (like a 486/33, pretty much) and port scanners are a cinch. Winnuke and anything else are just too easy to do. I can't say enough about it."

YOU CAN GO TO JAIL WARNING: Denial of service attacks such as ICMP and Winnuke as well as theft of passwords are against the law in the US and many other countries.

Next, would you like to learn how to subvert and break into your own Mac just like Win95 people can with their boxes? Sorry. Mac is way too good for those tricks. Your Mac is a powerful tool for messing with those hapless computers in the outside world, but is no good for torturing in front of your friends. Be grateful you're a Mac hacker.

Section 1, Chapter 5
How to Become a Hero in Computer Lab

They came for Daniel Gilkerson in the middle of class. He knew why. He was the school Überhacker.

But Daniel wasn't worried. He figured it would turn out to be good news, and he was right. They had come to make him security manager of the Rio Rancho High School computer system. Seven hundred computers and all networked.

Within days he had found one simple hack that was key to disabling security on all the Win95 boxes on their NT server system. On bootup, when the login screen appears, don't enter the password. Hold down the control key and hit the escape key (or, if the computer has a "hot" key, hit that). This brings up a task window. Click on "run" and you can run any program on that computer. You can edit and get rid of any controls, including the NT Server's "Policy Editor," which is supposed to control what programs students can run.

You've probably heard of lots of kids getting in big trouble for hacking school computers. Yet others, like Daniel, are also hackers, but end up being heroes. What makes the difference?

In this Chapter you will learn how to:
- Customize the animated logo on Internet Explorer
- Circumvent security programs through Internet Explorer
- Circumvent security programs through any Microsoft Office programs
- Circumvent FoolProof
- Circumvent Full Armor
- Solve the web babysitter problem
- Break into absolutely any school computer.
- Keep clueless kiddie hackers from messing up your school computer

This chapter will give you some tips for safely proving just how good you are, and maybe even showing your hacker teacher buddies a thing or two. Best of all, this chapter can help you become another hacker hero—to your teachers.

But I would feel really bad if someone were to use the tips in this chapter to mess up his or her life.

> **YOU CAN MESS UP YOUR LIFE WARNING: In most countries kids don't have nearly the legal protections that adults have. If you get involved in a hacker gang at school and you guys get caught, you can easily get expelled from school or even arrested. Even if the authorities don't have good proof of your guilt. Even if you are innocent. Arghhh!**

First task of this chapter, then, is how to find teachers who would love to play hacker games with you and give you free run of the school's computer systems. Whoa, you say, now this is some social engineering challenge! But actually this isn't that hard.

Coyote suggests, "in many cases you may find that if you prove yourself responsible (i.e., not acting like a jerk in class and not hacking to be cool) it will be easier to gain the trust of the teacher and subsequently gain the job of helping with the systems. And once you reach this level you are almost guaranteed that you will know more about system management, and of course hacking, than you could have learned by simply breaking in."

Here's the first thing you need to remember. Your teachers are overworked. If they get mad at hackers, it is because hackers keep on messing things up. Guess who gets to stay late at work fixing the mess students make when they break into school computers? Right, it's usually your computer lab teachers.

Think about it. Your computer lab teachers might really, really, like the idea of having you help with the work. The problem is—will they dare to trust you?

Karl Schaffarczyk warns, "I nearly got chucked out of school (many years ago) for pulling up a DOS prompt on a system that was protected against such things." Sheesh, for just getting a DOS prompt? But the problem is that your teachers go to a lot of effort to set school computers up so they can be used to teach classes. The minute they realize you know how to get to DOS, they know you could mess things up so bad they will have to spend a sleepless night putting that computer back together. Teachers hate to stay up all night. Imagine that!

So if you really want to work a deal where you become supreme ruler and hero-in-chief of your school's computers, don't start by getting caught! Don't start even by showing your teacher, "Look how easy it is to get a DOS prompt!" Remember, some authorities will immediately kick you out of school or call the cops.

Honest, many people are terrified of teenage hackers. You can't really blame them, either, when you consider those news stories. Here are some examples of stories your school authorities have probably read:

```
13 FEBRUARY 1997 Hackers are reported to be using servers at
Southampton University to circulate threatening emails (that) ...
instruct recipients to cancel credit cards, claiming their security
has been breached.
(c) VNU Business Publications Limited, 1997
```

```
NETWORK NEWS 7/5/97 P39 A teenager was fined an equivalent of US$350
for paralysing US telephone switchboards...The unnamed teenager made
around 60,000 calls...
```

Scary, huh? It's not surprising that nowadays some people are so afraid of hackers that they blame almost anything on us. For example, in 1997, authorities at a naval base at first blamed attackers using high-energy radio waves for computer screens that froze. Later investigators learned that ship radars, not hackers, were freezing screens.

So instead of getting mad at teachers who are terrified of hackers, give them a break. The media is inundating them with scare stories. Plus they have probably spent a lot of time fixing messes made by kiddie hackers. Your job is to show them that you are the good guy. Your job is to show them you can make life better for them by giving you free run of the school computers.

This same basic technique also will work with your ISP. If you offer to help for free, and if you convince them you are responsible, you can get the right to have root (or administrative) access to almost any computer system. For example, I was talking with the owner of the ISP one day, who complained how overworked he was. I told him I knew a high school sophomore who had been busted for hacking but had reformed. This fellow, I promised, would work for free in exchange for the root password on one of his boxes. Next day they did the deal.

So try it. Find an overworked teacher. Or overworked owner of an ISP. Offer to show him or her that you know enough to help take care of those computers.

But how do you prove you know enough for the job?

If you start out by telling your computer lab teacher that you know how to break into the school computers, some teachers will get excited and suspend you from school. Just in case your teacher is the kind who gets scared by all those hacker news stories, don't start out by talking about breaking in! Instead, start with showing them, with their permission, a few cheap tricks.

Cheap Internet Explorer Tricks

A good place to start is with Internet Explorer.

What could be more harmless—yet effective at showing off your talents—than changing the animated logos on Internet Explorer (IE) and Netscape?

You could do it the easy way with Microangelo, available from *ftp://ftp.im-pactsoft.com/pub/impactsoft/ma21.zip*. But since you are a hacker, you may want to impress your teachers by doing it the hacker way.

1) Bring up Paint.

2) Click "image," then "attributes."

3) Choose width = 40, height=480, units in pels.

4) Make a series of pictures, each 40x40 pels. One way to do this is to open a new picture for each one and set attributes to width = 40 and height = 40. Then cut and paste each one into the 40x480 image.

Figure 1: Here's where you control what animated logos show up in IE. "BackBitmap" holds a previous haxor graphic and "BrandBitmap" holds a new haxor graphic.

5) Make the top 40x40 image be the one you want to have sit there when IE is doing nothing. The next three are shown once when a download starts, and the rest are played in a loop until the download is done. You must have an even number of images for this to work.

6)Now run the Registry editor. See *Chapter 1* for instructions.

7) Click to highlight the subkey "HKEY_CURRENT_USER\Software\Microsoft\IE\Toolbar"

8) On the task bar above, click "Edit," then "Find." Type "Brandbitmap" in the find window.

9) Now double click on BrandBitmap to get a dialog window. Type the path and file name of your custom animated graphic into it.

So let's say you set up a flaming skull that rotates when you run IE. Your teacher is impressed. Now she wants you to put it back the way it was before. This is easy. Just open up BrandBitmap, and delete the name of your animation file. Windows Explorer will then automatically revert to the saved graphic in BackBitmap.

Let's now show your teacher something that is a little bit scary. Did you know that Internet Explorer (IE) can be used to break some Windows babysitter programs? Your school might be running one of them. If you play this right, you can win points by trashing that babysitter program.

Yes, you could just get to work on those babysitter programs using the tips of *Chapter 2*. But we will look at a new way to get around them in this chapter, using IE. The advantage of using IE when your teacher is anxiously looking over your shoulder is that you could just "accidentally" stumble on some cool stuff, instead of looking like a dangerous hacker. Then you could show that you know how to take advantage of that security flaw.

Besides, if it turns out the security program you try to override is well enough written to keep IE from breaking it, you don't look like a dummy.

Evil Genius tip: People are less afraid of you if you type sloowwwlllllyyyyyyyyyy.

The dirty little secret is that IE actually is a Windows shell program. That means it is an alternative to the Win95 desktop. From IE you may launch any program. IE operates much like the Program Manager and Windows Explorer that come with the Windows 95 and Windows NT operating systems.

Yes, from the IE shell you can run any program on your computer—unless the security program you are trying to break has anticipated this attack. With a little ingenuity you may be able to even gain control of your school's LAN. But don't try that just yet!

Newbie note: A shell is a program that mediates between you and the operating system.

The big deal about IE being a Windows shell is that Microsoft never told anyone that it was in fact a shell. The security problems that are plaguing IE are mostly a consequence of it turning out to be a shell. By contrast, the Netscape and Mosaic Web browsers are not quite such full-featured shells. This makes them safer to use. But you can still do some interesting things with them to break into a Win95 box. Experiment and have fun!

Evil Genius tip: Is your school network run from an NT server? Most of the hacks in this chapter may work if it is running Policy Editor. But as we saw above, you can get around Policy Editor.

To use IE as a Win95 shell, bring it up just like you would if you were going to surf the Web. If your computer is set to automatically initiate an Internet connection, you can kill it. You don't need to be online for this to work.

Now here are a few fun suggestions. In the space where you would normally type in the URL you want to surf, instead type in c:.

Whoa, look at all those file folders that come up on the screen. Now for fun, click "Program Files" then click "Accessories" then click "Paint." All of a sudden Paint is running. Now paint your teacher who is watching this hack surprised.

Next close all that stuff and get back to the URL window in IE. Click on the Windows folder, then click on Regedit.exe to start it up. Export the password file (it's in HKEY_CLASSES_ROOT). Open it in Word Pad. Remember, the ability to control the Registry of a server is the key to controlling the network it serves. Show this to your teacher and tell her that you're going to use IE to change all the school's password files. In a few hours the Secret Service will be fighting with the FBI on your front lawn over who gets to try to bust you. Okay, only kidding here.

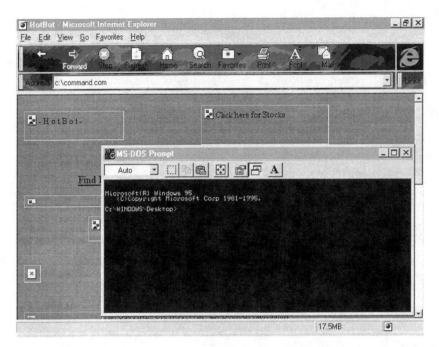

Figure 2: IE has just launched DOS 7.0. Now the computer is to-tally at your mercy, muhahaha.

No, maybe it would be a bit better to tell your teacher that if you can edit the registry, you can get total control over that computer. And maybe much more. Suggest that the school delete IE from all its computers and use Netscape instead. You are on the road to being a hero.

If you actually do edit the Registry, you had better know how to revert to its backup, or else undo your changes. Otherwise you will be making more work for the computer lab teacher instead of less work. Remember, the objective is to prove to your teachers you can cut how much work they have to do!

What if the school babysitter program won't let you run regedit.exe? Try typing c:/command.com. Then see *Chapter 2* for how to edit the Registry from DOS.

If you have gotten this far with IE, next try entering r:/ or w:/ or z: etc. to see if you can access the disk of a network server. Be sure to do this with your teacher watching and with her permission to try to access network computers. If you succeed, now you have a really good reason to ask her to take IE off all the school computers. This is because you have just taken over the entire school LAN. But you are a hero because you have done it to save your school from those mean kiddie hackers who change grades and class assignments. By now you have a great shot at getting a volunteer job running the school's computer systems. Before you know it, you and your friends will be openly playing Quake at school—and the authorities will consider it a small price to pay for your expertise.

Cheap Tricks with Microsoft Office

You also can run a Windows shell from several Microsoft Office programs. Remember, once you get a shell, you have a good shot at disabling security programs.

The following exploit works with Microsoft Word, Excel, and Powerpoint. To use them get into a Windows shell:

1) Click "help", then "About Microsoft (name of program inserted here)," then "System Info..."

2) This brings up a window which includes a button labeled "run." Click "run" and put in anything you want, for example regedit.exe! (That is, unless the security program you are trying to break has a way to disable this.)

Microsoft Access is a bit harder. The "run" button only gives a few choices. One of them is File Manager. But File Manager is also a Windows shell. From it you can run any program. (That is, unless the security program you are trying to break has a way to disable this.)

How to Circumvent FoolProof[1]

There is usually a hotkey to turn off FoolProof. One young hacker reports his school uses shift-alt-X (hold down the shift and alt keys at the same time, then press the "x" key.) Of course other schools may have other arrangements.

If you get the hotkey right, a sound may play, and a lock in the lower-right corner should open for 20-30 seconds.

Dante tells how he managed to get out of a hot spot with an even better hack of Fool Proof. "My computer science teacher asked me to show her exactly *how* I managed to print the 'the universe revolves around me' image I made to all the network printers in the school . . ." So he had her watch while he did the deed.

YOU CAN GET PUNCHED IN THE NOSE WARNING: Dante was lucky that his teacher was understanding. In some schools a harmless joke like this would be grounds for expulsion.

Here is how Dante was able to disable FoolProof.

1) First, break into the Windows box using one of the techniques of Chapter 2. Warning—don't try the soldering iron bit. Your teacher will faint.

3) Now you can edit the autoexec.bat and config.sys files. (Be sure to back them up.) In config.sys delete the line device=fp, and in autoexec.bat, delete fptsr.exe.

4) Run regedit.exe. You have to remove FoolProof from the Registry, too. Use the Regedit search feature to find references to Fool Proof.

5) Find the Registry backup files and make copies with different names just in case. Making a mistake with the Registry can cause spectacular messes!

---

1   FoolProof and Full Armor are babysitting programs popular in high schools and computer stores where people don't want you to mess with the computer.

6) Save the registry, and reboot. FoolProof won't load.

7) To put things back the way they were, rename the backup files.

You are now the school hero security expert.

How to Circumvent Full Armor

"I ran up against this program 8 months ago at school, they attempted to prevent people from writing to the hard drive. It presented itself as a challenge . . . for about 5 minutes."—Dave Manges.

Here's how Dave did the deed:

1) In the properties of the program it mentions the thread file (can't remember the name of the file) it was something.vbx

2) Okay . . . this is easy enough, open notepad, open something.vbx

3) Just because I can't write to the hard drive doesn't mean I can't edit something already there, delete the first character from the file.

4) The file (opened in notepad) looks like garbage, but if memory serves the first letter was M.

5) Save the File and restart the computer, it should come up with an error like "Unable to Initialize Full Armor".

6) Now you can go into add/remove programs and uninstall it.

Again, remember to back up all files before changing them so you can put the computer back the way you found it.

Solve the Web Babysitter Problem

Suppose your next goal is to get rid of Web babysitter programs. This can be a tough job. Think about it from the point of view of the teachers. If even one kid were to complain to her parents that she had seen dirty movies running on another kid's monitor in computer lab, your school would be in big trouble. So merely blasting your way through those babysitter programs with techniques such as those you learned in *Chapter 2* will solve the problem for only a short time—and get you and your teacher and your school in trouble.

But once again you can be a hero. You can help your teachers discover the Web sites that are being blocked by those babysitter programs. They may be surprised to find out they block lots more than naughty pictures. They often secretly censor certain political sites, too.

If your school is running CYBERsitter, you can really beat up on it. CYBERsitter has encrypted its list of banned sites, which include those with political beliefs they don't like. But you can download a program to decrypt this list at: *http://peace-fire.org. (This Web site is maintained by a teen organization, Peacefire, devoted to freedom of speech.)*

When your teacher discovers the hidden political agenda of CYBERsitter, you are a hero. Unless, of course, your teacher agrees with CYBERsitter's tactics. If so, you can probably find other teachers in your school who will be appalled by CYBERsitter.

How about IE's built-in site blocking system? It is harder to uncover what it blocks because it works by limiting the viewer to web sites that have "certificates" provided by a number of organizations. If a site hasn't gone to the effort of getting a certificate, IE can keep you from seeing it.

Of course, after reading *Chapter 2*, you can quickly disable the IE censorship feature. But instead of doing this, how about directing your teacher to *http://peace-fire.org* and let him or her follow the links? Then perhaps the authorities at your school will be ready to negotiate with you to find a way to give you freedom to surf without causing trouble with other kids in the computer lab or library who can't help but notice what may be on your monitor.

How to Break into Absolutely any School Computer

As you know from *Chapter 2*, you can break into any computer to which you have physical access. The trick is to figure out, once you have complete control, how to disable whatever program is giving you a hard time.

There are only a few possible ways for these programs to work. Maybe all you need to do is Control-Alt-Delete and remove it from the list of active programs that brings up.

If this doesn't work, if you can get into DOS, you can edit any files. See Chapter 2 for details on all the ways to get to DOS. Or you may only need to access regedit.exe. You can run it from either DOS or, depending on how good your problem program is, from Windows.

Once you can edit files, the ones you are likely to need to alter are autoexec.bat, config.sys, anything with the extension .pwl or .lnk, \windows\startm~1\pro-grams\startup, and the Registry. Look for lines with suspicious names that remind you of the name of the program you want to disable.

YOU CAN GET PUNCHED IN THE NOSE WARNING: Of course you could do something obvious like "format c:" and reinstall only what you want on that box. But this will make your teachers throw fits. Mega fits. If you want to be a hero, make sure that you can always return any school computer to the way it was before you hacked it.

When you are done, turn the victim computer off and then back on again instead of a reboot with power still on. This will get rid of anything lingering in RAM that could defeat your efforts.

Keep Clueless Kiddie Hackers from Messing up Your School Computers

Now that you have shown your teachers that you can break absolutely any security on any box to which you have physical access, what next? Do you just leave your teachers feeling awed and helpless? Or do you help them?

There is a reason why they have security systems on your school's computers. You would be amazed at all the things clumsy or malicious users can do.

You can do your school a world of good by using your hacking skills to fix things so that security works much better. Here are some basic precautions that you can offer to your teachers to lock down school computers. (See *Chapter 2* for instructions on most of these.)

1) Disable all boot keys.
2) Password the CMOS. If it already has a password, change it. Give your teacher the new password.
3) Remove or disable any programs that allow the user to get to regedit or dos.
4) Programs that allow hot keys to circumvent security should be changed, if possible, to disable hot keys.
5) Remove programs that can't be made safe.
6) Don't make it possible for Win95 computers to access sensitive data on a network disk. (The passwords can be easily grabbed and decoded.)
7) Try really, really hard to persuade the school administration to replace Win95 with WinNT.

With experimentation you will figure out much more for yourself.

Since Win95 is a totally insecure operating system, this will be a losing battle. But at least you will be able to keep secure enough that those students who do break in will know enough to not do anything disastrous by accident. As for malicious school hackers, sigh, there will always be kewl d00dz who think "format c:" shows they are, ahem, kewl d00dz.

You may also have a problem with school administrators who may feel that it is inconvenient to set up such a secure system. They will have to give up the use of lots of convenient programs. Upgrading to Windows NT will cost money. Try explaining to them how much easier it will be to keep those wannbe hacker vandals from trashing the school computers or using them to visit Bianca's Smut Shack.

Are you ready to turn your hacking skills into a great reputation at school? Are you ready to have the computer lab teachers begging to learn from you? Are you ready to have the entire school computer system under your control—legally? You will, of course, only use the tricks of this chapter under the supervision of an admiring teacher, right? It sure is more fun than expulsion and juvenile court!

Section 1, Chapter 6
Hacker Wars on Internet Relay Chat

What's the big deal about Internet Relay Chat (IRC) and hackers? Sheesh, IRC is sooo easy to use . . . until you get on a channel where hacker wars reign. What the heck do you do to keep from getting clobbered over and over again?

If you are already an IRC regular, this chapter may not tell you much that's new. But there may be a few new tips here that should help you hone your skills.

If you've never used IRC, now may be the time to start. Don't let its reputation for being a war ground rampant with flamers scare you off. IRC is a great place to meet hackers. Check out our Happy Hacker Web page at http://www.happy-hacker.org for the latest good channels to hang out on.

In this chapter you will learn:
- IRC basics
- Where good IRC servers are for meeting other hackers
- IRC wars—the small time skirmishes
- When IRC wars go nuclear
- Defending against IRC attack

IRC Basics

But before you venture forth into this new world, first let's cover the basics of IRC. It allows a group of people to type messages back and forth on a screen in almost real time. Some IRC programs also allow you to send sounds like bells, a flushing toilet—you get the picture. It can be more fun than Usenet where it can take from minutes to days for people's replies to turn up. And unlike Usenet, if you say something you regret, it's soon gone from the screen. Ahem. That is, it will soon be gone if no one is logging the session.

In some ways IRC is like CB radio, with lots of folks flaming and making fools of themselves in unique and irritating ways. So don't expect to always see timeless wisdom and wit scrolling down your computer screen.

But because IRC is such an inexpensive way for people from all over the world to quickly exchange ideas, it is widely used by hackers. Also, given the wars, you can fight for control of IRC channels. So it can give you a good hacker workout.

To get on IRC you need both an IRC client program and you need to connect to a Web site or Internet Service Provider (ISP) that is running an IRC server program.

 Newbie note: Any program that uses a resource is called a "client." Any program that offers a resource is a "server." Your IRC client program runs on either your home computer or shell account computer and connects you to an IRC server program which runs on a remote computer somewhere on the Internet.

You may already have a client program for your computer given to you by your ISP. But if you don't, there are plenty of places to download them.

How do you get onto IRC? We'll use an example of a hacker channel that, as of this writing, is lots of fun: #haphacker on dal.net.

1) Before you do anything else, first check your IRC client to see what commands you will be able to give.

- Typical commands include finger, ping and whois. Although these are superficially similar to the finger, ping and whois commands covered elsewhere in this book, they are not the same. You can only use these commands on your IRC connection, and not to get out into the Internet.
- You might also have the option of far more exotic commands, some of which are harmless fun, and others which may allow you to even commit computer crimes. It would be really dumb to accidentally commit computer crimes with an IRC program you don't fully understand. "But officer, I kept on hitting the wrong key!"
- The way your IRC program can tell that you are giving a command instead of typing in chat is for you to put a forward slash at the beginning of a new line. For example, to find out how long the delay is on someone's connection to your IRC channel, give the command "/ping."

2) Look for something that says "sign in." A typical IRC client program will have a sign-in screen that will ask you for your server, port, nick name and user name.

- You will usually find a list of servers you may choose from, or you can enter one not on the list.
- For port, the default is usually 6667. However, many IRC client programs are set up with a list of the well-known IRC servers and the ports they use. DALnet, for example, uses port 7000.
- You can pick any nickname before signing in. But if someone else on that server is already using it, you will have to choose another. You can change you nick while on an IRC channel, too. But people can abuse that power.

3) When you first log on, you will get a long message (usually) telling you the rules of the game. For example, the dal.net message carries the warning: "Flooding, nuking, spoofing, trading pirated software and/or kiddie porn are all FELONIES in the United States, and Banned on DALnet both inside and outside the United States.

They will cause you at least to lose your access to DALnet, but could result with you losing your Internet access and even going to jail. Please don't do ANY of them."

4) Now you can pick a channel.

- Different IRC nets may have channels with the same names as other IRC nets. But a channel in one net will not be connected to another. So if you find a channel you like, be sure to return to the same IRC net so you can get back together with the same folks on the right channel.
- You can either browse the available channels to find something that appeals to you, or pick one you know is good. Any channel called #hacker or #hack is usually really, really lame. When specifying a channel that is not on a menu, always put a # in front of the name.

5) You type your comments into one window, normally at the bottom, and send your messages by hitting Enter. Everyone's messages are displayed in another window. Scroll up this window to remind yourself of what people said awhile back, and down to make sure you don't miss new input. You can choose either to send your messages to everyone in the IRC channel, or send private messages.

6) A really good IRC client such as mIRC will let you be on several channels at the same time.

Where are good IRC servers for meeting other hackers?

Dalnet (specify irc.dal.net or dal.net as your server) is a network of IRC servers that hosts both #haphacker and #haphack. Try #haphacker first. It's a more friendly place, especially if you are a newbie. (Hope the neighborhood hasn't gone downhill by the time you read this.)

Undernet is one of the largest networks of IRC servers. The main purpose of Undernet is to be a friendly place with IRC wars under control. But this means, yes, lots of IRC cops! The operators of these IRC servers have permission to kill you not only from a channel but also from a server. Heck, they can ban you for good. They can even ban your whole domain.

 Newbie note: Here's why getting an entire domain banned is a Bad Thing. A domain is the last two (or sometimes three) parts of your email address. For example, aol.com is the domain name for America Online. If an IRC network were to ban the aol.com domain, that would mean every single person on America Online would be banned from it. If they find out it was you who made this happen . .

EFNet (Eris-Free Network) also links many IRC servers. It was originally started by the Eris FreeNet (ef.net). It is reputed to be a "war ground" where you might get a chance to really practice the IRC techniques we cover below. But even EFNet's IRC cops can get mad enough to kick and ban.

YOU CAN GET PUNCHED IN THE NOSE WARNING: If the sysadmins at your ISP were to find out that you had managed to get their entire domain banned from an IRC net on account of committing ICMP bombing or whatever, they will be

truly mad at you! You will be lucky if the worst that happens is that you lose your account. You'd better hope that word doesn't get out to all the IRC addicts on your ISP that you were the dude that got them all kicked out.

IRCNet is probably the same size if not larger than Undernet. IRCNet is basically the European/Australian split off from the old EFNet. But don't get the idea from this that IRC nets are only for locals. You will see people from all around the world on the larger nets. Yes, IRC is a world-wide phenomenon. Get on the right IRC network and you can be making friends with hackers on any continent of the planet.

There are at least 80 IRC networks in existence. To learn how to contact them, surf over to: *http://www.irchelp.org/*. You can locate additional IRC servers by surfing over to *http://hotbot.com* or *http://digital.altavista.com* and searching for "IRC server." Some IRC servers are ideal for the elite hacker, for example the l0pht server. (Note that is a "zero" not an "O" in l0pht.)

IRC War—the Small Time Skirmishes

But before you get too excited over trying out IRC, watch out. IRC is not always phun. Some d00dz aren't satisfied with using it to merely say naughty words and cast aspersions on people's ancestry and grooming habits. They get their laughs by kicking other people off IRC. Sometimes they even take down a entire IRC network. For example, in the summer of 1997, Undernet was wiped out for several days by incessant denial of service attacks.

The reason this goes on is because these 31337 IRC haxors are too chicken to start brawls in bars. So they beat up on people in cyberspace where they don't have to fret over getting ouchies.

Of course you could just decide your enemies can go to heck and abandon IRC. But let's say you'd rather hang in there. You may want to hang in there because if you want to make friends quickly in the hacker world, one of the best ways is over Internet Relay Chat (IRC).

We're going to show some simple, effective ways to keep these lusers from ruining your IRC sessions. However, first you'll need to know some of the ways you can get kicked off IRC by these bullies.

The simplest way to get in trouble is to accidentally give operator control ("op") of your IRC channel to an impostor whose goal is to kick you and your friends off. Remember, just because someone has the same nick as your friend doesn't mean it really is him or her. Not all IRC nets enforce a rule on not using other peoples' nicks.

To understand the op problem, you need to understand the powers of the op and how he or she gets them. The first person to start up a channel on an IRC server is automatically operator and has the power to kick people off or invite people in. Also, if the operator wants to, he or she may pass operator status on to someone else.

Ideally, when you leave the channel you would pass this status on to a friend your trust. You can't stay on IRC 24 hours seven days a week. (Some people try, though!)

Also, maybe someone who you think is your good buddy is begging you to please, please give him a turn being the operator. You may decide to op him or her to demonstrate friendship. But if you mess up and accidentally op a bad guy who is pretending to be someone you know and trust, your fun chat can become history.

One way to keep this all this obnoxious stuff from happening is to simply not op people you do not know. But this is easier said than done. It is a friendly thing to op to your buddies. You may not want to appear stuck up by refusing to op anyone. So if you are going to op a friend, how can you really tell that IRC dude is your friend?

Just because you recognize the nick (nickname), don't assume it's who you think it is! Check the host address associated with the nick by giving the command "/whois IRCnick" where "IRCnick" is the nickname of the person you want to check.

This "/whois" command will give back to you the email address belonging to the person using that nick. If you see, for example, "d***@wannabe.net" instead of the address you expected, say friend@cool.com, then DO NOT OP him. Make the person explain who he or she is and why the email address is different.

Warning! A really serious hacker could either spoof their email address or even join your IRC channel from a hacked account. So a whois alone will not always protect you.

But entering a fake nick when entering an IRC server is only the simplest of ways someone can sabotage an IRC session.

First let's consider the more innocuous types of flooding attacks on IRC. The purpose of flooding is to send so much garbage to a client that its connection to the IRC server either becomes useless or gets cut off.

Text flooding is the simplest attack. For example, you could just hold down the "x" key and hit enter from time to time. This would keep the IRC screen filled with your junk and scroll the others' comments quickly off the screen. However, text flooding is almost always unsuccessful because almost any IRC client (the program you run on your computer) has text flood control. Even if it doesn't, text must pass through an IRC server. Most IRC servers also have text flood filters.

Because text flooding is basically harmless, you are unlikely to suffer anything worse than getting banned or possibly K:lined for doing it. At least you can't go to jail for it!

Newbie note: "K:line" means to ban not just you, but anyone who is in your domain from an IRC server. For example, if you are a student at Giant State University with an email address of IRCd00d@giantstate.edu, then every person whose email address ends with "giantstate.edu" will also be banned. Obviously, getting k:lined is a Bad Thing.

Client to Client Protocol (CTCP) echo flooding is the most effective type of flood that isn't a felony. This is sort of like the ping you send to determine whether a host computer is alive. It is a command used within IRC to check to see if someone is still on your IRC channel.

How does the echo command work? To check whether someone is still on your IRC channel, give the command "/ctcp nick ECHO hello out there!" If "nick" (where "nick" is the IRC nickname of the person you are checking out) is still there, you get back "nick HELLO OUT THERE."

What has happened is that your victim's IRC client program has automatically echoed whatever message you sent.

But someone who wants to boot you off IRC can use the CTCP echo command to trick your IRC server into thinking you are hogging the channel with too much talking. This is because most IRC servers will automatically cut you off if you try text flooding.

So CTCP echo flooding spoofs the IRC server into falsely cutting someone off by causing the victim's IRC client to automatically keep on responding to a whole bunch of echo requests.

Of course your attacker could also get booted off for making all those CTCP echo requests. But a knowledgeable attacker will either be working in league with some friends who will be doing the same thing to you or else be connected with several different nicks to that same IRC server. So by having different versions of him or herself in the form of software bots making those CTCP echo requests, the attacker stays on while the victim gets booted off.

This attack is also fairly harmless, so people who get caught doing this will only get banned or maybe K:lined for their misbehavior.

 Newbie note: A "bot" is a computer program that acts kind of like a robot to go around and do things for you. Some bots are hard to tell from real people. For example, some IRC bots wait for someone to use bad language and respond to these naughty words in annoying ways.

YOU CAN GET PUNCHED IN THE NOSE WARNING: Bots are not permitted on the servers of the large networks. The IRC Cops who control hacker wars on these networks love nothing more than killing bots and banning the botrunners that they catch.

A similar attack is IRC ping flood. You can give the command "/ping nick" and the IRC client of the guy using that nick would respond to the IRC server with a message to be passed on to the guy who made the ping request saying "nick" is alive, and telling you how long it took for nick's IRC client program to respond.

The legitimate use of this command is to know the response time because sometimes the Internet can be so slow it might take ten seconds or more to send an IRC message to other people on that IRC channel. So if someone seems to be taking a long time to reply to you, it may just be a slow Internet.

But an IRC vandal will keep on pinging his victims until they are unable to use the channel.

Your attacker can also easily get the dynamically assigned IP (Internet protocol) address of your home computer and directly flood your modem. But just about every Unix IRC program has at least some CATCH flood protection in it. Again, we are looking at a fairly harmless kind of attack.

Another type of flood attack is the nick flood, where someone keeps on giving the command to change nick names. It fills the screen with so much text that no one can read anything else.

When IRC War Goes Nuclear

There are far more serious attacks that these. Your real trouble comes when people deploy "nukes" and "ICBMs" against you.

"Nuking" is also known as "ICMP Bombing." This includes forged messages such as EOF (end of file), dead socket, redirect, etc. ICMP stands for Internet Control Message Protocol. This is an class of IRC attacks that go beyond exploiting quirks in the IRC server program to take advantage of major league hacking techniques based upon the way the Internet works.

YOU CAN GO TO JAIL WARNING: ICMP attacks constitute illegal denial of service attacks. They are not just harmless harassment of a single person on IRC, but may affect an entire Internet host computer, disrupting service to all who are using it.

For example, ICMP redirect messages are used by routers to tell other computers "Hey, quit sending me that stuff. Send it to routerx.foobar.net instead!" So an ICMP redirect message could cause your IRC messages to go to bit heaven instead of your chat channel.

EOF stands for "end of file." "Dead socket" refers to connections such as your PPP session that you would be using to connect to the Internet. If your IRC enemy spoofs a message that your socket is dead, your IRC chat session can't get any more input from you. That's what the program "ICMP Host Unreachable Bomber for Windows" does.

One of the most devastating IRC weapons is the flood ping, known as "ICBM flood or ICMPing." But ICMPing is far more serious—and often illegal. A bully will find out what Internet host you are using, and then give the command "ping-f" to your host computer. Or even to your home computer. Yes, it is possible to identify the dynamically assigned IP address of your home computer and send stuff directly to your modem! If the bully has a decent computer, he or she may be able to ping yours badly enough to briefly knock you out of IRC. Then this character can take over your IRC session and may masquerade as you.

 Newbie note: When you connect to the Internet with a point-to-point (PPP) connection, your ISP's host computer assigns you an Internet Protocol (IP) address which may be different every time you log on. This is called a "dynamically assigned IP address." In some cases, however, the ISP has arranged to assign users the same IP address each time.

Defending against IRC Attack

So how do you handle IRC attacks? There are several programs that you can run with your Unix IRC program. Examples are the programs LiCe and Phoenix. These scripts will run in the background of your Unix IRC session and will automatically kick in some sort of protection (ignore, ban, kick) against attackers.

If you are running a Windows-based IRC client, you may assume that like usual you are out of luck. In fact, when I first got on an IRC channel recently, the first thing the denizens of #hackers did was make fun of my Win95 operating system. Yeah, thanks. But in fact there are great IRC war programs for Windows 95, too.

For Windows 95 you may wish to use the mIRC client program. You can download it from *http://www.mirc.co.uk.* It includes protection against ICMP ping flood.

But this program isn't enough to handle all the IRC wars you may encounter. So you may wish to add the protection of the most user-friendly, powerful Windows 95 war script around: 7th Sphere. You can get it from *http://www.localnet.com/~mar-craz/*. Warning: 7th Sphere is rumored to have a back door. If so, it won't protect you against people who know that back door.

If you surf IRC from a Unix box, you'll want to try out IRCII. You can download it from *ftp.undernet.org/pub/irc/clients/unix*, or *http://www.irchelp.org/*, or *ftp://cs-ftp.bu.edu/irc/*. For added protection, you may download the self defense program LiCe from *ftp://ftp.cibola.net/pub/irc/scripts*. Ahem, at this same site you can also download the attack program Tick from */pub/irc/tick*. But if you get Tick, just remember our "You can get punched in the nose" warning!

Newbie note: For detailed instructions on how to run these IRC programs, see *http://www.irchelp.org/*. Or go to Usenet and check out alt.irc.questions

Evil genius tip: Want to know every excruciating technical detail about IRC? Check out RFC 1459 (The IRC protocol). You can find this ever popular RFC (Request for Comments) at *http://cnswww.cns.cwru.edu/net/odds-ends/rfc* which has a searchable database of RFCs.

Now let's suppose you are set up with an industrial strength IRC client program and war scripts. Does this mean you are ready to go to war on IRC? Us Happy Hacker folks don't recommend attacking people who take over op status by force on IRC. Not even if they use ICMP attacks. Even if the other guys start it.

Remember this. If they were able to sneak into the channel and get ops just like that, or suddenly wipe you out —or even the entire IRC server net with ICMP attacks, then chances are they are much more experienced and dangerous than you are. Until you become an IRC master yourself, we suggest you do no more than ask politely for ops back.

Better yet, "/ignore nick" the l00zer and join another channel. For instance, if #evilhaxorchat is taken over, just create #evilhaxorchat2 and give the command "/invite IRCfriend" all your friends there. And remember to use what you learned in this Guide about the IRC whois command so that you *don't* OP people unless you know who they are.

As Patrick Rutledge says, this might sound like a wimp move, but if you don't have a fighting chance, don't try—it might be more embarrassing for you in the long run. And if you start IRC warrioring and get K:lined off the system, just think about that purple nose and black eye you could get when all the other IRC dudes at your ISP or school find out who was the luser who got everyone banned.

That's it for now. Now don't try any funny stuff, okay?

Our thanks for help in this chapter to Patrick Rutledge, Warbeast, Meltdown and k1neTiK, who all provided invaluable information on the burning question of the IRC world: *help, they're nuking meee* . . . .

Section 1, Chapter 7
How to Forge Email Using Eudora Pro

One of the most popular hacking tricks is forging email. People love to fake out their friends by sending them email that looks like it is from Bill_Gates@microsoft.com, santa@north.pole.org, or beelzebub@hell.mil. Unfortunately, spammers and other undesirables also love to fake email so it's easy for them to get away with flooding our email accounts with junk.

Thanks to these problems, most email programs are good Internet citizens. Pegasus, which runs on Windows, and Pine, which runs on Unix, are fastidious in keeping people from misusing them. Have you ever tried to forge email using Compuserve or AOL? I'm afraid to ever say something is impossible to hack, but those email programs have resisted my attempts. So flame me. See if I care, I can't hack everything.

Then there is Eudora Pro, Qualcomm's gift to the Internet, and the meanest, baddest email program around.

In this chapter you will learn how to use Eudora Pro to fake really hilarious email. This will include how to forge:
- Who sent the mail
- Extra headers to fake the route it took though the Internet
- Even the message ID!
- And anything else you can imagine
- Plus, how to use Eudora for sending your email from other people's computers—whether they like it or not.

Some Super Duper haxors will see this chapter and immediately start making fun of it. They will assume I am just going to teach the obvious stuff, like how to put a fake sender on your email.

No way. This is serious stuff. Don't believe me? Then check out the full headers of this email I composed in Eudora:

```
Return-Path: <cmeinel@techbroker.com>
Received: from kizmiaz.fu.org (root@kizmiaz.fu.org
[206.14.78.160])
 by Foo66.com (8.8.6/8.8.6) with ESMTP id VAA09915
 for <cpm@foo66.com>; Sat, 13 Sep 1997 21:54:34 -
0600 (MDT)
Received: from Anteros (pmd08.foo66.com
[198.59.176.41])
 by kizmiaz.fu.org (8.8.5/8.8.5) with SMTP id
UAA29704
 for <cpm@foo66.com>; Sat, 13 Sep 1997 20:54:20 -
0700 (PDT)
Date: Sat, 13 Sep 1997 20:54:20 -0700 (PDT)
Message-Id:
<2.2.16.19970913214737.530f0502@ayatollah.iq>
received: from emout09.mail.ayatollah.ir
(emout09.mx.aol.com [198.81.11.24]) by Foo66.com
(8.8.6/8.8.6) with ESMTP id MAA29967 for
<cpm@Foo66.com>; Mon, 8 Sep 1997 12:06:09 -0600 (MDT)
Favorite-color:turquoise
X-Sender: meinel@ayatollah.ir (Unverified)
X-Mailer: Windows Eudora Pro Version 2.2 (16)
Mime-Version: 1.0
Content-Type: text/plain; charset="us-ascii"
To: cpm@foo66.com
From: Carolyn Meinel  <cmeinel@techbroker.com>
Subject: Test of forged everything
```

I actually sent this email though a PPP connection with my account cpm@foo66.com to myself at that same address. Yes, this email began and ended up at the same computer. However, if you read the headers, this email looks like it was sent by a computer named Anteros, then went to kizmiaz.fu.org, then ayatollah.ir. Sender, it reports, is unverified but appears to be meinel@ayatollah.ir.

What is of particular interest is the message ID. Many people, even experienced sysadmins and hackers, assume that even with forged email, the computer name at the end of the message ID is the computer on which the email was written, and the computer that holds the record of who the guy was who forged it.

But you can quickly prove with Eudora Pro that you can forge a message ID that references almost any computer, including nonexistent computers.

Some of this chapter is clearly amateurish. For hundreds of dollars you can buy an email program from a spammer company that will forge email better and pump it out faster. Still, learning to forge email on Eudora illustrates some basic principles of email forgery that will come in handy in the chapter *Heroic Hacking in Half an Hour*.

YOU CAN GET PUNCHED IN THE NOSE WARNING: If you use the information in this chapter to spam from Eudora, I will personally punch you out.

Let's start with the sender's email address. I managed to call myself three different senders in this email: meinel@ayatollah.ir, cmeinel@techbroker.com, and cpm@foo66.com

Only the last of these, cpm@foo66.com, was "real." If I had used the right computer to forge this email on, even that one could have been faked. The other two senders I inserted myself.

There is a legitimate use for this power. In my case, I have several ISPs but like to have everything returned to my email address at my own domain, techbroker.com. But that ayatollah address is purely a joke. Here's how I put in those names.

1) In Eudora, click "tools" then "options." This will pull down a menu.

2) Click "Personal Information." For forging email, you can make every one of these entries fake.

3) The address you put under "Pop account" is where you tell Eudora where to look to pick up your email. But guess what? When you send email you can put a phony host in there. I put "ayatollah.ir." This generated the line in the header, "Message-Id: .16.19970913214737.530f0502@ayatollah.ir." Some people think the message ID is the best way to track down forged email. Just mail the sysadmin at ayatollah.ir, right? Wrong!

4) "Real name" and "Return address" are what showed up in the header lines "From: Carolyn Meinel <cmeinel@techbroker.com>" and "Return-Path: <cmeinel@techbroker.com>." I could have made them fake. If they are fake, people can't reply to you by giving the "reply" command in their email program.

5) Next, while still on the options pulldown, scroll down to "sending mail." Guess what, under "SMTP Server," you don't have to put in the one your ISP offers you to send your email out on. With a little experimentation you can find hundreds—thousands—millions—of other computers that you can use to send email on. However, this must be a real computer that will really send out your email. I picked kizmiaz.fu.org for this one. That accounts for the header lines:

```
Received: from kizmiaz.fu.org (root@kizmiaz.fu.org
[206.14.78.160])
 by Foo66.com (8.8.6/8.8.6) with ESMTP id VAA09915
 for <cpm@foo66.com>; Sat, 13 Sep 1997 21:54:34 -0600
(MDT)
Received: from Anteros (pmd08.foo66.com [198.59.176.41])
 by kizmiaz.fu.org (8.8.5/8.8.5) with SMTP id UAA29704
 for <cpm@foo66.com>; Sat, 13 Sep 1997 20:54:20 -0700
(PDT)
```

How to Make Extra Headers and Fake the Path through the Internet

But maybe this doesn't make a weird enough header for you. Want to make your email even phonier? Even really experienced Eudora users rarely know about how to make extra headers, so it's a great way to show off.

1) Open Windows Explorer by clicking "start," then "programs," then "Windows Explorer."

2) On the left hand side is a list of directories. Click on Eudora.

3) On the right hand side will be all the directories and files in Eudora. Scroll down them to the files. Click on "eudora.ini."

4) Eudora.ini is now in Notepad and ready to edit.

5) Fix it up by adding a line. Go to the line entitled "extra headers=" under [Dialup]. After the "=" type in something like this:

```
extraheaders=received:from emout09.mail.ayatollah.ir
(emout09.mx.aol.com [198.81.11.24])by Foo66.com
(8.8.6/8.8.6) with ESMTP id MAA29967 for @foo66.com;
Mon, 8 Sep 1997 12:06:09 -0600 (MDT)
```

With this set up, all your email going out from Eudora will include that line in the headers. You can add as many extra headers to your email as you want by adding new lines that also start with "extra headers=". For example, in this case I also added "Favorite_color=turquoise."

YOU CAN GO TO JAIL WARNING: There still are ways for experts to tell where you sent this email from. So if someone were to use forged email to defraud, threaten or mail bomb people, watch out for that cellmate named Spike.

Of course there are better ways to forge email with Eudora. But as you will see in the chapters on how to fight spam and email bombs, the ease with which one may forge perfect mail may well be the greatest threat the Internet faces today. By the time you finish reading this book, if you really want to, you will have figured out the secret to perfect forgery. The mail forgery problem is a deeply ingrained flaw in the Internet's basic structure, so it is almost impossible to explain the basics of hacking without revealing the pieces to the puzzle of the perfect forgery.

If you figure it out, be a good guy and don't abuse it, okay? Become one of us insiders who see the problem—and want to fix it rather than exploit it for greed or hatred.

Section 1, Chapter 8
How to Dig Up Hacker Information on the Web

Want to become really, really unpopular? Try asking your hacker friends too many questions of the wrong sort.

But, but, how do we know what are the wrong questions to ask? I sympathize with your problems because I get flamed a lot, too. That's partly because I sincerely believe in asking dumb questions. I make my living asking dumb questions. People pay me lots of money to go to conferences, call people on the phone and hang out on Usenet news groups asking dumb questions so I can find out stuff for them. And, guess what, sometimes the dumbest questions get you the best answers. So that's why you don't see me flaming people who ask dumb questions.

 Newbie note: Have you been too afraid to ask the dumb question, "What is a flame?" Now you get to find out! It is a bunch of obnoxious rantings and ravings made in email or a Usenet post by some idiot who thinks he or she is proving his or her mental superiority through use of foul and/or impolite language such as "you suffer from rectocranial inversion," f*** y***, d****, b****, and of course @#$%^&*! This newbie note is my flame against those flamers to whom I am soooo superior.

But even though dumb questions can be good to ask, you may not like the flames they bring down on you. Besides, it can be lots of fun to find something out by hunting it down yourself. So, how do you find out answers for yourself?

In this chapter you will learn:
- what are the best Web search engines
- how to use Web search engines
- good starting places on the Web to find hacker information
- where to find RFCs

This chapter covers one way to find out hacking information without having to ask people questions: by surfing the Web. The other way is to buy lots and lots of computer manuals, but that costs a lot of money. Also, in some parts of the world it is difficult to get manuals. Fortunately, however, almost anything you want to learn about computers and communications is available for free somewhere on the Web.

What Web Search Engines Are Best?

First, let's consider the Web search engines. Generally when the Super Dooper hackers flame people for asking dumb questions, they say "do a Web search." But this may be easier said than done.

There are two major considerations in using Web search engines. One is what search engine to use, and the other is the search tactics themselves.

I have used many Web search engines. But eventually I came to the conclusion that for serious research, you only need two: Hot Bot (*http://hotbot.com*)and Dejanews (*http://www.dejanews.com*). Hot Bot is, in my humble opinion, the best for the Web, while Dejanews is the best one for searching Usenet news groups. But, if you don't want to take me at my word, you may surf over to a site with links to almost all the Web and news group search engines at *http://sgk.tiac.net/search/*.

Why are some Web search engines better than others? The problem is, as this book is being written, there are already an estimated 100 million Web pages on the Internet. This is more than a search engine can efficiently cover. So you can guarantee no search engine can tell you everything. What you want from a good search engine is maximum coverage. Your objective is to learn all there is to learn, rather than have a Web search babysitter lead you by the hand to "cool sites."

Another problem is that some search engines, for example Altavista, arbitrarily limit the number of pages it will search under a given domain. Since most hacker Web sites are in user directories of ISPs such as Geocities, Altavista won't do much good for you.

Finally, hacker Web sites have a way of moving from one URL to another. Between hacker wars and general objections to hacker Web sites, ISPs are always shutting them down. So you need a Web search engine that keeps its information up to date. Otherwise you'll waste a lot of time following dead links.

How to Use Web Search Engines

Once you have chosen your search engine, just how do you efficiently use it? If you ask it to find "hacker" or even "how to hack," you will get bazillions of Web sites and news group posts to read. Okay, so you painfully surf through one hacker Web site after another. You get portentous-sounding organ music, skulls with red rolling eyes, animated fires burning, and each site has links to other sites with pretentious music and ungrammatical boastings about "I am 31337, d00dz!!! I am so *&&^%$ good at hacking you should bow down and kiss my $%^&&*!" But somehow they don't seem to have any actual information. Welcome to the wannabe hacker world!

You need to figure out some words that help the search engine of your choice get more useful results. For example, let's say you want to find out whether I, the Supreme R00ler of the Happy Hacker world, am an elite hacker chick or merely some poser. Now the luser approach would to simply go to *http://www.dejanews.com* and do a search of Usenet news groups for "Carolyn Meinel," being sure to click the "old" button to bring up stuff from years back. But if you do that, you get this huge long list of posts, most of which have nothing to do with hacking:

- CDMA vs GSM - carolyn meinel <cmeinel@unm.edu> 1995/11/17
- Re: October El Nino-Southern Oscillation info gonthier@usgs.gov (Gerard J. Gonthier) 1995/11/20
- Re: Internic Wars MrGlucroft@psu.edu (The Reaver) 1995/11/30
- shirkahn@earthlink.net (Christopher Proctor) 1995/12/16
- Re: Lyndon LaRouche - who is he? lness@ucs.indiana.edu (lester john ness) 1996/01/06
- U-B Color Index observation data - cmeinel@nmia.com (Carolyn P. Meinel) 1996/05/13
- Re: Mars Fraud? History of one scientist involved gksmiley@aol.com (GK Smiley) 1996/08/11
- Re: Mars Life Announcement: NO Fraud Issue twitch@hub.ofthe.net 1996/08/12
- Hackers Helper E-Zine wanted - rcortes@tuna.hooked.net (Raul Cortes) 1996/12/06
- Carolyn Meinel, Soooooooper Genius - nobody@cypherpunks.ca (John Anonymous MacDonald, a remailer node) 1996/12/12

Anyhow, this list goes on and on and on.

But if you specify "Carolyn Meinel hacker" and click "all" instead of "any" on the "Boolean" button, you get a list that starts with:

- Media: "Unamailer delivers Christmas grief" - Mannella@ipifidpt.difi.unipi.it (Riccardo Mannella) 1996/12/30 Cu Digest, #8.93, Tue 31 Dec 96 - Cu Digest (tk0jut2@mvs.cso.niu.edu)
- <TK0JUT2@MVS.CSO.NIU.EDU> 1996/12/31
- RealAudio interview with Happy Hacker - bmcw@redbud.mv.com (Brian S. McWilliams) 1997/01/08

etc. This way all those posts about my boring life in the world of science don't show up, just the juicy hacker stuff.

Now suppose all you want to see is flames about what a terrible hacker I am. You could bring those to the top of the list by adding (with the "all" button still on) "flame" or "f***" or "b****" being careful to spell out those bad words instead fubaring them with ****'s. For example, a search on "Carolyn Meinel hacker flame" with Boolean "all" turns up only one post. This important tome says the Happy Hacker list is a dire example of what happens when us prudish moderator types censor naughty words and inane diatribes.

Newbie note: "Boolean" is math a term. On the Dejanews search engine they figure the user doesn't have a clue of what "Boolean" means so they give you a choice of "any" or "all" and then label it "Boolean" so you feel stupid if you don't understand it. But in real Boolean algebra we can use the operators "and" "or" and "not" on word searches (or any searches of sets). "And" means you would have a search that turns up only items that have "all" the terms you specify; "or" means you would have a search that turns up "any" of the terms. The "not" operator would exclude items that included the "not" term even if they have any or all of the other search terms. Altavista has real Boolean algebra under its "advanced"" search option.

Good Starting Places to Find Hacker Information

But let's forget all those Web search engines for a minute. In my old-fashioned opinion, the best way to search the Web is to use it exactly the way its inventor, Tim Berners-Lee, intended. You start at a good spot and then follow the links to related sites. Imagine that!

Here's another of my old fogie tips. If you want to really whiz around the Web, and if you have a shell account, you can do it with the program lynx. At the prompt, just type "lynx" followed by the URL you want to visit. Because lynx only shows text, you don't have to waste time waiting for the organ music, animated skulls and pornographic JPEGs to load.

So where are good places to start? Simply surf over to the Web sites listed in this book. They carry a lot of valuable information for the newbie hacker, as well as links to other quality sites.

For example, where do you start if your question is "How do I break into a computer?"

You definitely don't want to ask this question on IRC or an email list or news group. You will get a truly rude reaction. Here's why. The world is full of many kinds of computers running many kinds of software on many kinds of networks. How you break into a computer depends on all these things. So to ask simply "How do I break into a computer" is like asking "How do I fix machinery."

So first you need to decide what kind of computer you want to break into. If Windows NT is your target, check out NT Bugtraq at *http://www.ntbugtraq.com*. For Unix, see the searchable Bugtraq archives at *http://www.netspace.org/lsv-ar-chive/bugtraq.html* or *http://geek-girl.com/bugtraq*. If you want somewhat outdated but easier to understand information on how to break into Unix computers, look for the *Hack FAQ*, which was written by Voyager. Because it is controversial, your best bet to find a live link to it is a web search or usenet search for "alt.2600/#hack FAQ".

For an eclectic survey of links to top hacker information on any operating system, see *http://underground.org*. For both information and ready-to-run hacking programs that won't destroy your computer, see *http://l0pht.com* (that's a number 0, not the letter O, and the letter "l" rather than the number one in l0pht). Another excellent archive is the back issues of the *Phrack* ezine at *http://www.phrack.com*. For the hottest new cracker exploits, see *http://www.rootshell.com*.

From these starting points you should be able to get the cream of the crop of hacker information. Of course, if you surf over to those Web sites, you won't instantly learn how to become an Übercracker. Unless you already are an excellent programmer and knowledgeable in Unix or Windows NT, you will discover the information you find on the Web won't instantly grant you access to any victim computer you may choose. It's not that easy. You are going to have to learn how to program. Learn at least one operating system inside and out.

Of course some people try to take the shortcut into being able to break into or crash any computer. They find these Web sites with the organ music and animated fires and skulls and places that say to click to download deadly haxor programs to mess up computers.

However, what these lazy wannabes forget is that the kinds of kewl d00dz who say they want to mess up computers often want to mess up the computers of the people who come to visit them. So run any program you find at a hacker Web site with the greatest caution. Be sure you have backed up your computer. If the source code is available, try to understand what it does before you run it. Better yet, stay away from malicious programs.

Now let's suppose you are really serious about learning everything you can about hacking. You want to be more than a kode kiddie who downloads ready-to-run exploits. You want to be a hacker badly enough to learn an operating system inside and out. You want to populate your dreaming hours with arcane communications protocol topics.

The old-fashioned, and super expensive way top become an uberhacker is to buy and study lots of manuals. [Geek mode on] I'm a real believer in manuals. I spend about $200 per month on them. I read them in the bathroom, while sitting in traffic jams, and while waiting for doctor's appointments. But the Web stuff is free! [Geek mode off]

RFCs!

The most fantastic Web resources for the aspiring geek, er, hacker, are the RFCs. RFC stands for "Request for Comment." Now this sounds like nothing more than a discussion group. But actually RFCs are the definitive documents that tell you how the Internet works. The funny name "RFC" comes from ancient history when lots of people were discussing how the heck to make that ARPAnet thingy work. But nowadays RFC means "Gospel Truth about How the Internet Works" instead of "Hey Guys, Let's Talk this Stuff Over."

Ideally you should simply read and memorize all the RFCs. But there are thousands of RFCs and some of us need to take time out to eat and sleep. So those of us without photographic memories and gobs of free time need to be selective about what we read. So how do we find an RFC that will answer whatever is our latest dumb question?

One good starting place is a complete list of all RFCs and their titles at *ftp://ftp.tstt.net.tt/pub/inet/rfc/rfc-index*. Although this is an ftp (file transfer protocol) site, you can access it with your Web browser. A searchable database of RFCs is at *http://cnswww.cwru.edu/odds-ends.rfc*.

Newbie note: ARPAnet was the US Advanced Research Projects Agency experiment launched in 1969 that evolved into the Internet. When you read RFCs you will often find references to ARPAnet and ARPA—or sometimes DARPA. That "D" stands for "defense." DARPA/ARPA keeps on getting its name changed between these two. For example, when Bill Clinton became US President in 1993, he changed DARPA back to ARPA because "defense" is a Bad Thing. Then in 1996 the US Congress passed a law changing it back to DARPA because "defense" is a Good Thing.

Or, how about the RFC on RFCs! That's right, RFC 825 is "intended to clarify the status of RFCs and to provide some guidance for the authors of RFCs in the future. It is in a sense a specification for RFCs." To find this RFC, or in fact any RFC for which you have its number, just go to Hot Bot and search for "RFC 825" or whatever the number is.

Whoa, these RFCs can be pretty hard to understand! Heck, how do we even know which RFC to read to get an answer to our questions? Guess what, there is solution, a fascinating group of RFCs called "FYIs" Rather than specifying anything, FYIs simply help explain the other RFCs. How do you get FYIs? Easy! I just surfed over to the RFC on FYIs (1150) and learned that:

```
FYIs can be obtained via FTP from NIC.DDN.MIL, with the pathname
FYI:mm.TXT, or RFC:RFCnnnn.TXT (where "mm" refers to the number of
the FYI and "nnnn" refers to the number of the RFC). Login with FTP,
username ANONYMOUS and password GUEST. The NIC also provides an
automatic mail service for those sites which cannot use FTP. Address
the request to SERVICE@NIC.DDN.MIL and in the subject field of the
message indicate the FYI or RFC number, as in "Subject: FYI mm" or
"Subject: RFC nnnn".
```

But even better than this is an organized set of RFCs hyperlinked together on the Web at *http://www.FreeSoft.org/Connected/*. I can't even begin to explain to you how wonderful this site is. You just have to try it yourself. It has a tutorial and a newbie-friendly set of links through the RFCs.

What about that NIC.DDN.MIL mentioned above? It is the Network Information Center for the US Department of Defense. It is full of free information on how the Internet works, as well as being the site from which you can search for interesting military computers on the Internet. (Of course you would not want to mess with any of those Internet hosts.) You can reach it at *http://nic.ddn.mil*.

Last but not least, you can check out two sites that offer a wealth of technical information on computer security: *http://csrc.nist.gov/secpubs/rainbow/*, and *http://GANDALF.ISU.EDU/security/security.html*.

I hope this is enough information to keep you busy studying for the next five or ten years. But please keep this in mind. Sometimes it's not easy to figure something out just by reading huge amounts of technical information. Sometimes it can save you a lot of grief just to ask a question. Even a dumb question.

Hey, how would you like to check out the Web site for those of us who make our living asking people dumb questions? Surf over to *http://www.scip.org*. That's the home page of the Society of Competitive Intelligence Professionals, the home organization for folks like me. So, go ahead, make someone's day. Have phun asking those dumb questions. Just remember to fireproof your phone and computer first, and be gracious to others who ask dumb questions!

Section 2
Hacking with Unix

When I first began writing the Guides to (mostly) Harmless Hacking and passing them around to my friends, I'd led a sheltered existence. I had enjoyed dialups to PDP and Data General computers, a Compuserve account in the era of X.25 and Telenet, an ARPAnet account using the UUCP protocol, and shell accounts with many varieties of Unix. All of these offered simple command line interfaces—delicious to the hacker mind.

That's why it shocked to me when so many beginner hackers told me how hard it can be to find an Internet Service Provider (ISP) that would give them a Unix shell account. The commercial online world wants you to just look at pretty pictures, point and click. Arghhh!

As a result, way too many folks tried to study the hacking techniques of this section—and got totally lost. They tried to type Unix commands into the URL boxes of their Web browsers. They searched AOL high and low for nslookup and whois.

Even so, kids handicapped by having only an AOL account and a Mac or Windows box amazed me with their ingenuity as they nevertheless found ways to hack. In the process they learned a great deal about Windows and the Mac. They also taught me a thing or two. Bravo to them.

But hacking without a Unix shell account is like paddling a canoe while standing on your head. It is possible. It is a cool stunt. But if you want to get somewhere fast, do it right.

Hacking with a Unix shell account is doing it right. That's what Section 2 of *The Happy Hacker* is all about. If you want to learn the material of Section 2, get a shell account. SHELL ACCOUNT!

In the first chapter of this section you will learn how to get a shell account no matter where you live. Read it. Get a shell account. Now. There. Have I said it enough times?

Section 2, Chapter 1
How to Get a Good Shell Account— and Keep it!

There are good hackers and bad hackers. But I learned the hard way that for most Internet Service Providers (ISPs), the only good hacker is one whose account they have just closed.

Thunderheads were building that humid August morning in 1996 when I picked up the phone to hear Stan Whooziz, the owner of New Mexico Internet Fubar, shouting in my ear. "You're inviting hackers to attack us!"

In this chapter you will learn how to:
- tell whether you may already have a Unix shell account
- get a shell account
- log on to your shell account
- explore your shell account
- decide whether your shell account is any good for hacking
- keep from getting kicked off your shell account

"Duh," I replied wittily. I had no idea what he meant, but then sometimes I'm a little slow.

"Yeah, listen to this. You wrote, 'I feel privileged to have been targeted by a sophisticated attack by the Gray Areas Liberation Front.' Privileged! You like to be hacked!"

"Duh?" I repeated. But my brain was finally coming up to speed.

"Don't get cute with me. Someone forwarded your email to me."

"Stan," I soothed, finally getting the picture. "You are quoting from email I sent out to everyone who got an obscene message from my account. You know, the one written by those GALF guys two days ago, when they rooted you."

I wondered whether Stan had been snooping in my file of copies of outgoing email, which back in those days I incautiously stored on one of New Mexico Internet Fubar's machines.

"You are supposed to keep it quiet that we got hacked!" Stan continued. "Now every hacker in the world will be descending on us. Thanks to you, already dozens of attempts are being made on us every hour!"

"Stan," I tried to reason. "Are you saying I should pretend that all the people on my address list got obscene email because I sent it to them? I think I'm being awfully nice not being mad at you for being so easy to hack." Humph, I thought, that dude had told me he was so good at computer security that he moonlighted helping banks keep the bad guys out of their computers.

"Look at our terms of service," Stan replied. "We make it clear the Internet is inherently insecure. We promise you nothing for security. Nothing. Yes, I want you to keep it quiet that we got hacked! I have a business to run. I can't have people spreading word that we got hacked!"

I looked out the window at that growing thunderhead. On our high plains of New Mexico, lightning storms are violent. Was that storm about to blow out the local power co-op again and dump a bunch more junk into temp files on my Windows box? Maybe I'd better log off my shell account and shut everything down. I entered "exit," the connection to my shell account broke, and I began shutting down Windows.

Stan paused. Then he almost whispered, "I was beginning to really like you. You're a fascinating woman. But," his voice grew louder, "You're an attractive nuisance. I've locked you out of your account. Get another ISP."

This was the first time, and certainly not the last, that I have been kicked off an ISP for being targeted by a hacker. The problem is, ISPs generally figure the best way to keep from getting attacked is to boot off anyone who is a victim of attack. It doesn't matter if you are Mother Teresa, if you get attacked too often, or maybe only once, you get booted off. Since hackers like to attack each other, most ISPs figure it's a good idea to boot out everyone they suspect of being one of us.

So the problems we tackle in this chapter are, what kind of Internet access is best for hacking? And, once we get what we want, how do we keep from getting the boot?

True, you can hack a teensy bit without Internet access. If you've been trying out the stuff in this book, by now you've already fixed up your Windows computer to boot up with a lurid hacker logo. You've renamed your "Recycle Bin" to "Hidden Haxor Secrets." When you run Netscape or Internet Explorer, instead of that boring corporate logo, you have a full-color animated Mozilla destroying New York City. Now your friends and neighbors are terrified and impressed.

But if you really have that hacker spirit, you want to go exploring. Without Internet access, of course, you could always try war dialing to get a phone connection to an unknown computer, or pester the few remaining public computer bulletin boards.

 Newbie note: War dialers are programs that automatically dial up phone numbers looking for ones that will give you entry to a computer.

You could go to jail warning: In the US, war dialing is illegal.

You could get punched in the nose warning: Mess with a bulletin board (bbs) and you will be sorry. Many are run by guys who can hack circles around you.

But in your heart of hearts you know Internet hacking is where it's at. Besides, there are many kinds of hacking that you can do with the Internet that are legal, fun and harmless.

Furthermore, you keep on hearing about those hairy hacker exploit programs with which people can go on the rampage—or do polite cybertourism—and guess what? Almost every one of them requires the Unix operating system.

You have developed a burning desire to become one of those Unix wizards yourself. Yes, you're ready for a Unix shell account. SHELL ACCOUNT!!!!

 Newbie note: A shell account allows you to use your home computer as a terminal on which you can give commands to a computer running Unix. The "shell" is the program that translates your keystrokes into commands that your computer can understand. With the right shell account you can enjoy the use of a far more powerful workstation than you could ever dream of owning yourself. It is also a great stepping stone to the day when you will be running some form of Unix on your home computer.

The problem is that you used to be able to simply phone an ISP, say "I'd like a shell account," and they would give it to you, just like that! But nowadays, especially if you sound like a teenage male, you'll run into something like this:

ISP guy: "You want a shell account? What for?"

Hacker dude: "Um, well, I like Unix."

"Like Unix, huh? You're a hacker, aren't you!"

Slam, ISP guy hangs up on you.

So how do you ask for a shell account without accidentally convincing the guy on the other end of the phone that you are some sort of cyber-terrorist? Actually, it's possible you may already have a shell account and not know it. So first we will answer the question, how do you tell whether you may already have a shell account? Then, if you are certain you don't have one, we'll explore the many ways you can get one, no matter what, no matter where you live in the world.

How Do I Know whether I Already Have a Shell Account?

Do you still have the original documentation you got when you signed up with your online service provider or Internet service provider? "Sure," you may answer, "but it doesn't say 'shell account' on it anywhere." But you still might already have a shell account. Here's how to find out.

You could, of course, just call tech support. But we're hackers and would never (well, almost never) subject ourselves to the humiliation of calling tech support. Besides, those tech support guys are usually busy explaining to people how to turn on their computers and not to put their coffee mug on the CD-ROM holder.

A key to finding out whether you have a shell account is that the user name and password you use to get email will usually be the same as what you use to log into your shell account.

To test this hypothesis, first you need to get a program running that will connect you to a shell account. There are two programs with Windows 95 that will do this, as well as many other programs, some of which are excellent and free.

We will start with the Windows 95 Telnet program. We start here not because it is a super-elite hacker tool, but because most people already have it, and it will always work—kindof. But it's a really limited program.

1) Find your Telnet program and make a shortcut to it on your desktop.
- One way is to click "Start", then "Programs", then "Windows Explorer".
- When Explorer is running, first resize it so it doesn't cover the entire desktop.
- Then click "Tools", then "Find", then "Files or Folders."
- Ask it to search for "Telnet."
- It will show a file labeled C:\windows\telnet (instead of C:\ it may have another drive). Right click on this file.
- This will bring up a menu that includes the option "create shortcut." Click on "Create shortcut" and then drag the shortcut to the desktop and drop it. Close Windows Explorer.

2) Depending on how your system is configured, there are two ways to connect to the Internet. The easy way is to configure Windows 95 so that it connects to the Internet automatically whenever you run a program that needs it. This option can give you trouble when you want to use several programs at once to access the Internet. If you have trouble, see page 30 for some suggestions. Once you are connected, minimize the program. Now try step three.

3) Bring up your Telnet program by double clicking on the shortcut you just made.
- First you need to configure Telnet so it actually is usable. On the toolbar click "terminal," then "preferences," then "fonts." Choose "Courier New," "regular" and 8 point size. You do this because if you have too big a font, the Telnet program is shown on the screen so big that the cursor from your shell program can end up being hidden off the screen. Okay, okay, you can pick other fonts, but make sure that when you close the dialog box that the Telnet program window is entirely visible on the screen.
- Now go back to the task bar to click "Connect", then under it click "Remote system". This brings up another dialog box.
- Under "Host name" in this box type in the last two or three parts of your email address. For example, if your email address is jane_doe@boring.ISP.com, type "ISP.com" or "boring.ISP.com" for host name.
- Under "port" in this box, leave it the way it is, reading "telnet."
- Under "terminal type," in this box, choose "VT100."
- Then click the "Connect" button and wait to see what happens.

If you have a shell account you should next get a message asking you to login. It may look something like this:

```
Welcome to Boring Internet Services, Ltd.
```

```
Boring.com S9 - login: cmeinel
Password:
Linux 2.0.0.
Last login: Thu Apr 10 14:02:00 on ttyp5 from pm20.kitty.net.
sleepy:~$
```

If you get something like this, you are in definite luck. The important thing here, however, is that the computer used the word "login" to get you started. If it asks for anything else, for example "logon," this is not a shell account. However, some shell accounts are hidden behind a menu system that begins with "logon" or some other prompt. In this case, since there are so many possible menus, all I can suggest is to act like a hacker and explore until hopefully you find something that lets you give Unix commands.

What if this shell login sequence doesn't let you get in? What if it hates your password? Many ISPs have different user names and passwords for PPP, email and shell accounts. Sometimes the difference is simply that your PPP account has the letter "P" to begin your user name. Try entering your user name just like it is in your email address, the part in front of the "@" and use your PPP password without the "P" in front. You just may get in.

As soon as you login, in the case of Boring Internet Services you have a Unix shell prompt on your screen. But instead of something this simple you may get something long and complicated like Figures 2 and 3.

Depending on the ISP you try out, there may be all sorts of different menus, all designed to keep the user from having to ever stumble across the shell itself. But if

Figure 1: You are ready to click on the "connect" button and find out if you have a shell account. (To the right you're getting a peek at my deadly haxor Win 95 desktop.)

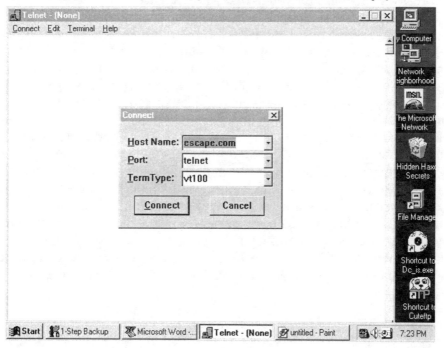

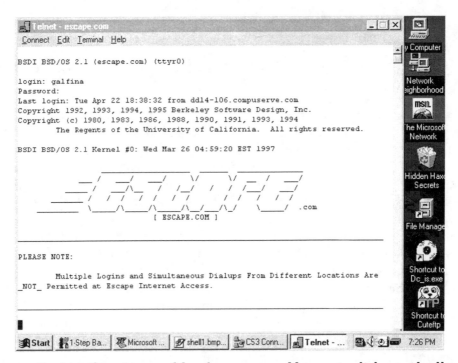

Figure 2: Another type of login screen. You aren't in a shell yet.

you have a shell account, you will probably find the word "shell" somewhere on the menu.

If you don't get something obvious like this, you may have to do the single most humiliating thing a wannabe hacker will ever do. Call tech support and ask whether you have a shell account and, if so, how to login. It may be that they just want to make it really, really hard for you to find your shell account.

If you own a Mac, you can make a direct dialup connection from your Mac with Zterm. Get it free, and many more goodies, at *http://www.lookoutgfx.com*. With Win95, you can make a direct dialup connection with Hyperterminal, which, like Telnet, comes free with the Windows 95 operating system. With both of these programs, instead of first making a PPP connection, we will do a simple phone dialup, the same sort of connection you use to get on most computer bulletin board systems (BBS).

1) First, find the program Hyperterminal and make a shortcut to your desktop. This one is easy to find. Just click Start, then Programs, then Accessories. You'll find Hyperterminal on the accessories menu. Clicking on it will bring up a window with a bunch of icons. Click on the one labeled "hyperterminal.exe."

2) This brings up a dialog box called "New Connection." Enter the name of your local dialup, then in the next dialog box enter the phone dialup number of your ISP.

3) Make a shortcut to your desktop.

4) Use Hyperterminal to dial your ISP. Note that in this case you are making a direct phone call to your shell account rather than trying to reach it through a PPP connection.

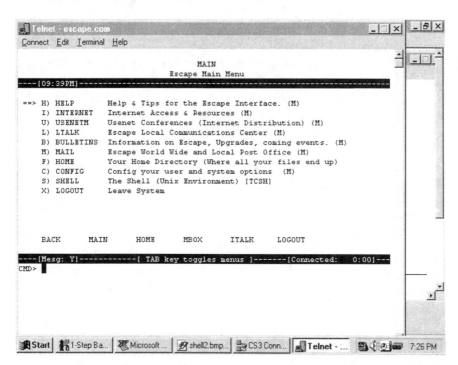

Figure 3: Next screen in the Escape.com login sequence. You aren't in a shell yet, but you can see an option on the menu to get to a shell. So hooray, you are in luck. Just enter "S" and you're into your shell account.

When you dial your ISP from Hyperterminal you might get a bunch of really weird garbage scrolling down your screen. But don't give up. What is happening is your ISP is trying to set up a PPP connection with Hyperterminal. That is the kind of connection you need in order to get pretty pictures on the Web. But Hyperterminal doesn't understand PPP. Unfortunately, since it is a problem with your ISP and not your system, there isn't a lot you can do to fix this problem.

But the good side of this picture is that the problem may go away the next time you use Hyperterminal to connect to your ISP. So if you dial again you may get a login sequence. I've found it often helps to wait a few days and try again. Of course you can complain to tech support at your ISP. But it is likely that they won't have a clue on what causes their end of things to try to set up a PPP session with your Hyperterminal connection. Sigh.

If all goes well, you will get the login sequence. But you may not be home free. Some ISPs uses modems that get befuddled when you try to login on a dialup shell account. Nowadays so many people just use PPP connections, tech support often hardly knows how to make a shell dialup work.

The way you can tell this is your problem is that you enter the correct user name and password over and over again but it doesn't work. If this happens, don't keep on trying the login sequence. Don't jump to the conclusion that you got hacked and your password changed. Break the connection, dial again and see if you are lucky enough to get a healthier modem.

If your ISP can handle Hyperterminal logins, try it out for awhile. See if you like it as much as I do.

There are a number of other terminal programs that are really good for connecting to your shell account. They include Qmodem, Quarterdeck Internet Suite, and Bitcom. My favorite hacker phriend/enemy jericho recommends Ewan, which also runs on Windows 95. Ewan is free, and has many more features than either Hyperterminal or Win 95 Telnet. Do a Web search to find the many free download sites.

There is also the Datafellows Secure Shell terminal program. It has lots of great features and gives you an encrypted tunnel into your shell account so sniffer programs can't snoop on you or steal your password. But this only works if your ISP runs the Secure Shell server. If you use it, you must use the "RSA" rather than the "password" option to remain secure.

Let's say you have logged into your ISP with your favorite program. But perhaps it still isn't clear whether you have a shell account. Here's your next test. At the prompt, give the command "ls - alK" (or "ls -alF" for some unixes). If you have a real, honest-to-goodness Unix shell account, you should get something like this:

```
>ls -alK
total 87
drwx—x—x     5 galfina    user     1024 Apr 22 21:45 ./
drwxr-xr-x  380 root       wheel    6656 Apr 22 18:15 ../
```

Figure 4: Hyperterminal is about to dial the Southwest Cyberport ISP. Note that in Hyperterminal you directly phone your ISP to get into your shell account. By contrast, Win 95 Telnet uses a PPP connection from a phone call that you have already made in order to reach your shell account.

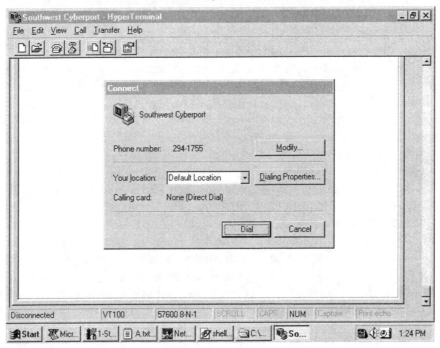

```
-rw-r—r—    1 galfina      user     2793 Apr 22 17:36 .README
-rw-r—r—    1 galfina      user      635 Apr 22 17:36 .Xmodmap
-rw-r—r—    1 galfina      user      624 Apr 22 17:36 .Xmodmap.USKBD
-rw-r—r—    1 galfina      user      808 Apr 22 17:36 .Xresources
drwx—x—x    2 galfina      user      512 Apr 22 17:36 www/
```

etc.

This is the listing of the files and directories in your home directory. Your shell account may give you a different set of directories and files than this (which is only a partial listing). In any case, if you see anything that looks sort of like this, congratulations, you already have a shell account!

 Newbie note: The first item in that bunch of dashes and letters in front of the file name tells you what kind of file it is. "d" means it is a directory, and "-" means it is a file. The rest are the permissions your files have. "r" = read permission, "w" = write permission, and "x" = execute permission (no, "execute" has nothing to do with murdering files, it means you have permission to run the program that is in this file). If there is a dash, it means there is no permission there.

The symbols in the second, third and fourth place from the left are the permissions that you have as a user, the following three are the permissions everyone in your designated group has, and the final three are the permissions anyone and everyone may have. For example, in galfina's directory the subdirectory "www/" is something she may read, write and execute, while everyone else may only execute. This is the directory where she can put her Web page. The entire world may browse ("execute") her Web page. But only you can read its HTML source code and write to it.

But let's say you were to someday discover your permissions looking like:

```
drwxrwxrwx        newbie user       512 Apr 22 17:36 www/
```

Whoa, all those "w's" mean anyone can hack your Web page!

Another command that will tell you whether you have a shell account is "man." This gives you an online Unix manual. Usually you have to give the man command in the form of "man <command>" where <command> is the name of the Unix command you want to study. For example, if you want to know all the different ways to use the "ls" command, type "man ls" at the prompt.

On the other hand, here is an example of something that, even though it is on a Unix system, is not a shell account:

```
BSDI BSD/386 1.1 (dub-gw-2.compuserve.com) (ttyp7)
Connected to CompuServe
Host Name: cis
Enter choice (LOGON, HELP, OFF):
```

The immediate tip-off that this is not a shell account is that it asks you to "logon" instead of "login:"

How to Get a Shell Account

What if you are certain that you don't already have a shell account? How do you find an ISP that will give you one?

The obvious place to start is your phone book. Unless you live in a really rural area or in a country where there are few ISPs, there should be a number of companies to choose from.

So here's your problem. You phone Boring ISP, Inc. and say, "I'd like a shell account." But Joe Dummy on the other end of the phone says, "Shell? What's a shell account?" You say "I want a shell account. SHELL ACCOUNT!!!" He says, "Duh?" You say "Shell account. SHELL ACCOUNT!!!" He says, "Um, er, let me talk to my supervisor." Mr. Uptight Supervisor gets on the phone. "We don't give out shell accounts, you dirty &%$*# hacker."

Or, worse yet, they claim the Internet access account they are giving you is a shell account but you discover it isn't one.

To avoid these embarrassing scenes, avoid calling big name ISPs. America Online, Compuserve and Microsoft Network don't give out shell accounts.

What you want to find is the seediest, tiniest ISP in town. The one that specializes in pasty-faced customers who stay up all night playing MOOs and MUDs. Guys who impersonate grrrls on IRC. Now that is not to say that MUD and IRC people are typically hackers. But these definitely are your serious Internet addicts. An ISP that caters to people like that probably also understands the kind of person who wants to learn Unix inside and out.

So you phone or email one of these ISPs and say, "Greetings, d00d! I am an evil haxor and demand a shell account pronto!"

No, no, no! Chances are you got the owner of this tiny ISP on the other end of the line. He's probably a hacker himself. Guess what? He loves to hack but he doesn't want hackers (or wannabe hackers) for customers. He doesn't want a customer who's going to be attracting email bombers and waging hacker war and drawing complaints from the sysadmins on whom you, the deadly dude, have been testing exploit code.

Say something like "Do you offer shell accounts? I really, really like to browse the Web with lynx. I hate waiting five hours for all those pretty pictures and Java applets to load. And I like to do email with Elm. Oooh, Emacs! Vi! C compiler!" you pant.

Start out like this and the owner of this tiny ISP may say something like, "Wow, dude, I know what you mean. What user name would you like?"

At this point, ask the owner for a guest account. If that isn't possible, in exchange for a valid credit card number, many ISPs will give you an account that you can cancel after a few days and not have to pay. As you will learn below, the next problem you are likely to encounter is that some shell accounts are so restricted that they are almost worthless.

 Evil Genius tip: Computer criminals and malicious hackers will often get a guest account on a distant ISP and do their dirty work during the few hours this account is available to them. Since this practice provides the opportunity to cause so much harm, eventually it may become really hard to get a test run on a guest account.

But let's say you can't find any ISP within reach of a local phone call that will give you a shell account. Or the only shell account you can get is worthless. Or you are well known as a malicious hacker and you've been kicked off every ISP in town. What can you do?

In that case, your best option is to get a shell account on some distant ISP, perhaps even in another country. Also, the few medium size ISPs that offer shell accounts (for example, Netcom) may even have a local dialup number for you.

But if they don't have local dialups, you can still access a shell account located *anywhere* in the world by setting up a PPP connection with your local dialup online service, and then accessing your shell account using a telnet program on your home computer.

 Evil Genius Tip: Sure, you can telnet into your shell account from another ISP account. But unless you have software that allows you to send your password in an encrypted form, someone may sniff your password and break into your account. If you become well known in the hacker world, lots of other hackers will constantly be making fun of you by sniffing your password and doing dastardly deeds with it. Unfortunately, almost all shell accounts are set up so you must expose your password to anyone who has hidden a sniffer between the ISP that provides your PPP connection and your shell account ISP.

One solution is to choose an ISP that can let you use Kerberos, a network authentication protocol which uses secret key cryptography. See *http://www.mit.edu/network/kerberos-form.html* for a freeware distribution, or *http://www.latticesoft.com*, *http://www.veritas.com* or *http://www.stonecast.net* for some commercial versions.

So where can you find these ISPs that will give you shell accounts? One good source that covers the entire planet is *http://www.celestin.com/pocia/*. It provides links to Internet Service Providers categorized by geographic region. They even have links to allow you to sign up with ISPs serving the Lesser Antilles!

But if you want to find a good shell account the hacker way, here's what you do. Start with a list of your favorite hacker Web sites. For example, let's try *http://ra.nilenet.com/~mjl/hacks/codez.htm*.

You take the beginning part of the URL (Universal Resource Locator) as your starting point. In this case it is "http://ra.nilenet.com." Try surfing to that URL. In many cases it will be the home page for that ISP. It should have instructions for how to sign up for a shell account. In the case of Nile Net we strike hacker gold:

```
Dial-up Accounts and Pricing
NEXUS Accounts
NEXUS Accounts include: Access to a UNIX Shell, full internet access,
Usenet newsgroups, 5mb of FTP and/or WWW storage space, and unlimited
time.
One Time Activation Fee: $20.00
Monthly Service Fee: $19.95 or Yearly Service Fee: $199.95
```

Plus they make a big deal over freedom of online speech. And they host a great hacker page full of my notorious Guides to (mostly) Harmless Hacking! (Note: there is no guarantee this Web site will still be up by the time you read this.)

How to Login to Your Shell Account

You finally have a guest shell account and are ready to test drive it. Now we need to figure out how to login. All you hacker geniuses reading this, hold the flames! Please remember that everyone has a first login. I'll bet even some Super Duper haxor geniuses had a hard time the first time they ever logged in. If you have never used Unix, this first time can be intimidating. In any case, if you are a Unix genius who makes phun of newbie hackers, you have no business reading this book. Humpf!

 Newbie note: "Flames" are insulting, obnoxious rantings and ravings done by people who are severely lacking in social skills and are a bunch of &$%@#!! but who think they are brilliant computer savants. For example, this newbie note is my flame against &$%@#!! flamers.

The first thing you need to know in order to get into your shell account is your user name and password. You need to get that information from the ISP that has just signed you up. The second thing you need to remember is that Unix is "case sensitive." That means if your login name is "JoeSchmoe" the shell will think "joeschmoe" is a different person than "JoeSchmoe" or "JOESCHMOE."

Okay, so you have just connected to your shell account for the first time. You may see all sorts of different stuff on that first screen. But the one thing you will always see is the prompt:

```
login:
```

Here you will type your user name. In response you will always be asked:

```
Password:
```

Here you type in your password. After this you will get some sort of a prompt. It may be a simple as:

```
%
```

Or as complicated as:

```
sleepy:~$
```

Or it may even be some sort of complicated menu where you have to choose a "shell" option before you get to the shell prompt. Again, it may be a simple as:

```
#
```

Newbie note: The prompt "#" usually means you have the superuser powers of a "root" account. The Unix superuser has the power to do anything to the computer. But you won't see this prompt unless either the systems administrator has been really careless—or someone is playing a joke on you. Sometimes a hacker thinks he or she has broken into the superuser account because of seeing the "#" prompt. This may just be a trick the sysadmin is playing. So the hacker goes playing around in what he or she thinks is the root account while the sysadmin and his friends are all laughing at the hacker.

How to Explore Your Shell Account

So you're in your shell account. You've tried the "ls -alK" command and are pretty sure this really, truly is a shell account. What do you do next?

A good place to start is to find out what kind of shell you have. There are many shells, each of which has slightly different ways of working. To do this, at your prompt give the command "echo $SHELL." Be sure to type in the same lower case and upper case letters as in this example. (If instead you were to give the command "ECHO $shell," this command won't work.) If you get the response:

```
/bin/sh
```

That means you have the Bourne shell. If you get:

```
/bin/bash
```

Then you are in the Bourne Again (bash) shell. If you get:

```
/bin/ksh
```

You have the Korn shell.

If the "echo $SHELL" command doesn't work, try the command "echo $shell," remembering to use lower case for "shell." This may get you the answer:

```
/bin/csh
```

This means you have the C shell.

Why is it important to know which shell you have? For right now, you'll probably want a shell that is easy to use. For example, when you make a mistake in typing, it's nice to hit the backspace key and not see ^H^H^H on your screen. Bash will make it easy to fix typing mistakes. Later, though, for running those super hacker exploits, the C shell may be better for you.

If you are a beginner, you will probably find bash to be the easiest shell to use. You may be able to get the bash shell by simply typing the word "bash" at the prompt. If this doesn't work, ask tech support at your ISP for a shell account set up to use bash. (If you want to get really expert at using this shell, get *Learning the Bash Shell.*[1])

If you want to find out what other shells you have the right to use, try "csh" to get the C shell; "ksh" to get the Korn shell, "sh" for Bourne shell, "tcsh" for the Tcsh shell, and "zsh" for the Zsh shell. If you don't have one of them, when you give the command to get into that shell you will get back the answer "command not found."

Evil genius tip: Later on, when you are trying to compile and run programs, you will discover that some programs don't run on all shells. A simple example of this is the "set prompt = " command. On my SunOS csh or tcsh shells I can give the command:

```
set prompt = "Your wish is my command, O master#"
```

and it works. This is really neat if a neighbor drops by and sees this prompt on my monitor. But the bash shell ignores this command, smugly sitting there with a "bash#" prompt. That #, by the way, doesn't mean I'm root. It means the sysadmins at this shell account provider think it is cool to make the "#" a default prompt for all users.

Now that you have chosen your shell, the next thing is to explore. See what riches your ISP has allowed you to use. For that you will want to learn, and I mean really learn, your most important Unix commands and auxiliary programs. Because I am supreme arbiter of what goes into this book (that's what you think, Carolyn—ed.), I get to decide what the most important commands are. Hmm, "ten" sounds like a famous number. So you're going to get the:

Ten Meinel Hall 'O Fame Shell Account Exploration Tools

1) **man <command name>** This magic command brings up the online Unix manual. Use it on each of the commands below, today! Wonder what all the *man* command options are? Try "man -k".

2) **ls** lists files. Jericho suggests "Get people in the habit of using 'ls - alK'. This will come into play down the road for security-conscious users." You'll see a huge list of files that you can't see with the "ls" command alone, and lots of details. If you see such a long list of files that they scroll off the terminal screen, one way to solve the problem is to use "ls -alK|more".

3) **pwd** shows what directory you are in.

4) **cd <directory>** changes directories. Kewl directories to check out include /usr, /bin and /etc. For laughs, jericho suggests exploring /temp.

---

1   by Cameron Newham and Bill Rosenblatt, published by O'Reilly.

5) **more** **<filename>** This shows the contents of text files. Also you might be able to find "less" and "cat," which are similar commands.

6) **whereis <program name>** Think there might be a nifty program hidden somewhere? Maybe a game you love? This will find it for you. Similar commands are "find" and "locate." Try them all for extra fun.

7) **vi** An editing program. You'll need it to make your own files and when you start programming while in your shell account. You can use it to write a really lurid file for people to read when they finger you. Or try "emacs." It's another editing program and IMHO more fun than vi. Other editing programs you may find include "ed" (an ancient editing program which I have used to write thousands of lines of Fortran 77 code), "ex," "fmt," "gmacs," "gnuemacs," and "pico." Pico is probably the easiest of these.

8) **grep** Extracts information from files, especially useful for seeing what's in syslog and shell log files. Similar commands are "egrep," "fgrep," and "look."

9) **chmod** **<filename>** Change file permissions.

10) **rm** **<filename>** Delete file. If you have this command you should also find "cp" for copy file, and "mv" for move file.

How to Tell Whether Your Shell Account Is any Good for Hacking

Alas, not all shell accounts are created equal. Your ISP may have decided to cripple your budding hacker career by forbidding your access to important tools. But you absolutely must have access to the top ten tools listed above. In addition, you will need tools to explore both your ISP's local area network (LAN) and the Internet. So in the spirit of being Supreme Arbiter of Haxor Kewl, here are my:

Ten Meinel Hall 'O Fame LAN and Internet Exploration Tools

1) **telnet hostname <port number or name>** If your shell account won't let you telnet into any port you want either on its LAN or the Internet, you are totally crippled as a hacker. Dump your ISP now!

2) **who** shows you who else is currently logged in on your ISP's LAN. Other good commands to explore the other users on your LAN are "w," "rwho, " "users."

3) **netstat** All sorts of statistics on your LAN, including all Internet connections. For real fun, try "netstat -r" to see the kernel routing table. However, jericho warns "Be careful. I was teaching a friend the basics of summing up a Unix system and I told her to do that and 'ifconfig'. She was booted off the system the next day for 'hacker suspicion' even though both are legitimate commands for users."

4) **whois <hostname>** Get lots of information on Internet hosts outside your LAN.

5) **nslookup** Get a whole bunch more information on other Internet hosts.

6) **dig** Even more info on other Internet hosts. whois, nslookup and dig are not redundant. Try to get a shell account that lets you use all.

7) **finger** Not only can you use finger inside your LAN. It will sometimes get you valuable information about users on other Internet hosts.

8) **ping** Find out if a distant computer is alive and run diagnostic tests—or just plain be a meanie and clobber people with pings. (However, I strongly advise against using ping to annoy or harm others.)

9) **traceroute** Kind of like ping with attitude. Maps Internet connections, reveals routers and boxes running firewalls. Also doubles as a cheapie weapon.

10) **ftp** Use it to upload and download files to and from other computers.

If you have all these tools, you're in great shape to begin your hacking career. Stay with your ISP. Treat him well.

Once you get your shell account, you will probably want to supplement the "man" command with a good Unix book . Jericho recommends the book *Unix in a Nutshell* published by O'Reilly.[2] I like *The Unix Companion* by Harley Hahn.

How to Keep from Losing Your Shell Account

So now you have a hacker's an account on a powerful computer running Unix. How do you keep this dream account? If you are a hacker, that is not so easy. The problem is that you have no right to keep that account. You can be kicked off for suspicion of being a bad guy, or even if you become inconvenient, at the whim of the owners. So what are the things you shouldn't do if you want to keep your account?

Meinel Hall 'O Shame Top Five Ways to Get Kicked out of Your Shell Account

1) **Abusing Your ISP** Let's say you are reading Bugtraq and you see some code for a new way to break into a computer. Panting with excitement, you run emacs and paste the code into a new file and use chmod to make the file executable. You debug until you have fixed up the purposely crippled stuff someone put in to keep total idiots from running it. You tweak it until it runs under your flavor of Unix. You compile and run the program against your own ISP. It works! You are looking at that "#" prompt and jumping up and down yelling "I got root! I got root!" You have lost your hacker virginity, you brilliant dude, you! Only, next time you go to log in, your password doesn't work. You have been booted off your ISP. *Never, never abuse your own ISP!*

> **You can go to jail warning: If you want to break into another computer, you must have the permission of the owner. Otherwise you are breaking the law.**

---

2   O'Riley has a lot of good books on Unix, and Unix-related programs. You can view their online catalog at *http://www.oreilly.com*, or write O'Reilly, 101 Morris St. Sebastopol, CA 95472.

2) **Ping Abuse** Another temptation is to use the powerful Internet connection of your shell account (usually a T1 or maybe even a T3) to ping the crap out of the people you don't like. This is especially common on Internet Relay Chat. Thinking of ICBMing or nuking that dork? Resist the temptation to abuse ping or any other Internet Control Message Protocol attacks. Use ping only as a diagnostic tool, okay? Please? Or else!

3) **Excessive Port Surfing** Port surfing is telnetting to a specific port on another computer. Usually you are okay if you just briefly visit another computer via telnet, and don't go any further than what that port offers to the casual visitor. But if you keep on probing and playing with another computer, the sysadmin at the target computer will probably email your sysadmin records of your little visits. (These records of port visits are usually stored in "syslog" depending on the configuration of your target computer—and assuming it is a Unix system.)

Even if no one complains about you, some sysadmins habitually check the shell log files that keep a record of everything you or any other user on the system has been doing in their shells. If your sysadmin sees a pattern of excessive attention to one or a few computers, he or she may assume you are plotting a break-in. Boom, your account is dead.

4) **Running Suspicious Programs** If you run a program whose primary use is as a tool to commit computer crime, you are likely to get kicked off your ISP. For example, many ISPs have a monitoring system that detects the use of the program SATAN. Run SATAN from your shell account and you may be history.

 Newbie note: SATAN stands for Security Administration Tool for Analyzing Networks. It basically works by connecting to one port after another of the victim computer. It determines what program (daemon) is running on each port, and figures out whether that daemon has a vulnerability that can be used to break into that computer. SATAN can be used by a sysadmin to figure out how to make his or her computer safe. Or it may be just as easily used by a computer criminal to break into someone else's computer.

5) **Storing Suspicious Programs** It's nice to think that the owners of your ISP mind their own business. But oftentimes they don't. In fact, in the US they actually have a legal right to snoop on their users. They may prowl around your files. They may laugh at your email. Okay, maybe they are really high-minded and resist the temptation to snoop in your email. But don't count on it.

One solution to this problem is to give your evil hacker tools innocuous names. For example, you could rename SATAN to ANGEL. But your sysdamin may try running your programs to see what they do. If any of your programs turn out to be commonly used to commit computer crimes, you are history.

Wait, wait, you are saying. Why get a shell account if I can get kicked out even for legal, innocuous hacking? After all, SATAN is legal to use. In fact, you can learn lots of neat stuff with SATAN. Most hacker tools, even if they are primarily used to commit crimes, are also educational. Certainly if you want to become a sysadmin someday you will need to learn how these programs work.

Sigh, you may as well learn the truth. Shell accounts are kind of like hacker training wheels. They are okay for beginner stuff. But to become a serious hacker, you need to find an ISP run by hackers who will accept you and let you do all sorts of suspicious things right under their nose. Yeah, sure.

Your alternative is to install some form of Unix on your home computer. If you have Unix on your home computer and use a PPP connection to get into the Internet, your ISP is much less likely to be successful at snooping on you. But that is a topic of another chapter: *Linux!*

Section 2, Chapter 2
Hacking with Finger

How would you like to move ahead in your hacking career with one of the simplest, yet most potentially hairy hacks of the Internet? Guess what, it's *finger*, a seemingly simple class of programs with hidden powers. That is, it has hidden powers if you are using one of the fingers programs that you run from a Unix shell account. If you try the techniques of this chapter using a Win95 or Mac finger program, you may not be able to get the same results. But the many different results you can get are part of the excitement of finger.

In this chapter you will learn:
- What is finger?
- Why hackers use finger
- Finger's .project and .plan files, and how you can set them up
- The normal way to finger
- The hacker way to finger—and why

What is Finger?

Finger will sometimes give you useful information about other people on the Internet. It may be as simple as a one line reply, or as complicated as screen after screen of usage statistics, users lists, or even jokes.

Here's what you might get when you finger me from your shell account. I gave this command on a shell account with Sun SPARC running SunOS:

```
-finger cpm
Login name: cpm    In real life: Carolyn Meinel
Directory: /home3/user/cpm      Shell: /bin/csh
On since Sep 12 20:36:42 on ttype from pmd01.Foo66.com
New mail received Fri Sep 12 19:49:09 1997;
   unread since Fri Sep 12 17:10:05 1997
Project: Writing the Happy Hacker book
Plan:
Top Ten Signs You Might Be A Sysadmin
```

— by Jonathan Kalbfeld
10. You see a bumper sticker that says "Users are Losers" and you have no idea it is referring to drugs.
9. Your sleep schedule is similar to that of the great horned owl.
8. You make more than all of the MBAs you know who actually finished college.
7. You have enough computing power in your house or apartment to render obscene pictures of upper management people.
6. Your idea of a social event is going to a Non-Disclosure Discussion.
5. The last time you wore a tie was your high school graduation.
4. The last time you kissed someone was in high school.
3. "What? No raise? No Backups, then!"
2. You have a vanity plate on your car that names part of the Unix File System.
And the number one sign you might be a Sysadmin...
1. You have ever uttered the phrase "I will be working from home today so I can avoid wearing pants."
— Jonathan Kalbfeld   jonathan@thoughtwave.com

The finger command we are studying today is not the IRC finger. Here's how you can prove this. While on the same computer, but running Mirc, I use the Mirc finger command and get:

```
-[cmeinel FINGER]
-
[cmeinel FINGER reply]: Carolyn Meinel
(cmeinel@techbroker.com) Idle 48 seconds
-
```

What happens if you try the Windows program WSFinger? To use it, first get a PPP connection running. With this program I enter the command "Cpm@Foo66.com" and get the exact same information as the finger program running under SunOS.

So why get a shell account if you can get the same results from a Windows or Mac finger program? The answer is, in this case we just did the simplest thing possible with finger. There are far more interesting ways to use finger.

Finger does not work the same everywhere. Because the Internet consists of tens of millions of computers with many different operating systems all linked together, you can expect that a lot of different finger programs are out there. Since the finger command will bring together finger programs running on two or more computers— results will vary.

It is these varying results that make finger a serious hacker tool. In fact, it is so serious, that that in 1988 Robert Tappan Morris used a bug in one type of finger program (along with a sendmail bug) to crash the entire Internet.

How to Create Your Finger Info

You are probably wondering how you can set things up so when people finger you, they get something that makes you look like a hacker.

First you need to have a shell account. Honest, this chapter is not going to be fun unless you get a shell account!

Next, you need to figure out whether your ISP even allows finger. Try fingering yourself. Just give the command "finger myname@myisp," substituting your email address for "myname@myisp." If this doesn't work, be happy, because if finger is disabled, this will make it harder for bad guy hackers to beat up on you.

If your ISP does allow finger, and if you have a shell account, you get to create two files, one named .project, and the other .plan. (The dot in front of each file means you won't see it if you give the plain "ls" command.) Both of these files will be sent to anyone who fingers you.

To create or edit each of these files, the easiest way is to type "pico .plan" or "pico .project." A screen will come up that has all the commands for this editor at the bottom. Put in whatever you like and save the file. Note that only the first line of .project will show when people finger you.

Why Hackers Use Finger

One of the first things you might notice when you try out finger is that it is hard to find computers on which this command works. The biggest reason for this is because finger might give away important information such as lists of user names and who is logged on to a computer at any given time.

Suppose a cracker were to be able to get a password file from a computer and crack a few passwords. He still needs to know what user names are there so he can match user names with passwords.

Also, a computer criminal doesn't want to try to break in when the system administrator is logged on. If finger is running on that computer, anyone can see whether the sysadmin is on.

Here's how the finger command can get information that is useful for hacking. Instead of fingering a particular user, I simply give the command:

```
-finger
Login      Name              TTY Idle    When     Where
support    Foo66 Support      p0   16 Fri 20:09  poqito.Foo66.com
ammann     Cheryl Foolady     p1   4d Mon 11:39  128.165.56.123:0
mfooggs    M. Fooggs          p4 8:19 Fri 12:20  vectra.fulabs.gov
reay       Kat                p5      Fri 19:54  puerta.Foo66.com
Ujmail     Fu Corporation U   p6      Fri 20:59  puerta.Foo66.com
swestart   Santa Fo Fine Art  p8 1:21 Fri 17:21  pmc10.Foo66.com
anaconda   David Fuling       pc 4:22 Mon 14:33  lugosi.fulabs.gov
sdl        sdl                pd    3 Fri 16:42  rio.Foo66.com
cpm        Carolyn Meinel     pe      Fri 20:36  pmd01.Foo66.com
hankypnk   Hank Fubar         q0   16 Fri 20:21  mack.Foo66.com
msix       Foo W7ZFB         *q1      Fri 20:17  puerta.Foo66.com
jalpha     Charlie Fooless    P0   31 Fri 08:25  pmd09:S.0
jalpha     Charlie Fooless    P1      Wed 17:54  pmd09:S.1
```

The WSFinger program can get the same result. However, it needs a different command. In its window for the finger command you enter the name of my ISP, Foo66.com.

The Hacker Way to use Finger

But there is a more elite way to finger people. Sometimes a finger command will not get you nearly as much information as a telnet directly into your target computer's finger port.

What's this finger port stuff? When you finger joe@boring.isp.net, this causes your computer to connect to port 79 on the host boring.ISP.net. It gets whatever is in the .plan and .project files in Joe Blow's account and displays them on your computer screen. If his account is also set up to reveal things like whether he has unread mail and when he last logged in, you will also see that.

But the hacker way is to first telnet to boring.ISP.net's port 79, from which we can then run its finger program directly from your home computer, instead of having your ISP's finger program control the interaction.

Here's how to do it. Give the command:

```
telnet boring.ISP.net 79
```

Now you are actually on a computer at boring.isp.net. If you are a good Internet citizen you would then give this boring.isp.net box the command:

```
Joe_Blow
```

This should give you the same results as just staying on your own computer and giving the command "finger Joe_Blow@boring.ISP.net."

So why bother doing it? The reason is, there are lots of other things to try after gaining control of the finger program of boring.ISP.net by telnetting to port 79.

For example, some finger programs will respond to the command:

```
@
```

Another command to which a finger port might respond is simply:

```
finger
```

If this command works, it will give you a complete list of the users of this host. These user names then can be used to try to break into that computer.

There are plenty of other commands that also will work on some finger programs on other computers.

Why is it so interesting to get a list of user names? Sometimes a system will have no restrictions on how lame a password can be. Common password problems are caused by users who use no password at all, choose a password that is the same as the user name, passwords that are the user's first or last name, and "guest." Even choosing a password that is a word or a common name can create a welcome mat for someone who wants to break in.

Someone who is trying to break into boring.isp.net might first try all the user names and then just hit enter for the password. Next the would-be intruder would try each user name and simply give the user name again for the password. Next tries are the first and last names of the users. If these don't work, there are widely circulated programs which find passwords by trying out every word of the dictionary and every name in the typical phone book.

You can go to jail warning: With just the information in this chapter alone, and finger, you could break into the user accounts on many of computers. But this is against the law almost everywhere. In the United States, if you break into a computer across state lines, it is a Federal felony. Newbie computer crackers often assume it is easy to get away with breaking in. But the headers on the packets that carry your commands tell the sysadmin of the victim computer who you are.

Newbie Note: Is your password easy to crack? If you have a shell account, you may change it with the command:

```
passwd
```

Choose a password that isn't in the dictionary or phone book, is at least 6 characters long, and includes some characters that are not letters of the alphabet. A password that is found in the dictionary but has one extra character is *not* a good password.

But presumably you don't want to run around committing felonies. Even though many Internet Service providers are out there creating an attractive nuisance by running the finger service, you can resist the temptation. What is there to do with finger that is legal?

How about experimenting with unusual variations in the finger command?

```
finger -l @hostname   (that's a letter l, not a minus one, you sub stitute the name of the
                        computer for hostname)
finger 0              (that's the number zero)
finger root
finger bin
finger ftp
finger system
finger guest
finger demo
finger manager
```

Or, even just hitting <Enter> once you are into port 79 may give you something interesting.

By telneting to finger you can sometimes discover really funny things. For example, one time I checked out one of my favorite victims, er, host computers, thales.nmfoobar.com (named after an ancient Greek philosopher).

```
-telnet thales.nmfoobar.com 79
Trying 198.59.166.10 ...
Connected to thales.nmfoobar.com.
```

```
Escape character is '^]'.
I just forgot my whole philosophy of life!!!
Connection closed by foreign host.
```

Gosh, I guess I had been port surfing Thales too much! Later I paid him another visit, and this time merely got:

```
Welcome to Linux version 2.0.30 at thales.nmfoobar.com !
9:29pm  up 1 day,  7:33,  2 users,  load average: 0.08, 0.13, 0.12
Login     Name         Tty  Idle  Login Time   Office    Office Phone
root      root          1d  Sep 11 13:56
Fupia     Ron Fupia    p0   4:28  Sep 11 14:34 (russell.nmfoobar.net)
```

There are plenty of other commands that may or may not work. However, most commands on most finger programs will give you little or nothing. This is because most system administrators don't want people breaking into their computers. In fact, a really cautious sysadmin will disable finger entirely. So you'll never even manage to get into port 79 of some computers.

Because it is so excruciatingly dangerous to keep the finger port open, some day it may become impossible to finger or be fingered. But today there are still many out there. So happy fingering while the fun lasts!

Section 2, Chapter 3
Heroic Hacking in Half an Hour

How would you like to totally blow away your friends? Okay, what is the hairiest thing you hear that super hackers do?

It's gaining access to a computer on which you don't have an account, right?

We'll explore how to run a powerful class of programs that run on most of the millions of computers hooked up to the Internet. How would you like to access these Internet computers in the same way as the most notorious hacker in history: Robert Tappan Morris? How would you like to do this without breaking the law and while causing no harm?

It was the "Morris Worm" which forced the National Science Foundation to briefly shut down the Internet in 1988. One flaw he exploited was in a once-common finger program. The other was in sendmail, which is one of the programs we will learn how to exploit in this chapter. Of course, the flaws Morris used to fill up 10% of the computers on the Internet with his self-mailing worm have been fixed now—on most Internet hosts. But other problems keep on taking their place.

What you will discover today holds the seeds of the biggest threat to the Internet today: denial of service attacks using the mail forging vulnerabilities of most Internet hosts. The tactics you will learn today are used by spammers (people who send out unsolicited email) and many types of criminals. But you can also use these tactics for fun and exploration of the mysteries of how email works.

In this chapter you will learn:
- How to forge simple email
- How to read the readers of your email to see how good the forgery is
- How to tell if a computer is good for forging email
- How to forge complicated headers for email
- How to forge Usenet news group posts

In addition, what we are about to learn is the first step of several ways that hackers break into the root accounts of unsuspecting computers, exploiting flaws in the sendmail program.

 Newbie note: Root! It is the Valhalla of the hard-core cracker. "Root" is the account on a multi-user Unix computer which allows you to play god. It is the account from which you can enter and use any other account, read and modify any file, run any program. With root access, you can completely destroy all data on boring.ISP.net. (I am *not* suggesting that you do so!)

However, even though what you are about to learn looks to some people like you have broken into a computer, it is legal, harmless, and fun—as long as you do not choose to misuse this information. In this chapter we will be careful not to step over the bounds of safe hacking. No pulling the blinds and swearing blood oaths among your buddies who will witness you doing this hack.

This chapter assumes you have a shell account. If you don't (shame, shame!), you could use a telnet program for your Mac or Win95 box.[1]

But your best way to do this is with a SHELL ACCOUNT! If you don't have one yet, get it now! See Section 2, Chapter 1 for instructions on how to get one. Get a shell account now! There, have I said it enough!?

 Newbie note: A shell account is an Internet account that lets you give Unix commands. Unix is a lot like DOS. You get a prompt on your screen and type out commands. Unix is the most common and most powerful language of the Internet. If you want to be a serious hacker, you have to learn Unix. I mean it!

How to Forge Simple Email

Even if you have never telneted before, this hack is super simple. In fact, even though what you are about to learn will look like, and is, hacking of the most heroic sort, you can master it in half an hour—or less. You only need to memorize two commands: "telnet hostname 25" (where *hostname* is the name of the computer on which you want to forge email), and "help."

Let's give this command:

```
->telnet callisto.uoffoo.edu 25
```

If you have ever done telnet before, you probably just put in the name of the computer you planned to visit, but didn't add in any numbers afterward. But those numbers afterward are what makes the first distinction between the good, boring

---

1   See Section 1, Chapter 3 for Win95 instructions, and Section 1, Chapter 4 for Mac instructions.

Internet citizen and someone slaloming down the slippery slope of hackerdom, muhahaha!

What that 25 means is that you are commanding telnet to take you to a specific port on your intended victim, er, computer. Just like you did with port 79.

 Newbie note: A computer port is a place where information goes in or out of it. On your home computer, examples of ports are your monitor, which sends information out, your keyboard and mouse, which send information in, and your modem, which sends information both out and in. But an Internet host computer such as callisto.uoffoo.edu has many more ports than a typical home computer. The ports we talk about in this book that are identified by numbers are not physical ports, like a keyboard or RS232 serial port (for your modem). They are virtual (software) ports specified by the TCP/IP protocol.

Whenever you telnet to a computer's port 25, you will get one of two results. Once in awhile, you'll get a message saying "connection refused" as you hit a firewall or a closed port. If this happens, just try another hostname. But, more often than not, you get something like this:

```
Trying 999.24.96.10...
Connected to callisto.uoffoo.edu.
Escape character is '^]'.
220 callisto.uoffoo.edu Smail3.1.28.1 #41 ready at Fri, 12 Jul  96
12:17 MDT
```

Get a look at this! It didn't ask us to log in. It just says . . . ready! Notice it is running Smail 3.1.28.1, a program used to compose and send email.

Ohmygosh, what do we do now? Ask callisto.uoffoo.edu to tell you what commands you can use. In general, when you get on a strange computer, at least one of three commands will get you information: "help," "?", or "man." In this case I type in:

```
help
250-The following SMTP commands are recognized:
250-
250-    HELO hostname              - startup and give your hostname
250-    MAIL FROM: <sender-address> - start transaction from sender
250-    RCPT TO: <recipient-address>   - name recipient for message
250-    VRFY address              - verify deliverability of address
250-    EXPN address               - expand mailing list address
250-    DATA                      - start text of mail message
250-    RSET                     - reset state, drop transaction
250-    NOOP - do nothing
250-    DEBUG [level]             - set debugging level,default 1
250-    HELP                     - produce this help message
250-    QUIT                    - close SMTP connection
250-
250-The normal sequence of events in sending a message is to state
the
```

```
250-sender address with a MAIL FROM command, give the recipients
with
250-as many RCPT TO commands as are required (one address per command)
250-and then to specify the mail message text after the DATA command.
250 Multiple messages may be specified.  End the last one with a
QUIT.
```

Getting this list of commands makes you look really kewl to your friends because you know how to get the computer to tell you how to hack it. And it means that all you have to memorize is the "telnet <hostname> 25" and "help" commands. For the rest, you can simply check up on the commands while on-line. So even if your memory is as bad as mine, you really can learn and memorize this hack in only half an hour. Heck, maybe half a minute.

What do we do with these commands? Yes, you figured it out, this is an email program. And guess why you can get on it without logging in? Guess why it was a point of vulnerability that allowed Robert Tappan Morris to crash the Internet?

Port 25 moves email from one node to the next across the Internet. It automatically takes incoming email, and if the email doesn't belong to someone with an email address on that computer, it sends it on to the next computer on the net, eventually to wend its way to the person to whom this email belongs.

Sometimes email will go directly from sender to recipient, but if you email to someone far away, it may go through several computers.

There are millions of computers on the Internet that forward email. If you telnet to the right ports, you can get access to many of these computers without a password! Most of these run the sendmail program. Furthermore, as you will soon learn, it is easy to get the Internet addresses of these millions of computers. So if someone finds a vulnerability in sendmail, they can beat up on one heck of a bunch of computers.

 Evil genius tip: Are you a sysadmin or owner of an ISP? You probably don't want your computers to forward email or allow people from outside your system to use them to compose email. Nowadays we have Internet backbones to pipe all that mail around. Make it impossible to forge or forward email on your computers and you will not only get rid of the readers of this book, you will also stymie spammers and other email bad guys.

If you must allow outsiders to use your mail programs, run identd and keep logs of mail use. That way you can help the authorities catch criminals.

Over and over again, hackers have discovered new ways to use bugs in this program to break into computers.

There are three major programs commonly found running on port 25. Besides sendmail, there are smail and qmail. Neither smail or qmail have the history that sendmail has of bugs that allow users to take over the entire computer. Qmail is especially easy to configure to prevent mail forging or forwarding.

However, the problems of sendmail don't necessarily mean it is less secure than smail or qmail. Sendmail has been around much longer than the other two. As Smail and qmail have more hackers play around with them, serious vulnerabilities may be discovered in them. Also, sendmail is more powerful in many respects than smail or qmail. As the latter two programs get more code added to them in order to make them able to do as much as sendmail, they may become complicated enough to become as easy for hackers to exploit them.

The sendmail, smail and qmail programs can be configured in many ways. This means you will get many different responses when you telnet about to different port 25s. One of the joys of hacking is exploring these computers to find those that suit ones fancy. Now that we are in Morris Worm country, what can we do?

 Evil Genius tip: The Morris worm exploited the "DEBUG" command. Don't try this at home. Nowadays if you find a program running on port 25 with the DEBUG command, it is probably a trap. Trust me. When I went to Callisto and saw "debug," I kept my hands to myself.

 Evil Genius tip: Are you waging hacker war? Are you trying to find out whether your enemy has an account on a certain computer? You know his user name, but finger is turned off on the computer you want to search. Instead, you can telnet to port 25 and use the vrfy or expn command to see if anyone by that user name is on that box. Are you a sysadmin? Turn off vrfy and expn.

Here's what I did with Callisto. (My commands have no numbers in front of them, whereas the computer's responses are prefixed by numbers.)

```
helo santa@north.pole.org
250 callisto.uoffoo.edu Hello santa@north.pole.org
mail from:santa@north.pole.org
250 <santa@north.pole.org> ... Sender Okay
rcpt to:cmeinel@nmfoobar.com
250  <cmeinel@nmfoobar.com> ... Recipient Okay
data
354 Enter mail, end with "." on a line by itself
It works!!!
.
250 Mail accepted
```

How to Read the Headers of your Email

Let's see what that email looked like when it arrived in my mailbox, showing the complete header. First, we use the free version of Eudora:

```
X-POP3-Rcpt: cmeinel@socrates
```

This line tells us that POP3 is the program of my ISP that received my email, and that my incoming email is handled by the computer Socrates.

 Evil Genius Tip: email which comes into your email reading program is handled by port 110. Try telnetting there someday. But usually POP3, the program running on 110, won't give you help with its commands and boots you off the minute you make a misstep.

```
Return-Path: <santa@north.pole.org>
```

This line above is my fake email address.

```
Apparently-From: santa@north.pole.org
Date: Fri, 12 Jul 96 12:18 MDT
```

Note that the header lines above say "Apparently-From." This is important because it alerts me to the fact that this might be fake mail.

```
Apparently-To: cmeinel@nmfoobar.com
X-Status:
It works!!!
```

   Different email reading programs show different headers. So how good your fake email is depends in part on what email program your recipient uses to read it. Here's what Pine, which runs in a shell account, shows:

```
Return-Path: <santa@north.pole.org>
Received:
    from callisto.uoffoo.edu by nmfoobar.com
      with smtp
    (Linux Smail3.1.28.1 #4)
    id m0uemp4-000LFGC; Fri, 12 Jul 96 12:20 MDT
```

This identifies the computer on which I ran the smail program. It also tells what version of the smail program was running.

```
Apparently-From: santa@north.pole.org
```

Here is the "apparently-from" message again. So both Pine and Eudora show this might be fake mail.

```
Received: from santa@north.pole.org by
callisto.uoffoo.edu with smtp
      (Smail3.1.28.1 #41) id m0uemnL-0000HFC; Fri, 12 Jul 96 12:18
MDT
Message-Id: 0uemnL-0000HFC@callisto.uoffoo.edu
```

Oh, oh! Not only does it show that it may be fake mail—it has a message ID! This means that somewhere on Callisto there might be a log of message IDs telling who has used port 25 and the smail program. Every time someone logs on to port 25 on that computer, their email address is left behind on the log along with that message ID.

```
Date: Fri, 12 Jul 96 12:18 MDT
Apparently-From: santa@north.pole.com
Apparently-To: cmeinel@nmfoobar.com
It works!!!
```

If someone were to use this email program to do a dastardly deed, that message ID is what will put the cops on his or her tail.

How Can you Tell Whether a Computer Is Good for Forging Email?

But—the email programs on port 25 of many Internet hosts are not as well defended as callisto.uoffoo.edu. Some are better defended, and some are not defended at all. In fact, it is possible that some may not even keep a log of the users of port 25, making them perfect for criminal email forgery. Or, even worse, they might not run a program called ident, which identifies the user name and host name of anyone who uses any port of that computer.

 Evil genius tip: An Internet host computer that doesn't run ident is a gold mine for bad guys. No one can trace back to the true users of port 25 on a host that doesn't run ident. On these computers, spammers, email bombers, extortionists and nasty pranksters can run rampant.

You can go to jail warning: If you are thinking of using fake email to commit a crime, think again. You probably don't know enough to forge email well enough to elude arrest.

What this means is that email with perfect-looking headers could still be fake. You need some sort of encrypted verification scheme, for example a PGP signature, to be certain email is genuine.

Let's check out how well port 25 is defended on various computers:

```
-telnet ns.Fulink.Net 25
Trying 198.999.73.8...
Connected to NS.FULINK.NET.
Escape character is '^]'.
220 Fulink.NET Sendmail AIX 3.2/UCB 5.64/4.03 ready at Fri, 12 Jul
1996 15:45
helo santa@north.pole.org
250 Fulink.NET Hello santa@north.pole.org
(plato.nmfoobar.com)
```

Oh, oh! This sendmail version isn't fooled at all! See how it puts "(plato.nmfoobar.com)"—the computer I was using for this hack—in there just to let me know it knows from what computer I've telnetted? But what the heck. I'll just bull ahead and send fake mail anyhow. Again, my input has no numbers in front, while the responses of the computer are prefaced by numbers:

```
mail from:santa@north.pole.com
250 santa@north.pole.com... Sender is valid.
rcpt to:cmeinel@nmfoobar.com
250 cmeinel@nmfoobar.com... Recipient is valid.
```

```
data
354 Enter mail. End with the . character on a line by
itself.
It works!
.
250 Ok
quit
221 Fulink.NET: closing the connection.
```

What kind of email did that computer generate? Here's what I saw using Pine:

```
Return-Path: <santa@north.pole.org>
Received:
from Fulink.NET by nmfoobar.com
 with smtp
(Linux Smail3.1.28.1 #4)
id m0ueo7t-000LEKC; Fri, 12 Jul 96 13:43 MDT
Received: from plato.nmfoobar.com by Fulink.NET (AIX
3.2/UCB 5.64/4.03)
   id AA23900; Fri, 12 Jul 1996 15:43:20 -0400
```

Oops. Here the Fulink.NET computer has revealed what computer I was on when I telnetted to its port 25. However, many people use that Internet host computer. So I'm still somewhat hidden.

```
Date: Fri, 12 Jul 1996 15:43:20 -0400
From: santa@north.pole.org
Message-Id:<9607121943.AA23900@Fulink.NET>
Apparently-To: cmeinel@nmfoobar.com
It works!
```

Here it doesn't say "Apparently-From," so now I know the computer ns.Fulink.Net is a pretty good one to send fake mail from. However, an experienced email aficionado would know from the Received: line that this is fake mail. But its phoniness doesn't just jump out at you.

Let's try another computer. Hmmm, the University of California at Fubaru is renowned for its computer sciences research. I wonder what their hosts are like? I give the command:

```
->telnet remarque.fubaru.edu
Trying 999.32.152.164...
Connected to 999.32.152.164.
Escape character is '^]'.
220 remarque.fubaru.edu ESMTP Sendmail 8.7.3/1.31 ready
at Thu, 11 Jul 1996 12
help
214-This is Sendmail version 8.7.3
214-Commands:
214-    HELO     EHLO     MAIL     RCPT     DATA
214-    RSET     NOOP     QUIT     HELP     VRFY
214-    EXPN     VERB     _____
214-For more info use "HELP        ".
```

```
214-To report bugs in the implementation send email to
214-     sendmail@CS.Fubaru.EDU.
214-For local information send email to Postmaster at your site.
214 End of HELP info
```

Oh, boy, a slightly different sendmail program! I wonder what more it will tell me about these commands?

```
HELP mail
214-MAIL FROM:
214-     Specifies the sender.
214 End of HELP info
```

Big deal! Oh, well, let's see what this computer will do to fake mail.

```
MAIL FROM:santa@north.pole.org
250 santa@north.pole.org... Sender ok
```

Heyyy ... this is interesting ... I didn't say "helo" and this sendmail program didn't slap me on the wrist! Wonder what that means ...

```
RCPT TO:cmeinel@techbroker.com
250 Recipient ok
DATA
354 Enter mail, end with "." on a line by itself
This is fake mail on a Fubaru computer for which I do not have a
password.
.
250 MAA23472 Message accepted for delivery quit
221 remarque.fubaru.edu closing connection
```

Now we go to Pine and see what the header looks like:

```
Return-Path: <santa@north.pole.org>
Received:
from nmfoobar.com by nmfoobar.com
 with smtp
(Linux Smail3.1.28.1 #4)
id m0ueRnW-000LGiC; Thu, 11 Jul 96 13:53 MDT
Received:
from remarque.fubaru.edu by nmfoobar.com
 with smtp
(Linux Smail3.1.28.1 #4)
id m0ueRnV-000LGhC; Thu, 11 Jul 96 13:53 MDT
Apparently-To:  <cmeinel@techbroker.com>
Received: from merde.food.org by remarque.fubaru.edu
(8.7.3/1.31)
id MAA23472; Thu, 11 Jul 1996 12:49:56 -0700 (PDT)
```

Look at the three "received" messages. My ISP's computer received this email not directly from Remarque.fubaru.edu. It came from merde.food.com, which in turn got the email from Remarque.

Let's see what email from remarque looks like using Pine again:

```
Date: Thu, 11 Jul 1996 12:49:56 -0700 (PDT)
From: santa@north.pole.org
Message-Id: 7111949.MAA23472@remarque.fubaru.edu
This is fake mail on a Fubaru computer for which I do not have a
password.
```

This program doesn't warn that the Santa address is phony! Even better (or worse, if you don't like computer crime), it keeps secret the name of the originating computer: plato.nmfoobar.com. Thus remarque.fubaru.edu is a really good computer from which to send fake mail.

But not all sendmail programs are so friendly to fake mail. Check out the email I created from atropos.c3pfu.org.

```
->telnet atropos.c3pfu.org 25
Trying 999.174.185.14...
Connected to atropos.c3pfu.org.
Escape character is '^]'.
220 atropos.c3pfu.org ESMTP Sendmail 8.7.4/CSUA ready
at Fri, 12 Jul 1996 15:41:33
help
502 Sendmail 8.7.4—HELP not implemented
```

Gee, you're pretty snippy today, aren't you . . . What the heck, let's plow ahead anyhow . . .

```
helo santa@north.pole.org
501 Invalid domain name
```

Hey, what's it to you, buddy? Other sendmail programs don't give a darn what name I use with "helo." Okay, okay, I'll give you a valid domain name. But not a valid user name!

```
helo satan@uoffoo.edu
250 atropos.c3pfu.org Hello cmeinel@plato.nmfoobar.com
[198.59.166.165], pleased to meet you
```

Verrrry funny, pal. I'll just bet you're pleased to meet me. Why the #%&@ did you demand a valid domain name when you knew who I was all along?

```
mail from:santa@north.pole.com
250 santa@north.pole.com... Sender ok
rcpt to: cmeinel@nmfoobar.com
250 Recipient ok
data
354 Enter mail, end with "." on a line by itself
Oh, crap!
.
250 PAA13437 Message accepted for delivery
quit
```

```
221 atropos.c3pfu.org closing connection
```

Okay, what kind of email did that obnoxious little sendmail program generate? I rush over to Pine and take a look:

```
Return-Path: <santa@north.pole.com>
Received:
from atropos.c3pfu.org by nmfoobar.com
 with smtp
(Linux Smail3.1.28.1 #4)
id m0ueqxh-000LD9C; Fri, 12 Jul 96 16:45 MDT
Apparently-To: <cmeinel@nmfoobar.com>
Received: from satan.uoffoo.edu
(cmeinel@plato.nmfoobar.com     [198.59.166.165])
by atropos.c3pfu.org (8.7.4/CSUA) with SMTP id PAA13437
for     cmeinel@nmfoobar.com; Fri, 12
Jul 1996 15:44:37 -0700 (PDT)
Date: Fri, 12 Jul 1996 15:44:37 -0700 (PDT)
From: santa@north.pole.com
Message-Id: 7122244.PAA13437@atropos.c3pfu.org
Oh, crap!
```

How truly special! Not only did the computer atropos.c3pfu.org blab out my true identity, it also revealed that satan.uoffoo.edu thing. Grump . . . that will teach me.

The moral of that little hack is that there are lots of different setups on port 25 of Internet hosts. So if you want to have fun with them, it's a good idea to check them out first before you use them to show off with.

Meanwhile you are probably wondering, was Robert Tappan Morris's exploit using sendmail debug the only way to use it to get root access? It turns out that sendmail has a long history of bugs that have allowed people to get root access to a computer by tricks as simple as just emailing the right thing. For this reason, many responsible sysadmins don't run sendmail. They use smail or qmail, which have much better histories (at least as of this writing).

How to Forge Complicated Headers for Email

Suppose you want to add things to your forged email? You'll notice in the examples above that there was no subject line in the forged email. It is easy to make as many headers as we want to make.

Here's the trick. After the data command, make your first line be "Subject: This is my forged subject header." Only put the subject you want in place of "This is my forged subject header." Then hit enter and put in your next header, for example "From: Santa Claus <santa@north.pole.org>". For each header you use just one word followed by a colon, then followed by whatever you want to be in that header. For example, it could be "Favorite-color: flamingo." Then hit enter and write the next one. You can keep this up indefinitely.

When someone opens your forged email, it will look really cool. You can even fake a bunch of those "Received:" headers to make it look like your forgery went around the world and to and from several planets, and they will stay hidden until someone hits the "full headers" command.

How about forging Usenet news group posts? This can be pretty serious business, as with a little imagination you can not only forge posts, but also forge cancel messages that can obliterate posts you don't like from the entire Usenet.

 Newbie Note: Usenet is a part of the Internet consisting of the system of on-line discussion groups called "news groups." Examples of news groups are rec.humor, comp.misc, news.announce.newusers, sci.space.policy, and alt.sex. There are well over 20,000 news groups. Usenet started out in 1980 as a Unix network linking people who wanted—you guessed it— to talk about Unix. Then some of the people wanted to talk about stuff like physics, space flight, barroom humor, and sex. The rest is history.

Here's a quick summary of how to forge Usenet posts. Once again, we use the technique of telneting to a specific port. The Usenet port usually is open only to those with accounts on that system. So you will need to telnet from your ISP shell account back into your own ISP as follows:

```
telnet news.myISP.com nntp
```

where you substitute the part of your email address that follows the @ for "myISP.com." You also have the choice of using "119" instead of "nntp."

With my ISP I get this result:

```
Trying 198.59.115.25 ...
Connected to sloth.Swfooport.com.
Escape character is '^]'.
200 sloth.Swfooport.com InterNetNews NNRP server INN
1.4unoff4 05-Mar-96 ready (posting)
```

Since we are suddenly in a program that we don't know too well, we ask for:

```
help
```

And we get:

```
100 Legal commands
auth info user Name|pass Password|generic <prog> <args>
article [MessageID|Number]
body [MessageID|Number]
date
group newsgroup
head [MessageID|Number]
help
ihave
last
list [active|newsgroups|distributions|schema]
listgroup newsgroup
mode reader
```

```
newgroups yymmdd hhmmss ["GMT"] [<distributions>]
newnews newsgroups yymmdd hhmmss ["GMT"]
  [<distributions>]
next
post
slave
stat [MessageID|Number]
xgtitle [group_pattern]
xhdr header [range|MessageID]
xover [range]
xpat header range|MessageID pat [morepat...]
xpath MessageID
Report problems to  <usenet        @Swfooport.com>
```

Use your imagination with these commands. Also, if you want to forge posts from an ISP other than your own, keep in mind that few Internet host computers have an nntp port that requires no password or an easily guessed password such as "post." So it can be quite an effort to find an undefended nntp port. Because of this, you usually have to do this on your own ISP, which makes it harder to hide your identity.

You can go to jail warning: Both faked email and Usenet posts can be easily detected—if you know what to look for. And it is possible to tell where they were forged. That means people who use these techniques to commit crimes can easily be caught.

This lesson is only a beginning explanation of forging. To learn more, how about experimenting with it yourself? So long as you don't do it for the wrong reasons, forging email is legal in most places, and can be harmless fun. Wait until your friends start getting email from aliens living on Jupiter! And if you discover yet another deadly sendmail exploit, be a good guy and don't use it for a computer crime spree, okay?

SECTION 2, CHAPTER 4
HOW TO DECIPHER HEADERS
— EVEN FORGED HEADERS

"Pleeeeze give me the names of Internet computers so I can hack them." Get control of yourself and stop laughing. I actually get email like that all the time. But it really is true that some people who call themselves hackers do not know how to get Internet host computer names from headers of email and Usenet posts.

But there are good guy uses of headers, too. If you want to become a vigilante who hunts down people who abuse email or Usenet news groups by forging headers, you absolutely must get good at deciphering forged headers.

Also, I want to make sure that the deady haxor d00dz who just read the previous chapter on forging email get anxiety attacks when they read this chapter and realize how easy it is to get caught.

In this chapter you will learn:
- what is a header
- why headers are fun
- how to see full headers
- what all that stuff in headers means
- how to get the names of Internet host computers from your headers
- what forged headers may look like

In this chapter we will concentrate on email headers. But headers on Usenet posts are almost identical to those on email. So most of what you learn here can be applied to Usenet posts.

All you need to use the techniques you will learn from this chapter is to be able to send and receive email. However, if you have a shell account, you can do much more with deciphering headers. Viva Unix!

Headers may sound like a boring topic. Heck, the Eudora email program named the button you click to read full headers "blah blah blah." But all those guys who tell you headers are boring are either ignorant—or else afraid you'll open a wonderful chest full of hacker insights. Yes, every email header you check out has the potential to unearth a treasure hidden in some back alley of the Internet.

Headers may seem simple enough to be a topic for one of the beginner chapters in section one of this book. But when I went to look up the topic of headers in my library of manuals, I was shocked to find that most of them don't even cover the topic. Two of the three I found that did cover headers said almost nothing about them. The best manual I could find is *Sendmail* by Costales and Allman, published by O'Reilly.

Technical tip: Information relevant to headers may be extracted from Requests for Comments (RFCs) 822 (best), as well as 1042, 1123, 1521 and 1891 (not a complete list). To read them, take your Web browser to http://hotbot.com and search for "RFC 822" etc.

Lacking much help from manuals, and finding that RFC 822 didn't answer many questions, the main way I researched this chapter was to send email back and forth among some of my accounts, trying out many variations (including many types of forgeries) in order to see what kinds of headers they generated. Hey, that's how real hackers are supposed to figure out stuff when RTFM (read the fine manual) or RTFRFC (read the fine RFC) doesn't tell us as much as we want to know.

What are Headers?

If you are new to hacking, the headers you are used to seeing may be incomplete. Chances are that when you get email it looks something like this:

```
From: Vegbar Fubar <fooha@ifi.foobar.no>
Date: Fri, 11 Apr 1997 18:09:53 GMT
To: hacker@techbroker.com
```

But if you know the right command, suddenly, with this same email message, we are looking at tons and tons of stuff:

```
Received: by o200.fooway.net
(950413.SGI.8.6.12/951211.SGI)
for techbr@fooway.net id OAA07210; Fri, 11 Apr
1997 14:10:06 -0400
Received: from ifi.foobar.no by o200.fooway.net via
ESMTP (950413.SGI.8.6.12/951211.SGI)
for <hacker@techbroker.com> id OAA18967; Fri, 11
Apr 1997 14:09:58 -0400
Received: from gyllir.ifi.foobar.no
(2234@gyllir.ifi.foobar.no [129.999.64.230]) by
ifi.foobar.no with ESMTP (8.6.11/ifi2.4)
id <UAA24351@ifi.foobar.no> for
<hacker@techbroker.com> ; Fri, 11 Apr 1997 20:09:56
+0200
From: Vegbar Fubar <fooha@ifi.foobar.no>
Received: from localhost (Vegbarha@localhost) by
gyllir.ifi.foobar.no ; Fri, 11 Apr 1997 18:09:53 GMT
Date: Fri, 11 Apr 1997 18:09:53 GMT
```

```
Message-Id: <199704111809.13156.gyllir@ifi.foobar.no>
To: hacker@techbroker.com
```

Have you ever wondered why all that stuff is there and what it means? We'll return to this example later in this tutorial. But first we must consider the burning question of the day:

Why are headers fun?

Why bother with those "blah blah blah" headers? Some people say they are boring, right? Wrong!

Ever hear a wannabe hacker complaining he or she doesn't have the addresses of any good computers to explore? Have you ever used one of those IP scanner programs that find valid Internet Protocol addresses of Internet hosts for you? You can find gazillions of valid addresses without the crutch of one of these programs simply by reading the headers of emails or Usenet posts.

Ever wonder who really mailed that "Make Money Fast" spam? Or who is that klutz who email bombed you? The first step to learning how to spot email forgeries and spot the culprit is to be able to read headers.

Want to learn how to convincingly forge email? Do you aspire to write spam or email bomber programs? (I disapprove of spam and email bomb programs, but let's be honest about the kinds of knowledge their creators must draw upon.) The first step is to understand headers.

Want to attack someone's computer? Find out where best to attack from the headers of their email. I disapprove of this use, too. But I'm dedicated to telling you the truth about hacking, so like it or not, here it is.

How can you see full headers?

So you look at the headers of your email and it doesn't appear to have any good stuff whatsoever. Want to see all the hidden stuff? The way you do this depends on what email program you are using.

The most popular email program today is Eudora. To see full headers in Eudora, just click the "blah, blah, blah" button on the far left end of the tool bar.

The Netscape web browser includes an email reader. To see full headers, click on Options, then click the "Show All Headers" item.

Another popular email program is Pegasus. Hit control-H to see full headers.

The Compuserve and AOL email programs automatically show full headers.

To see the full headers with Microsoft Exchange in Windows-95, simply choose Archive and then Preferences.

Pine is the most popular email program used with Unix shell accounts. Since in order to be a real hacker you will sooner or later be using Unix, now may be a great time to start using Pine.

If you have never used Pine before, you may find it isn't as easy to use as those glitzy Windows email programs. But aside from its amazing powers, there is a really good reason to learn to compose email in Pine: you get practice using pico editor commands (or whatever is the editor with your configuration of Pine). If you want to be a real hacker, you will be using the pico editor (or another editor that uses similar commands) someday when you are writing programs in a Unix shell.

To bring up Pine, at the cursor in your Unix shell simply type in "pine."

In Pine, while viewing an email message, you may be able to see full headers by simply hitting the "h" key. If this doesn't work, you will have to go into the Setup menu to enable this command. To do this, go to the main menu and give the command "s" for Setup. Then in the Setup menu choose "c" for Config. On the second page of the Config menu you will see something like this:

```
PINE 3.91   SETUP CONFIGURATION   Folder: INBOX  2
Messages
[ ]  compose-rejects-unqualified-addrs
    [ ]   compose-sets-newsgroup-without-confirm
    [ ]   delete-skips-deleted
    [ ]   enable-aggregate-command-set
    [ ]   enable-alternate-editor-cmd
    [ ]   enable-alternate-editor-implicitly
    [ ]   enable-bounce-cmd
    [ ]   enable-flag-cmd
    [X]   enable-full-header-cmd
    [ ]   enable-incoming-folders
    [ ]   enable-jump-shortcut
    [ ]   enable-mail-check-cue
    [ ]   enable-suspend
    [ ]   enable-tab-completion
    [ ]   enable-unix-pipe-cmd
    [ ]   expanded-view-of-addressbooks
    [ ]   expanded-view-of-folders
    [ ]   expunge-without-confirm
    [ ]   include-attachments-in-reply
? Help        E Exit Config P Prev       - PrevPage
    X [Set/Unset] N Next     Spc NextPage  W
WhereIs
```

You first highlight the line that says "enable-full-header-command" and then press the "x" key. Then give "e" to exit saving the change. Once you have done this, when you are reading your email you will be able to see full headers by giving the "h" command.

Elm is another Unix email reading program. It actually gives slightly more detailed headers than Pine. In some cases your sysadmin may have configured it to automatically show full headers. If not, hit h to get them.

What does all that stuff in your headers mean?

We'll start by taking a look at a mildly interesting full header. Then we'll examine two headers that reveal some interesting shenanigans. Finally we will look at a forged header.

Let's return to that fairly ordinary full header we looked at above. We will decipher it piece by piece. First we look at the simple version:

```
From: Vegbar Fubar <fooha@ifi.foobar.no>
Date: Fri, 11 Apr 1997 18:09:53 GMT
To: hacker@techbroker.com
```

The information within any header consists of a series of fields separated from each other by a "newline" character. Each field consists of two parts: a field name, which includes no spaces and is terminated by a colon; and the contents of the field. In this case the only fields that show are "From:", "Date:", and "To:".

In every header there are two classes of fields: the "envelope," which contains only the sender and recipient fields; and everything else, which is information specific to the handling of the message. In this case the only field that shows which gives information on the handling of the message is the Date field.

When we expand to a full header, we are able to see all the fields of the header. We will now go through this information line by line.

```
Received: by o200.fooway.net
(950413.SGI.8.6.12/951211.SGI)for techbr@fooway.net id
OAA07210; Fri, 11 Apr 1997 14:10:06 -0400
```

This line tells us that I downloaded this email from the POP server at a computer named o200.fooway.net. This was done on behalf of my account with email address of techbr@fooway.net. The (950413.SGI.8.6.12/951211.SGI) part identifies the software name and version running that POP server.

 Newbie note: POP stands for Post Office Protocol. Your POP server is the computer that holds your email until you want to read it. Usually your the email program on your home computer or shell account computer will connect to port 110 on your POP server to get your email. A similar, but more general protocol is IMAP, for Interactive Mail Access Protocol. Trust me, you will be a big hit at parties if you can hold forth on the differences between POP and IMAP! (Hint: for more info, RTFRFCs.)

Now we examine the second line of the header:

```
Received: from ifi.foobar.no by o200.fooway.net via
ESMTP (950413.SGI.8.6.12/951211.SGI)for
hacker@techbroker.com id OAA18967; Fri, 11 Apr 1997
14:09:58 -0400
```

I didn't promise that this header would be totally ordinary. This line tells us that a computer named ifi.foobar.no passed this email to the POP server on o200.fooway.net for someone with the email address of hacker@techbroker.com. This is because I am piping all email to hacker@techbroker.com into the account techbr@fooway.net. Under some Unix systems this is done by setting up a file in your home directory named ".forward" with the address to which you want your email sent. Now there is a lot more behind this, but I'm not telling you. Heh, heh. Can any of you evil geniuses out there figure out the whole story?

"ESMTP" stands for "extended simple mail transfer protocol." The "950413.SGI.8.6.12/951211.SGI" designates the program that is handling my email.

Now for the next line in the header:

```
Received: from gyllir.ifi.foobar.no
(2234@gyllir.ifi.foobar.no [129.999.64.230]) by
ifi.foobar.no with ESMTP (8.6.11/ifi2.4) id
<UAA24351@ifi.foobar.no> for hacker@techbroker.com ;
Fri, 11 Apr 1997 20:09:56 +0200
```

This line tells us that the computer ifi.foobar.no got this email message from the computer gyllir.ifi.foobar.no. These two computers appear to be on the same LAN or subnet. In fact, note something interesting. The computer name gyllir.ifi.foobar.no has a number after it, 129.999.64.230. This is the numerical representation of its name. (I substituted ".999." for three numbers in order to fubar the IP address.) But the computer ifi.foobar.no didn't have a number after its name. How come?

If you are working with Windows 95 or a Mac you may have hard going to figure out this little mystery. But hacking is all about noticing these little mysteries and probing them.

But since I am trying to be a real hacker, I go to my trusty Unix shell account and give the command:

```
nslookup ifi.foobar.no
Server:   Fubarino.com
Address:  198.6.71.10

Non-authoritative answer:
Name:    ifi.foobar.no
Address:  129.999.64.2
```

Notice the different numerical IP addresses between ifi.foobar.no and gyllir.ifi.foobar.no. Hmmm, I begin to think that the domain ifi.foobar.no may be a pretty big deal. Probing around with dig and traceroute leads me to discover lots more computers in that domain. Probing with nslookup in the mode "set type=any" tells me yet more.

Say, what does that ".no" mean, anyhow? A quick look at the International Standards Organization (ISO) records of country abbreviations, I see "no" stands for Norway. Aha, it looks like Norway is an arctic land of fjords, mountains, reindeer, and lots and lots of Internet hosts. A quick search of the mailing list for Happy Hacker reveals that some 5% of its email addresses have the .no domain. So now we know that this land of the midnight sun is also a hotbed of hackers! Who said headers are boring?

On to the next line, which has the name and email address of the sender:

```
From: Vegbar Fubar <fooha@ifi.foobar.no>
Received: from localhost (Vegbarha@localhost) by
gyllir.ifi.foobar.no ; Fri, 11 Apr 1997 18:09:53 GMT
```

I'm going to do some guessing here. This line says the computer gyllir.ifi.foobar.no got this email message from Vegbar Fubar on the computer "localhost." Now "localhost" is what a Unix computer calls itself. While in a Unix shell, try the command "telnet localhost." You'll get a login sequence that gets you right back into your own account.

So when I see that gyllir.ifi.foobar.no got the email message from "localhost," I assume that means the sender of this email was logged into a shell account on gyllir.ifi.foobar.no, and that this computer runs Unix. I quickly test this hypothesis:

```
> telnet gyllir.ifi.foobar.no
Trying 129.999.64.230...
Connected to gyllir.ifi.foobar.no.
Escape character is '^]'.
IRIX System V.4 (gyllir.ifi.foobar.no)
```

Irix is a Unix-type operating system for Silicon Graphics Inc. (SGI) machines. This fits with the name of the POP server software on ifi.foobar.no in the header of (950413.SGI.8.6.12/951211.SGI). So, wow, we are looking at a large network of Norwegian computers that includes SGI boxes. We could find out just how many SGI boxes with patience, scanning of neighboring IP addresses, and use of the Unix dig and nslookup commands.

You don't see SGI boxes just every day on the Internet. SGI computers are optimized for graphics and scientific computing.

So I'm really tempted to learn more about this domain. Oftentimes an ISP will have a Web page that is found by directing your browser to its domain name. So I try out *http://ifi.foobar.no*. It doesn't work, so I try *http://www.ifi.foobar.no*. I get the home page for the University of Fubar Institutt for Informatikk. The Informatikk division has strengths in computer science and image processing. No wonder people with ifi.foobar.no get to use SGI computers.

Next I check out www.foobar.no and learn the University of Fubar has some 39,000 students. No wonder we find so many Internet host computers under the ifi.foobar.no domain!

But let's get back to this header. The next line is pretty simple, just the date:

```
Date: Fri, 11 Apr 1997 18:09:53 GMT
```

But now comes the most fascinating line of all in the header, the message ID:

```
Message-Id: <199704111809.13156.gyllir@ifi.foobar.no>
```

The message ID is a key to tracking down forged email. Conversely, avoiding the creation of a valid message ID is the key to using email for criminal purposes. Computer criminals go to a great deal of effort to find Internet hosts on which to forge email that will leave no trace of their activities through these message IDs.

The first part of this ID is the date and time. 199704111809 means 1997, April 11, 18:08 (or 6:08 PM). Some message IDs also include the time in seconds. Others may leave out the " 19" from the year. The 13156 is a number identifying who wrote the email, and gyllir@ifi.foobar.no refers to the computer, gyllir within the domain ifi.foobar.no, on which this record is stored.

Where on this computer are the records of the identities of senders of email stored? Unix has many variants, so I'm not going to promise these records will be in a file of the same name in every Unix box. But often they will be in either or both the syslog files or usr/spool/mqueue. Some sysadmins will archive the message IDs in case they need to find out who may have been abusing their email system. But the default setting for some systems, for example those using sendmail, is to not archive. Unfortunately, an Internet host that doesn't archive these message IDs is creating a potential haven for email criminals.

Now we will leave the University of Norway and move on to a header that hides a surprise.

```
Received: from NIH2WAAF (mail6.foo1.csi.com
[149.999.183.75]) by Fubarino.com (8.8.3/8.6.9) with
ESMTP id XAA20854 for <galfina@Fubarino.com>; Sun, 27
Apr 1997 23:07:01 GMT
Received: from CISPPP - 199.999.193.176 by csi.com with
Microsoft SMTPSVC; Sun, 27 Apr 1997 22:53:36 -0400
Message-Id: <2.2.16.19970428082132.2cdf544e@fubar.com>
X-Sender: cmeinel@fubar.com
X-Mailer: Windows Eudora Pro Version 2.2 (16)
Mime-Version: 1.0
Content-Type: text/plain; charset="us-ascii"
To: galfina@Fubarino.com
From: "Carolyn P. Meinel"  <cmeinel@techbroker.com>
Subject: Sample header
Date: 27 Apr 1997 22:53:37 -0400
```

Let's look at the first line:

```
Received: from NIH2WAAF (mail6.foo1.csi.com
[149.999.183.75]) by Fubarino.com (8.8.3/8.6.9) with
ESMTP id XAA20854 for galfina@Fubarino.com; Sun, 27
Apr 1997 23:07:01 GMT
```

This first line tells us that it was received by the email account "gal-fina@Fubarino.com". That's the "for <galfina@Fubarino.com>" part. The Internet host computer that sent the email to galfina was mail6.foo1.csi.com [149.999.183.75]. This computer name is given first in a form easily (ha, hah!) read by humans followed by the version of its name that a computer can more easily translate into the 0's and 1's that computers understand.

"Galfina" is one of my user names. I chose it in order to irritate G.A.L.F. (Gray Areas Liberation Front), a gang of computer criminals that has taken credit for some pretty ugly attacks on three New Mexico and one Texas ISPs and two state universities—that I know of.

"Fubarino.com (8.8.3/8.6.9)" is the name of the computer that received the email for my galfina account. But notice it is a very partial computer name. All we get is a domain name and not the name of the computer from which I download my email. We can guess that Fubarino.com is not the full name because Fubarino is a big enough ISP to have several computers on a LAN to serve all its users.

Evil genius tip: Want to find out the names of some of the computers on your ISP's LAN? Commands that can dredge some of them up include the Unix commands traceroute, dig, and who. Experiment. Don't make me tell you everything!

For example, I explored the Fubarino.com LAN and found free.Fubarino.com (from command "dig Fubarino.com"); and then dialin.Fubarino.com and milnet.Fubarino.com (from "who" given while logged in my galfina account)

Then using the numerical addresses given from the dig command with these names of Fubarino.com computers I was able, by checking nearby numbers, to find a whole bunch more names of Fubarino.com computers.

The number after Fubarino.com is not a numerical IP address. It is the designation of the version of the mail program it runs. We can guess from these numbers 8.8.3/8.6.9 that it refers to the Sendmail program. But just to make sure, we try the command "telnet Fubarino.com 25." This gives us the answer:

```
220 Fubarino.com ESMTP Sendmail 8.8.3/8.6.9 ready at Mon, 28 Apr
1997 09:55:58 GMT
```

From this we know for sure Fubarino.com is running the Sendmail program.

Evil genius tip: Sendmail is notorious for flaws that you can use to gain root access to a computer. So even though Fubarino.com is using a version of sendmail that has been fixed from its most recently publicized security holes, if you are patient, a new exploit will almost certainly come out within the next few months. The cure for this problem may be to run qmail, which so far hasn't had embarrassing problems.

Now let's look at the next "received" line in that header:

```
Received: from CISPPP - 199.999.193.176 by csi.com with
Microsoft SMTPSVC; Sun, 27 Apr 1997 22:53:36 -0400
```

CISPPP stands for Compuserve Information Services point to point protocol (PPP) connection. This means that the mail was sent from a PPP connection I set up through Compuserve. We also see that Compuserve uses the Microsoft SMTPSVC mail program.

However, we see from the rest of the header that the sender (me) didn't use the standard Compuserve mail interface:

```
Message-Id: <2.2.16.19970428082132.2cdf544e@fubaretta.com>
```

The number 2.2.16. was inserted by Eudora, and means I am using Eudora Pro 2.2, 16-bit version. The 19970428082132 means the time I sent the email, in order of year (1997), month (04), day (28) and time (08:31:32).

The portion of the message ID "2cdf544e@fubaretta.com" is the most important part. That is provided by the Internet host where a record of my use of fubaretta's mail server has been stored.

Did you notice this message ID does not designate Compuserve, but rather fubaretta.com? This is, first of all, because the message ID is created with the POP server that I specified with Eudora. Since Compuserve does not yet offer POP servers, I can only use Eudora to send email over a Compuserve connection but not to receive Compuserve email. So, heck, I can specify an arbitrary POP server when I send email over Compuserve from Eudora. I picked the Fubaretta ISP. So there!

If I were to have done something bad news with that email such as spamming, extortion or email bombing, the sysadmin at fubaretta.com would look up that message ID and find information tying that email to my Compuserve account. That assumes, of course, that fubaretta.com is archiving message Ids.

When you read this part of the header you might think that the computer where I pick up my email is with the Fubaretta.com ISP. But all this really means is that I specified to Eudora that I was using a mail account at Fubar. But if I had put a different account name there, then I would have generated a different message ID.

Did I need to have an account at Fubaretta? No. The mail server did not ask for a password. In fact, I don't have an account at Fubaretta. I could even have created a totally false domain name for the message ID. This is why people who tell you the record of a forged email will be found on the computer shown in the message ID are not always right.

The rest of the header is information provided by Eudora:

```
X-Sender: cmeinel@fubar.com
X-Mailer: Windows Eudora Pro Version 2.2 (16)
Mime-Version: 1.0
Content-Type: text/plain; charset="us-ascii"
```

The "X-Mailer" information tells you I was using the 16 bit version of Windows Eudora Pro Version 2.2. Some people have asked me why I don't use the 32 bit version (which runs on Win 95) instead of the 16 bit version. Answer: better error handling! That's the same reason I don't normally use Pegasus. Also, Eudora lets me get away with things.

Mime (Multipurpose Internet Mail Extensions) is a protocol to view email. The character set "us-ascii" tells us what character set this email will use. Some email, especially if it originates outside the US, uses ISO ascii instead.

How to get Internet host computer names from your headers

An email header can give you valuable information about the full names of host computers and even the operating systems they run. For example, in the first example in this chapter, we could look at just one line to tell the full Internet address of the computer from which that email was sent:

```
Received: from gyllir.ifi.foobar.no
```

Some email headers will have a whole series of "Received" lines, each identifying yet another full Internet name of a computer.

However, an email header does not necessarily reveal the names of all the computers through which it is relayed. For example, a good firewall will strip out all "Received" lines from the computers inside its LAN so that hackers won't be able to learn this information. Also, an asynchronous transfer mode (ATM) network hides the names of all the computers within the ATM network through which email is relayed.

Reading forged headers

Now let's look at a slightly more exciting header. In fact, this is a genuine muhahaha header. In early 1997 I declared war on Web sites that provide downloads of email bombing programs. You know, those Windows 95 for lusers programs that run from a few mouse clicks? Here's a header that reveals my tiny contribution toward making life unpleasant for the ISPs that used to distribute these programs. This copy is from the Happy Hacker Digest, April 12, 1997, from a copy that reached a test email address I had on the list:

```
Received: by o200.fooway.net
(950413.SGI.8.6.12/951211.SGI)for techbr@fooway.net id
MAA07059; Mon, 14 Apr 1997 12:05:25 -0400
Date: Mon, 14 Apr 1997 12:05:22 -0400
Received: from mocha.icefubarnet.com by o200.fooway.net
via ESMTP (950413.SGI.8.6.12/951211.SGI) for
<pettit@techbroker.com> id MAA06380; Mon, 14 Apr 1997
12:05:20 -0400
Received: from cmeinel (hd14-211.foo.compuserve.com
[206.999.205.211]) by mocha.icefubarnet.com (Netscape
Mail Server v2.01) with SMTP id AAP3428; Mon, 14 Apr
```

```
1997 08:51:02 -0700
Message-Id: <2.2.16.19970414100122.4387d20a@mail.fooway.net>
X-Sender: techbr@mail.fooway.net (Unverified)
X-Mailer: Windows Eudora Pro Version 2.2 (16)
Mime-Version: 1.0
Content-Type: text/plain; charset="iso-8859-1"
To: (Recipient list suppressed)
From: "Carolyn P. Meinel"  <cmeinel@techbroker.com>
Subject: Happy Hacker Digest April 12, 1997
```

If you wonder what was so "muhahaha" about this header, it reveals that I was using the mail server of the ISP that was knowingly distributing email bomber programs to send mailings out to the rather large Happy Hacker list. To see how this header proves I was doing this, let's examine the first field:

```
Received: by o200.fooway.net
(950413.SGI.8.6.12/951211.SGI)for techbr@fooway.net id
MAA07059; Mon, 14 Apr 1997 12:05:25 -0400
Date: Mon, 14 Apr 1997 12:05:22 -0400
```

We already looked at this computer o200.fooway.net above. But, heck, let's probe a little more deeply. Since I suspect this is a POP server, I'm going to telnet to port 110, which is normally the POP server port.

```
> telnet o200.fooway.net 110
Trying 207.999.192.57...
Connected to o200.fooway.net.
Escape character is '^]'.
+OK QUALCOMM Pop server derived from UCB (version 2.1.4-R3) at mail
starting.
```

Now we know more about Fooway Technology's POP server. If you have ever run one of those port scanner programs that tell you what programs are running on each port of a computer, there is really no big deal to it. They just automate the process that we are doing here by hand. But in my humble opinion you will learn much more by strobing ports by hand the same way I am doing here.

We could do lots more probing, but I'm getting bored. So we check out the second field in this header:

```
Date: Mon, 14 Apr 1997 12:05:22 -0400
```

That -0400 is a time correction. But what is it correcting? The difference from Greenwich Mean Time.

Let's see the next field in the header:

```
Received: from mocha.icefubarnet.com by o200.fooway.net
via ESMTP (950413.SGI.8.6.12/951211.SGI) for
hacker@techbroker.com id MAA06380; Mon, 14 Apr 1997
12:05:20 -0400
```

Hmmm, why is mocha.icefubarnet.com in the header? If this header isn't forged, it means this mail server was handling the Happy Hacker Digest mailing. So where is mocha.icefubarnet.com located? A quick use of the whois command tells us:

```
> whois icefubarnet.com
ICEFUBARNET INTERNET, INC (ICEFUBARNET-DOM)
   2178 Fooway
   North Bar, Oregon 97999
   USA
```

The next field in the header iss:

```
Received: from cmeinel (hd14-211.foo.compuserve.com
[206.999.205.211]) by mocha.icefubarnet.com (Netscape
Mail Server v2.01) with SMTP id AAP3428; Mon, 14 Apr
1997 08:51:02 -0700
```

This tells us that the Happy Hacker Digest was delivered to the mail server (SMTP stands for simple mail transport protocol) at mocha.icefubarnet.com by Compuserve. But, and this is very important to observe, once again I did not use the Compuserve mail system. This merely represents a PPP session I set up with Compuserve. How can you tell? Playing with nslookup shows that the numerical representation of my Compuserve connection isn't an Internet host. But you can't learn much more without great effort because Compuserve has great security—one reason I use it. But take my word for it, this is another way to see a Compuserve PPP session in a header.

Now we get to the biggie, the message ID:

```
Message-Id: <2.2.16.19970414100122.4387d20a@mail.fooway.net>
```

Whoa, how come that ID is at the computer mail.fooway.net? It's pretty simple. In Eudora I specified my POP server as mail.fooway.net. But if you were to do a little port scanning, you would discover that while fooway.net has a POP server, it doesn't have an SMTP or ESMTP server. You can get mail from Fooway, but you can't mail stuff out from Fooway. But the marvelous workings of the Internet combined with the naïveté of the Eudora Pro 2.2 program created a message ID claiming it was at mail.fooway.net anyhow.

The remaining fields of the header were all inserted by Eudora:

```
X-Sender: techbr@mail.fooway.net (Unverified)
X-Mailer: Windows Eudora Pro Version 2.2 (16)
Mime-Version: 1.0
Content-Type: text/plain; charset="iso-8859-1"
To: (Recipient list suppressed)
From: "Carolyn P. Meinel"  <cmeinel@techbroker.com>
Subject: Happy Hacker Digest April 12, 1997
```

Notice Eudora does let us know that techbr@mail.fooway.net is unverified as sender. And in fact, it definitely is not the sender. This is a very important fact. The message ID of an email is not necessarily stored with the computer that is in the message ID.

So how was I able to use Icefubarnet Internet's mail server to send out the Happy Hacker Digest? Fortunately Eudora's naïveté makes it easy for me to use any mail server that has an open SMTP or ESMTP port. You may be surprised to discover that there are uncountable Internet mail servers that you may easily commandeer to send out your email—if you have the right program—or if you know how to telnet to port 25 (which runs using the SMTP or ESMTP protocols) and give the commands to send email yourself.

However, as more sysadmins wise up, you will find it harder to find Internet hosts that will let you send out your email on them. Smail, qmail and sendmail can be configured to automatically reject relaying from nonlocal hosts.

Why did I use Icefubarnet? Because at the time it was hosting an ftp site that was being used to download email bomber programs (*http://www.icefubarnet.com/~astorm/uy4beta1.zip*). Last time I checked the owner of the account from which he was offering this ugly stuff was unhappy because Icefubarnet Internet had made him take it down.

But—back to how to commandeer mail servers while sending your message IDs elsewhere. In Eudora, just specify your victim mail server under the hosts section of the options menu (under tools). Then enter the computer for which you want to specify your message ID under "POP Server."

But if you try any of this monkey business with Pegasus, it gives a nasty error message accusing you of trying to forge email.

Of course you may do even more convincing forging of email by simply telneting into port 25 of a cooperating Internet host computer and using the sendmail program. See the chapter *Heroic Hacking in Half an Hour* for details on how this is done. The bottom line is—it is ridiculously easy.

In fact, if the computer on which one forges email is not running the ident program, or if it is not keeping logs of outgoing email, a computer criminal can operate totally undetected.

For example, there have been several email bomber programs written which are incredibly destructive. They send their victim tens of thousands or more emails per day. This flood of mail may sometimes fill up the disk space of the entire mail spool of an Internet Service Provider, crashing the system and denying email service to all the users of that ISP.

The way these email bomber programs kept their users from getting caught was that the writers of these programs (mostly members of the gang Global kOS) found several Internet host computers that were configured to allow email to be forged on them and also were not running the ident program. (Note: sendmail 8.8 also tracks true identity of the user regardless of whether ident is running.)

Ident determines the email address of the person who composes email and logs a record of that person writing that particular email message into a file named syslog. This syslog file is what you look for if you want to track down email criminals. Syslog is a file that can only be read by the sysadmin of the computer on which the message was forged. So to tracking down these criminals ususally requires the cooperation of sysadmins on the computers used to commit these bad guy deeds.

These mail bomber programs went out of vogue when the sysadmins of the computers these programs were exploiting were alerted by the ISPs that had been attacked that mailbombings were originating from their computers. Once ident was installed, the users of these programs began to get arrested and Global kOS withdrew these programs from their download sites.

For more information on headers, see *http://www.stopspam.org* and click on the "headers" button.

In conclusion, you can see that it is pretty easy to forge email headers. People can do it with no hacking skills whatsoever, simply using commercial software whose coders wrote it with no concern for how it might be abused. However, if the computer they use to forge email is running ident or sendmail 8.8, and if it logs email activity—and if the sysadmin of the computer used for the forgery will let you read the syslog file—then the bad guys can be caught.

Section 2, Chapter 5
Linux!

So far we have assumed that you have been hacking using a shell account that you get through your Internet Service Provider (ISP). A shell account allows you to give Unix commands on one of your ISP's computers. But you don't need to depend on your ISP for a machine that lets you play with Unix. You can run Unix on your own computer and with a PPP connection be directly connected to the Internet.

In this chapter you will learn:
- what kind of computer is the best for the home Unix user
- what kinds of Unix are available for PCs and Macs
- what is Linux
- how to install Linux
- where to get further help

Top ten reasons to install Linux on your PC:

10. When Linux is outlawed, only outlaws will own Linux.
9. When installing Linux, it is so much fun to run fdisk without backing up first.
8. The flames you get from asking questions on Linux newsgroups are of a higher quality than the flames you get for posting to alt.sex.bestiality.
7. No matter what flavor of Linux you install, you'll find out tomorrow there was a far more elite version you should have gotten instead.
6. People who use Free BSD or Solaris will not make fun of you. They will offer their sympathy instead.
5. When you go to a hacker convention you'll be able to say stuph like "so then I su-ed to his account and grepped all his files for 'kissyface'."
4. Port surf in privacy.
3. Raw sockets!
2. Installing Linux on your office PC is like being a postal worker and bringing an Uzi to work.
1. But—if you install Linux on your office computer, you boss won't have a clue what that means.

Newbie note: Serial Line Internet Protocol (SLIP) and Point-to-Point Protocol (PPP) connections give you a temporary Internet Protocol (IP) address that allows you to be hooked directly to the Internet. You have to use either SLIP or PPP connections to get to use a Web browser that gives you pictures instead on text only. So if you can see pictures on the Web, you already have one of these available to you. The advantage of using one of these direct connections for your hacking activities is that you will not leave behind a shell log file for your ISP's sysadmin to pore over. Even if you are not breaking the law, a log file that shows you doing lots of hackerish stuph can be enough for some sysadmins to summarily close your account.

What Kind of Computer is Best for the Home Unix User?

What is the best kind of computer to run Unix on? Unless you are a wealthy hacker who thinks nothing of buying a Sun SPARC workstation, you'll probably do best with some sort of PC. There are almost countless variants of Unix that run on PCs. Most of them are free for download, or inexpensively available on CD-ROMs. However, in the chapter *Mac Hacking* you can find places to get forms of Unix that will run on your Mac.

What Kinds of Unix Will Run on Home Computers?

The three primary variations of Unix that run on PCs are Sun's Solaris, FreeBSD and Linux. Solaris is expensive. Enough said. FreeBSD is really, really good but doesn't have as big a community of users as Solaris or Linux. Linux, however, has the advantage of being available in many variants (so you can have fun mixing and matching programs from different Linux offerings). Most important, Linux is supported by many news groups, mail lists and Web sites. If you have hacker friends in your area, most of them probably use Linux and can help you out.

What Is Linux?

Linux was created in 1991 by a group led by Linus Torvalds, at the time a student at the University of Helsinki. Linux is copyrighted under the GNU General Public License. Under this agreement, Linux may be redistributed to anyone along with the source code. Anyone can sell any variant of Linux and modify it and repackage it. But even if someone modifies the source code he or she may not claim copyright for anything created from Linux. Anyone who sells a modified version of Linux must provide source code to the buyers and allow them to reuse it in their commercial products without charging licensing fees. This arrangement is known as a "copyleft."

Linux! 133

Under this arrangement the original creators of Linux receive no licensing or shareware fees. Linus Torvalds and the many others who have contributed to Linux have done so from the joy of programming and a sense of community with all of us who will hopefully use Linux in the spirit of good guy hacking. Viva Linux! Viva Torvalds!

Linux consists of the operating system itself (called the "kernel") plus a set of associated programs.

The kernel, like all types of Unix, is a multitasking, multi-user operating system. Although it uses a different file structure, and hence is not directly compatible with DOS and Windows, it is so flexible that many DOS and Windows programs can be run while in Linux. So a power user will probably want to boot up in Linux and then be able to run DOS and Windows programs from Linux.

Associated programs that come with most Linux distributions may include:

- At least one shell program (Bourne Again Shell — BASH — is most common);
- Compilers for programming languages such as Fortran-77 (my favorite!), C, C++, Pascal, Perl, LISP, Modula-2, Ada, Basic (the best language for a beginner), and Smalltalk.;
- X (sometimes called X-windows), which is a graphical user interface that many people think is better than Windows
- Utility programs such as the email reader Pine (my favorite) and Elm

What types of Linux work best? It depends on what you really want. Redhat Linux is famed for being the easiest to install. The Walnut Creek Linux CD-ROM set is also really easy to install — easy for Linux, that is! My approach has been to get lots of Linux versions and mix and match the best from each distribution. I like the Walnut Creek version best because with my brand X hardware, its hardware autodetection feature is a life-saver.

How to Install Linux

Installing Linux is not for the faint of heart! Several tips for surviving installation are:

1) Although you can, in theory, run Linux on a 386 with 4 MB RAM and two floppy drives, it is much easier with at least a 486 or above with 8 MB RAM, a CD-ROM, and at least 200 MB free hard disk space. However, watch out for a system with really new types of hardware. You may not be able to find Linux device drivers for them.

2) Know as much as possible about what type of mother board, modem, hard disk, CD-ROM, and video card you have. If you have any documentation for these, have them on hand to reference during installation.

3) It works better to use hardware that is name-brand and somewhat out of date on your computer. Because Linux is freeware, it doesn't offer device drivers for all the latest hardware. And if your hardware is like mine—lots of Brand X and El Cheapo stuph, you can take a long time experimenting to find what drivers will work.

4) Before beginning installation, back up your hard disk(s)! In theory you can install Linux without harming your DOS/Windows files. But we are all human.

5) Get more than one Linux distribution. The first time I successfully installed Linux, I finally hit on something that worked by using the boot disk from one distribution with the CD-ROM for another. In any case, each Linux distribution had different utility programs, operating system emulators, compilers and more. Add them all to your system and you will be set up to become beyond elite.

6) Buy a book or two or three on Linux. I didn't like any of them! But they are better than nothing. Most books on Linux come with one or two CD-ROMs that can be used to install Linux. But I found that what was in the books did not exactly coincide with what was on the CD-ROMs.

7) I recommend drinking while installing. It may not make debugging go any faster, but at least you won't care how hard it is.

Where to Get Further Help

I can almost guarantee that even following all these 6 pieces of advice, you will still have problems installing Linux. Oh, do I have 7 advisories up there? Forget number 7. But be of good cheer. Since everyone else also suffers mightily when installing and using Linux, the Internet has an incredible wealth of resources for the Linux-challenged.

If you are allergic to getting flamed, you can start out with Linux support Web sites. The best I have found is *http://sunsite.unc.edu:/pub/Linux/*. It includes the Linux Frequently Asked Questions list (FAQ), available from sunsite.unc.edu/pub/Linux/docs/FAQ.

In the directory /pub/Linux/docs on sunsite.unc.edu you'll find a number of other documents about Linux, including the Linux INFO-SHEET and META-FAQ. The Linux HOWTO archive is on sunsite.unc.edu/pub/Linux/docs/HOWTO. The directory /pub/Linux/docs/LDP on sunsite.unc.edu contains the current set of LDP manuals.

You can also get "Linux Installation and Getting Started" from sunsite.unc.edu in /pub/Linux/docs/LDP/install-guide. The README file there describes how you can order a printed copy of the book of the same name (about 180 pages).

If you don't mind getting flamed, you may want to post questions to the amazing number of Usenet news groups that cover Linux. These include:

- *comp.os.linux.advocacy* Benefits of Linux compared
- *comp.os.linux.development.system*Linux kernels, device drivers
- *comp.os.linux.x* Linux X Window System servers
- *comp.os.linux.development.apps* Writing Linux applications
- *comp.os.linux.hardware* Hardware compatibility
- *comp.os.linux.setup* Linux installation
- *comp.os.linux.networking* Networking and communications
- *comp.os.linux.answers* FAQs, How-To's, READMEs, etc.
- *linux.redhat.misc*
- *alt.os.linux* Use comp.os.linux.* instead

- *alt.uu.comp.os.linux.questions* Usenet University helps you
- *comp.os.linux.announce* Announcements important to Linux
- *comp.os.linux.misc* Linux-specific topics

Sindekated has pointed out "A lot of the Linux newsgroups have been purged from Usenet recently. They are now on a Majordomo mailing list site. For information on the Linux mailing lists available (and there are a lot of them . . .), write to the following address:"

```
majordomo@vger.rutgers.edu
body of message: lists
```

If you live near a computer swap meet, Fry's, Microcenter, or other such place, look for Linux CD's there. They are usually under $20, which is an excellent investment. I personally like the Linux Developer's Resource by Infomagic, which is now up to a seven CD set, I believe, which includes all major Linux distributions (Slackware, Redhat, Debian, Linux for DEC Alpha to name a few) plus mirrors of tsx11.mit.edu and sunsite.unc.edu/pub/linux plus much more. You should also visit *http://www.linux.org/*. You might also want to check out *http://www.redhat.com/* and *http://www.caldera.com/* for more information on commercial versions of Linux (which are still freely available under GNU)."

How about Linux security? Yes, Linux, like every operating system, is imperfect. Eminently hackable, if you really want to know. So if you want to find out how to secure your Linux system, or if you should come across one of the many ISPs that use Linux and want to go exploring (oops, forget I wrote that), here's where you can go for info:

- *ftp://info.cert.org/pub*
- *ftp://info.cert.org/pub/tech_tips/root_compromise*
- *http://bach.cis.temple.edu/linux/linux-security/*

Last but not least, you may subscribe to the Happy Systems Administrator Digest (Happy-SAD), which covers Linux questions only, by emailing majordomo@happyhacker.org with message "subscribe happy-sad."

Section 2, Chapter 6
Port Surf's Up!

In October 1996 I had a lady friend visiting. She's 42 and at the time didn't own a computer. However, she was taking a class on personal computers at a community college. She also wanted to know what all this hacking stuph is about. So I introduced her to port surfing.

Port surfing is so easy anyone can do it—if you have a shell account or a good telnet program for Windows or Mac. It is also legal, yet is also used as part of the process of committing many computer crimes.

In this chapter you will learn:
- What is port surfing?
- Why scan ports by hand?
- How to scan ports by hand
- Fun ports to scan

In a nutshell, port scanning is simply telneting into any port that suits your fancy, and then exploring.

Port surfing takes advantage of the structure of TCP/IP (Transfer Control Protocol/Internet Protocol). This is the protocol (set of rules) used for computers to talk to each other over the Internet. One of the basic principles of TCP/IP is to assign a "port" to every service that one computer might command another to perform.

 Newbie note: An Internet host computer has many more ports than a typical home computer. Most of these ports are identified by numbers, and represent virtual (software) ports. These ports are used to connect to the Internet or other networks using TCP/IP protocol.

A "service" is the activity that is conducted on a "port." For example, a service might be as complicated as supporting connections to a Web site or as simple as telling you the time of day. Common services are those that send and receive email, read Usenet newsgroups, telnet, transfer files, and offer Web pages.

For example, if you want to read a Web page, your browser contacts port number 80 and tells the computer that manages that Web site to let you in. And, sure enough, you get into that Web server computer without a password.

Okay, big deal. That's pretty standard for the Internet. Many—most—computers on the Internet will let you do some things with them without needing a password, for example Web sites, anonymous ftp sites, and even email programs.

However, the essence of hacking is doing things that aren't obvious, that don't just jump out at you from the manuals. One way you can move a step up from the run of the mill computer user is to learn how to port surf.

Why Scan Ports by Hand?

Super Duper hackers will laugh at port surfing. They run automated port scanning programs that tell them what ports are in use. These programs also probe these ports for the presence of daemons with known security flaws, and tell them what they are.

 Newbie note: A daemon is not some sort of grinch or gremlin or 666 guy. It is a program that runs in the background on many (but not all) numbered ports. When you telnet to a port, that program is up and running, just waiting for your input. If you find a daemon on a port, it just may be hackable.

But running a port scanner is like using a surveillance satellite to prepare for invading a peaceful country. If you run one of these programs without the permission of the owner of the computer you scan, you may mark yourself as a probable computer criminal and get kicked off your ISP.

By contrast, port surfing—scanning ports by hand—is like hiking in the mountains and enjoying the birds and flowers. I have never once gotten in trouble for port surfing.

Here are some of the other reasons to surf ports by hand instead of automatically:

- You will learn something. By probing manually you get a gut feel for how the daemon running on that port behaves.
- You can impress your friends. If you run a canned hacker tool like Satan, your friends will look at you and say, "Big deal. I can run programs, too." They will immediately catch on to the dirty little secret of the hacker world. Most hacking exploits are just lamerz running programs they picked up from some BBS or ftp site. But if you enter commands keystroke by keystroke, they will see you using your brain. And you can help them play with daemons, too.
- Truly elite hackers surf ports and play with daemons by hand because it is the only way to discover something new. Very few hackers discover new exploits. The rest just run canned exploits over and over and over again. Boring.

Here's what my middle-aged friend and I discovered just messing around. First, we decided we didn't want to waste our time messing with some minor little host computer. Hey, let's go for the big time!

How do you find a big kahuna computer on the Internet? We started with a domain which consisted of a LAN of PCs running Linux that I happened to already know about, used by the New Mexico Internet Fubar ISP, nmfubar.com.

 Newbie Note: A domain is an Internet address. You can use it to look up who runs the computers used by the domain, and also to look up how that domain is connected to the rest of the Internet.

So to do this we first logged into my shell account with Southwest Fooport. I gave the command:

```
->whois nmfubar.com
New Mexico Internet Fubar (NMFUBAR-DOM)
   2201 Good Fubar SE
   Albuquerque, NM 87106

   Domain Name: NMFUBAR.COM

   Administrative Contact, Technical Contact, Zone
Contact:
      Whosis, Stan  (SO11)  SAO@NMFUBAR.COM
      (505) 877-xxxx
   Record last updated on 11-Mar-94.
   Record created on 11-Mar-94.
   Domain servers in listed order:
   NS.NMFUBAR.COM                  999.59.999.10
   GRANDE.NEWFOO.ORG               999.121.1.2
```

It's a good bet that grande.newfoo.org is serving a lot of other Internet hosts beside nmfubar.com. Here's how we port surf our way to find this out:

```
-telnet grande.newfoo.org 15
Trying 999.121.1.2 ...
Connected to grande.newfoo.org.
Escape character is '^]'.
TGV MultiNet V3.5 Rev B, VAX 4000-400, OpenVMS VAX V6.1

Product           License   Authorization       Expiration Date
_____           ___.      _____.            _____

MULTINET          Yes       A-137-1641          (none)
NFS-CLIENT        Yes       A-137-113237        (none)

*** Configuration for file "MULTINET:NETWORK_DEVICES.CONFIGURATION" ***
Device                              Adapter    CSR Address
Flags/Vector
                                    ___.       _____.       _____

se0    (Shared VMS Ethernet/FDDI)   -NONE-     -NONE-       -NONE-
MultiNet Active Connections, including servers:
Proto Rcv-Q Snd-Q  Local Address (Port)    Foreign Address (Port) State
- - - - - - - - - - - - - - - - - - - - - - - - - - - - - - - - - - -
TCP     0    822   GRANDE.NEWFOO.ORG(NETSTAT)  999.59.115.24(1569) ESTABLISHED
TCP     0     0    GRANDE.NEWFOO.ORG(POP3)     164.64.201.67(1256) ESTABLISHED
TCP     0     0    GRANDE.NEWFOO.ORG(4918)     999.121.254.5(TELNET) ESTABLISHED
TCP     0     0    GRANDE.NEWFOO.ORG(TELNET)   AVATAR.NEWFOO.ORG(3141) ESTABLISHED
TCP     0     0    *(NAMESERVICE)              *(*)  LISTEN
TCP     0     0    *(TELNET)                   *(*)  LISTEN
TCP     0     0    *(FTP)                      *(*)  LISTEN
```

```
TCP      0      0    *(FINGER)                *(*)  LISTEN
TCP      0      0    *(NETSTAT)               *(*)  LISTEN
TCP      0      0    *(SMTP)                  *(*)  LISTEN
TCP      0      0    *(LOGIN)                 *(*)  LISTEN
TCP      0      0    *(SHELL)                 *(*)  LISTEN
TCP      0      0    *(EXEC)                  *(*)  LISTEN
TCP      0      0    *(RPC)                   *(*)  LISTEN
TCP      0      0    *(NETCONTROL)            *(*)  LISTEN
TCP      0      0    *(SYSTAT)                *(*)  LISTEN
TCP      0      0    *(CHARGEN)               *(*)  LISTEN
TCP      0      0    *(DAYTIME)               *(*)  LISTEN
TCP      0      0    *(TIME)                  *(*)  LISTEN
TCP      0      0    *(ECHO)                  *(*)  LISTEN
TCP      0      0    *(DISCARD)               *(*)  LISTEN
TCP      0      0    *(PRINTER)               *(*)  LISTEN
TCP      0      0    *(POP2)                  *(*)  LISTEN
TCP      0      0    *(POP3)                  *(*)  LISTEN
TCP      0      0    *(KERBEROS_MASTER)       *(*)  LISTEN
TCP      0      0    *(KLOGIN)                *(*)  LISTEN
TCP      0      0    *(KSHELL)                *(*)  LISTEN
TCP      0      0    GRANDE.NEWFOO.ORG(4174)  OSO.NEWFOO.ORG(X11)  ESTABLISHED
TCP      0      0    GRANDE.NEWFOO.ORG(4172)  OSO.NEWFOO.ORG(X11)  ESTABLISHED
TCP      0      0    GRANDE.NEWFOO.ORG(4171)  OSO.NEWFOO.ORG(X11)  ESTABLISHED
TCP      0      0    *(FS)                    *(*)  LISTEN
UDP      0      0    *(NAMESERVICE)           *(*)
UDP      0      0    999.0.0.1(NAMESERVICE)   *(*)
UDP      0      0    GRANDE.NM.OR(NAMESERV)   *(*)
UDP      0      0    *(TFTP)                  *(*)
UDP      0      0    *(BOOTPS)                *(*)
UDP      0      0    *(KERBEROS)              *(*)
UDP      0      0    999.0.0.1(KERBEROS)      *(*)
UDP      0      0    GRANDE.NM.OR(KERBEROS)   *(*)
UDP      0      0    *(*)                     *(*)
UDP      0      0    *(SNMP)                  *(*)
UDP      0      0    *(RPC)                   *(*)
UDP      0      0    *(DAYTIME)               *(*)
UDP      0      0    *(ECHO)                  *(*)
UDP      0      0    *(DISCARD)               *(*)
UDP      0      0    *(TIME)                  *(*)
UDP      0      0    *(CHARGEN)               *(*)
UDP      0      0    *(TALK)                  *(*)
UDP      0      0    *(NTALK)                 *(*)
UDP      0      0    *(1023)                  *(*)
UDP      0      0    *(XDMCP)                 *(*)
MultiNet registered RPC programs:
Program    Version    Protocol    Port
- - - - - - - - - - - - - - - - - - - - - - -
PORTMAP       2         TCP        111
PORTMAP       2         UDP        111


MultiNet IP Routing tables:
Destination       Gateway             Flags         Refcnt Use Interface  MTU
- - - - - - - - - - - - - - - - - - - - - - - - - - - - - - - - - - - - - - -
999.59.167.1      LAWRII.NEWFOO.ORG    Up,Gateway,H 0        2       se0 1500
999.45.0.1        ENSS365.NEWFOO.ORG   Up,Gateway,H 0        4162    se0 1500
999.138.138.1     ENSS365.NEWFOO.ORG   Up,Gateway,H 0        71      se0 1500
999.999.999.1     ENSS365.NEWFOO.ORG   Up,Gateway,H 0        298     se0 1500
999.0.0.1         999.0.0.1           Up,Host   5      1183513 lo0 4136
999.59.167.2      LAWRII.NEWFOO.ORG    Up,Gateway,H 0        640     se0 1500
999.132.89.2      ENSS365.NEWFOO.ORG   Up,Gateway,H 0        729     se0 1500
999.77.56.2       ENSS365.NEWFOO.ORG   Up,Gateway,H 0        5       se0 1500
999.97.213.2      ENSS365.NEWFOO.ORG   Up,Gateway,H 0        2641    se0 1500
999.90.74.66      ENSS365.NEWFOO.ORG   Up,Gateway,H 0        1       se0 1500
999.252.102.2     ENSS365.NEWFOO.ORG   Up,Gateway,H 0        109     se0 1500
999.999.243.2     ENSS365.NEWFOO.ORG   Up,Gateway,H 0        78      se0 1500
999.213.4.2       ENSS365.NEWFOO.ORG   Up,Gateway,H 0        4       se0 1500
999.216.224.66    ENSS365.NEWFOO.ORG   Up,Gateway,H 0        113     se0 1500
999.132.89.3      ENSS365.NEWFOO.ORG   Up,Gateway,H 0        1100    se0 1500
999.203.196.67    ENSS365.NEWFOO.ORG   Up,Gateway,H 0        385     se0 1500
999.999.13.3      ENSS365.NEWFOO.ORG   Up,Gateway,H 0        78      se0 1500
999.247.107.131   ENSS365.NEWFOO.ORG   Up,Gateway,H 0        19      se0 1500
999.59.167.4      LAWRII.NEWFOO.ORG    Up,Gateway,H 0        82      se0 1500
```

```
(snip)
MultiNet IPX Routing tables:
Destination       Gateway          Flags        Refcnt Use Interface   MTU
- - - - - - - - - - - - - - - - - - - - - - - - - - - - - - - - - - - - - - -
MultiNet ARP table:
Host Network Address                              Ethernet Address
Arp Flags
- - - - - - - - - - - - - - - - - - - - - - - - - - - - - - - - - - - - - - -
GLORY.NEWFOO.ORG (IP 999.121.1.4)               AA:00:04:00:61:D0 Temporary
[UNKNOWN] (IP 999.121.251.1)                     00:C0:05:01:2C:D2 Temporary
NARANJO.NEWFOO.ORG (IP 999.121.1.56)            08:00:87:04:9F:42 Temporary
CHAMA.NEWFOO.ORG (IP 999.121.1.8)               AA:00:04:00:0C:D0 Temporary
[UNKNOWN] (IP 999.121.251.5)                  AA:00:04:00:D2:D0 Temporary
LAWRII.NEWFOO.ORG (IP 999.121.254.10)           AA:00:04:00:5C:D0 Temporary
[UNKNOWN] (IP 999.121.1.91)                      00:C0:05:01:2C:D2 Temporary
BRAVO.NEWFOO.ORG (IP 999.121.1.6)               AA:00:04:00:0B:D0 Temporary
PENNY.NEWFOO.ORG (IP 999.121.1.10)              AA:00:04:00:5F:D0 Temporary
ARRIBA.NEWFOO.ORG (IP 999.121.1.14)             08:00:2B:BC:C1:A7 Temporary
AZUL.NEWFOO.ORG (IP 999.121.1.51)               08:00:87:00:A1:D3 Temporary
ENSS365.NEWFOO.ORG (IP 999.121.1.3)             00:00:0C:51:EF:58 Temporary
AVATAR.NEWFOO.ORG (IP 999.121.254.1)            08:00:5A:1D:52:0D Temporary
[UNKNOWN] (IP 999.121.253.2)                  08:00:5A:47:4A:1D Temporary
[UNKNOWN] (IP 999.121.254.5)                  00:C0:7B:5F:5F:80 Temporary
CONCHAS.NEWFOO.ORG (IP 999.121.1.11)            08:00:5A:47:4A:1D Temporary
[UNKNOWN] (IP 999.121.253.10)                 AA:00:04:00:4B:D0 Temporary
MultiNet Network Interface statistics:
Name Mtu    Network     Address          Ipkts    Ierrs Opkts Oerrs Collis
- - - - - - - - - - - - - - - - - - - - - - - - - - - - - - - - - - - - - - -
se0  1500   999.121.0   GRANDE.NEWFOO.ORG   68422948 0     53492833 1     0
lo0  4136   999.0.0     999.0.0.1           1188191  0     1188191  0 0
MultiNet Protocol statistics:
       65264173 IP packets received
             22 IP packets smaller than minimum size
           6928 IP fragments received
              4 IP fragments timed out
             34 IP received for unreachable destinations
         704140 ICMP error packets generated
           9667 ICMP opcodes out of range
           4170 Bad ICMP packet checksums
         734363 ICMP responses
         734363 ICMP "Echo" packets received
         734363 ICMP "Echo Reply" packets sent
          18339 ICMP "Echo Reply" packets received
         704140 ICMP "Destination Unreachable" packets sent
         451243 ICMP "Destination Unreachable" packets received
           1488 ICMP "Source Quench" packets received
         163911 ICMP "ReDirect" packets received
         189732 ICMP "Time Exceeded" packets received
         126966 TCP connections initiated
         233998 TCP connections established
         132611 TCP connections accepted
          67972 TCP connections dropped
          28182 embryonic TCP connections dropped
         269399 TCP connections closed
       10711838 TCP segments timed for RTT
       10505140 TCP segments updated RTT
        3927264 TCP delayed ACKs sent
            666 TCP connections dropped due to retransmit timeouts
         111040 TCP retransmit timeouts
           3136 TCP persist timeouts
              9 TCP persist connection drops
          16850 TCP keepalive timeouts
           1195 TCP keepalive probes sent
          14392 TCP connections dropped due to keepalive timeouts
       28842663 TCP packets sent
       12714484 TCP data packets sent
     1206060086 TCP data bytes sent
          58321 TCP data packets retransmitted
       22144036 TCP data bytes retransmitted
        6802199 TCP ACK-only packets sent
           1502 TCP window probes sent
            483 TCP URG-only packets sent
```

```
    8906175 TCP Window-Update-only packets sent
     359509 TCP control packets sent
   38675084 TCP packets received
   28399363 TCP packets received in sequence
 1929418386 TCP bytes received in sequence
      25207 TCP packets with checksum errors
     273374 TCP packets were duplicates
  230525708 TCP bytes were duplicates
       3748 TCP packets had some duplicate bytes
     493214 TCP bytes were partial duplicates
    2317156 TCP packets were out of order
 3151204672 TCP bytes were out of order
       1915 TCP packets had data after window
     865443 TCP bytes were after window
       5804 TCP packets for already closed connection
        941 TCP packets were window probes
   10847459 TCP packets had ACKs
     222657 TCP packets had duplicate ACKs
          1 TCP packet ACKed unsent data
 1200274739 TCP bytes ACKed
     141545 TCP packets had window updates
         13 TCP segments dropped due to PAWS
    4658158 TCP segments were predicted pure-ACKs
   24033756 TCP segments were predicted pure-data
    8087980 TCP PCB cache misses
        305 Bad UDP header checksums
         17 Bad UDP data length fields
   23772272 UDP PCB cache misses

MultiNet Buffer Statistics:
        388 out of 608 buffers in use:
                30 buffers allocated to Data.
                10 buffers allocated to Packet Headers.
                66 buffers allocated to Socket Structures.
                57 buffers allocated to Protocol Control Blocks.
                163 buffers allocated to Routing Table Entries.
                2 buffers allocated to Socket Names and Addresses.
                48 buffers allocated to Kernel Fork-Processes.
                2 buffers allocated to Interface Addresses.
                1 buffer allocated to Multicast Addresses.
                1 buffer allocated to Timeout Callbacks.
                6 buffers allocated to Memory Management.
                2 buffers allocated to Network TTY Control Blocks.
        11 out of 43 page clusters in use.
        11 CXBs borrowed from VMS device drivers
        2 CXBs waiting to return to the VMS device drivers
        162 Kbytes allocated to MultiNet buffers (44% in use).
        226 Kbytes of allocated buffer address space (0% of maximum).
        Connection closed by foreign host.
```

Whoa! This hit the jackpot! What is all this?

What we did was telnet to port 15, which until 1994 was designated as the netstat port. This may run a daemon that tells anybody who cares to drop in just about everything about the connections made by all the computers linked to the Internet through this computer, the LAN it was on, the open ports, and on and on.

What is fascinating is that netstat tells so much information of value to computer criminals that this is no longer an assigned port IETF (Internet Engineering Task Force) function. So almost no Internet host computers leave that port open any more. This was a rare find of a clueless Internet backbone provider.

 Newbie note: An Internet backbone usually provides high speed connections to the Internet to entire ISPs and large companies, rather than selling accounts to individuals.

Another discovery is that this is a Vax running VMS. Back in the days of X.25 networks, when what was to become the Internet was just a gleam in the eyes of the people developing ARPAnet, Vax/VMS was common. But nowadays they are rare.

So from port 15 we discovered that grande.newfoo.org is a busy and important computer, and that even a very busy and important computer can have sysdmins that might let a port surfer play with sensitive information.

My lady friend wanted to try out another port. I suggested the finger port, number 79. So she gave the command:

```
->telnet grande.newfoo.org 79
Trying 999.121.1.2 ...
Connected to grande.newfoo.org.
Escape character is '^]'.
```

Next the simplest command is to just try "enter." This gives:

```
Sunday, November 9, 1997 9:17PM-MST    Up 43 05:24:17
1+0 Jobs on GRANDE   Load ave   0.15 0.16 0.17
User     Personal Name Job    Subsys        Terminal  Console Location
DONORNET New Mexico Donor P   60262E3D MAIL LTA5632SIENNA/DONORNET
TMLINFO TML Information Se 20612428 *DCL* BRAVO$NTY311tml-fw.tml.com
                             20612D31  *DCL*  BRAVO$NTY307tml-
fw.tml.com
                      20605FDF  *DCL* BRAVO$NTY314tml-fw.tml.com
Connection closed by foreign host.
```

If you look back at the chapter on finger, you will see this finger program gives different output than most other finger programs. That is because we are on one of those rare Vaxes, rather than a common Unix or Windows NT Internet host.

So what did we do next? We could have gotten some of those old hacker files about how to break into Vax/VMS, especially one that was so badly administered as this one. But we are good Internet citizens and also allergic to jail. We decided we'd better log off.

But there was one last hack we decided to do: leave our mark on a log file. (We presumed the sysadmin did keep a log file of all outside connections.)

A good sysadmin keeps a record of comings and goings on a computer's ports. The administrator of an obviously important computer such as grande.newfoo.org will probably scan the records of what commands are given by whom to his computer. Especially on a port important enough to be running a mystery daemon. So everything we typed while connected was presumably saved on a log.

So my friend giggled and left a few messages on port 79 before logging off. Stuff like "Hi, papa-san." Oh, dear, I do believe she's hooked on hacking. Hmmm, it could be a good way to meet cute sysadmins . . .

How to Port Surf

Port surf's up! If you want to surf, too, here are the basics:

1) Get logged on to a shell account. That's an account with your ISP that lets you give Unix commands. Or—run Linux or some other kind of Unix on your PC and hook up to the Internet. Or, get a telnet program that you understand intimately and run it on your Windows or Mac box. But Unix is by far the easiest to make work.

2) With Unix, give the command "telnet <hostname> <port number>" where <hostname> is the Internet address of the computer you want to visit and <port number> is whatever looks phun to you.

3) If you get the response "connected to hostname," then surf's up!

You can get punched in the nose warning: Even though port surfing is legal, if you do too much of it, especially by running a program that automates port scanning, this may be considered a hostile act by the systems administrator of your target computer. He or she may contact the company that gives you Internet access and get your account closed. So you may want to explain in advance that you are merely a harmless hacker looking to have a good time, er, um, learn about TCP/IP. Yeh, that sounds good . . .

Fun Ports to Surf

```
Port      Service        Why it's phun!
7         echo           Whatever you type in, the host repeats back
9         discard/null   How fast can you figure out this one?
11        systat         Lots of info on users
13        daytime        Time and date at computer's location
15        netstat        Tremendous info on networks—super rare find!
19        chargen        Pours out a stream of ASCII characters. Use
                         ^C to stop. On some computers even ^C doesn't
                         work - you may even have to reboot your
                         computer. Great for playing jokes on newbies.
21        ftp            Transfers files
23        telnet         Where you normally log in to your
                         shell account
25        smpt           Forge email from Bill.Gates@Microsoft.org.
37        time           Time
39        rlp            Resource location
43        whois          Info on hosts and networks
53        domain         Nameserver
70        gopher         Out-of-date info hunter
79        finger         Lots of info on users
80        http           Web server
110       pop            Where your email program picks up email
119       nntp           Usenet news groups—forge posts, cancels
443       shttp          Another web server
512       biff           Mail notification
513       rlogin         Remote login, or...
          who            Remote who and uptime
514         shell              Remote command, no password used! or...

          syslog         Remote system logging
520       route          Routing information protocol
```

This numbering system is voluntarily offered by the Internet Engineering Task Force (IETF). That means that an Internet host may use other ports for these services. More than one service may also be assigned simultaneously to the same port. Expect the unexpected!

If you are in a shell account, you can get a list of many IETF assignments of port numbers from the file /etc/services. A place to get a complete listing is from *http://ds2.internic.net/rfc/rfc1700.txt*. Read it and you'll be in for happy port surfing!

Section 2, Chapter 7
How to Map the Internet

Carl was on the phone. Yes, Carl, the fellow who was man enough to take a turn hosting one of the most hated domain names in computer criminaldom, my techbroker.com. "They managed to break into a DNS server and change the listing for techbroker to something obscene," he told me. The message used the spelling, grammar and vocabulary of a foul-mouthed seven-year-old. It was the trademark of my chronic nemesis, the Gray Areas Liberation Front (GALF).

 Newbie note: DNS stands for the Internet's Domain Name System. It makes sure that no two computers have the same name. It also tells you a lot about each domain name. When hacked, a DNS server may tell you rude things about a domain name.

The next day they managed to break into a computer where Carl was root and wipe out his account. Again. The day after that they rooted another computer, broke into a user's account and from it sent me the message "I lub ewe. G.A.L.F."

This was getting ridiculous. Couldn't those guys ever figure out where my Web page or mail server were kept? They normally preferred to break into my account and send obscene email to hacker email lists from it. Kewl d00dz, huh? But this time they weren't managing to find their usual mass audience.

"What shall we do next," Carl asked. He was tiring of the harassment. After all, he was giving me free services for which most ISPs charge over $100 per month. I asked him to route techbroker.com over to an Internet host run by another masochist, er, brave person.

GALF is a competent, if emotionally immature, hacker gang. They've hidden their tracks well enough that, as of this writing, none of them have been caught. They are good enough to break into lots of computers. But judging from their attacks, they are terrible at figuring out how a group of computers can share the various functions of one domain name, especially one they hate as much as techbroker.com.

When you finish this chapter, you, however, will know enough to find your way around the Internet pretty darn well. However, I'm not revealing everything—leave my POP server alone, guys!

If you are defending a computer system, this will give you an idea of the tools your attackers have. If you are a member of GALF, tough luck, after reading this you will still have lots more hurdles between you and your goal of bashing techbroker.com.

In this chapter you will learn how to:
- Explore the unknown vastness of cyberspace. The Internet is so huge, and it changes so fast, that no one today has a complete map and no one ever will again.
- If you can't make contact with someone in a distant place, you can help your ISP trouble shoot broken links in the Internet. Yes, I did that once when email failed to a friend in Northern Ireland.
- If you don't want people to sniff your telnet sessions, you can check to see whether your PPP connection connects directly to your destination.
- If you want to be a computer criminal, your map of the connections to your intended victim and layout of the victim's LAN gives you valuable information. Better read up, GALF.
- Since this is a lesson on legal hacking, we're not going to show how to determine the best box in which to install a sniffer or how to tell what IP address to spoof to get past a packet filter.

For this lesson, you can get some benefit even if all you have is Windows. But to take full advantage of this lesson, you should either have some sort of Unix on your personal computer, or a shell account! SHELL ACCOUNT!

If you are a Windows user, for this lesson you will need to install an nslookup program. Global Solutions, Inc. of Columbia, SC offers one. John A. Junod also has written an nslookup program that runs in DOS. However, don't expect your Windows or DOS nslookup program to have all the functionality of a Unix version. If you are unable to get the results in this lesson, don't email me with your questions. Get a shell account. SHELL ACCOUNT!

Let's start our mapping expedition by visiting the Internet in Botswana. Wow, is Botswana even on the Internet? It's a lovely landlocked nation in the southern region of Africa, famous for cattle ranching, diamonds and abundant wildlife. The language of commerce in Botswana is English, so there's a good chance that we could understand messages from their computers.

Our first step in learning about Botswana's Internet hosts is to use the nslookup program.

 Newbie note: Are you a Windows or Mac user? Are you trying out this lesson on anything other than a shell account? Like some of my correspondents, your curiosity may lead you to try entering the nslookup command in the window of your web browser, or some other goshawful place other than a program plainly labeled "nslookup." This is commendable hacker experimentation. However, if your experiments at using anything other than a program plainly labeled "nslookup" don't work, don't email me to complain. I *will* flame you.

Evil genius tip: nslookup—as brought to you as a Unix program—is one of the most powerful Internet mapping tools in existence. We can hardly do it justice here. If you want to explore to the max, get the book *DNS and BIND* by Paul Albitz and Cricket Liu, published by O'Reilly, 1997 edition.

If you are using a shell account, when you enter the command "nslookup," you may get the message "command not found." If this happens, give the command "whereis nslookup." (Or your computer may use the "find" command.) On the account I'm using for this example I find it in /usr/etc/nslookup. So at the prompt I simply enter:

```
-> /usr/etc/nslookup
Default Server:  southwestfoobar.com
Address:  198.59.999.2
```

This tells me that my local ISP is using a Domain Name Server on the computer 198.59.999.2. Now we are in the program, so I have to remember that my bash commands don't work any more. Our next step is to tell the program that we would like to know what computers handle any given domain name.

```
set type=ns
```

Now we need to know the domain name for Botswana. To do that I look up the list of top level domain names on page 379 of the 1997 edition of *DNS and BIND*. For Botswana it's .bw. So I enter it at the prompt, remembering—this is VERY important—to put a period after the domain name:

```
bw.
Server:  southwestfoobar.com
Address:  198.59.999.2
Non-authoritative answer:
```

This "non-authoritative answer" stuff tells me that this information has been stored for awhile, so it is possible that it has changed.

```
bw        nameserver = FOOFLOWER.EE.FOO.BAR.ZA
bw        nameserver = SLEET.PSG.COM
bw        nameserver = NS.UU.NET
bw        nameserver = HIPBAR.RU.AC.ZA
Authoritative answers can be found from:
FOOFLOWER.EE.FOO.BAR.ZA       inet address = 146.999.999.18
SLEET.PSG.COM                 inet address = 147.28.999.34
NS.UU.NET                     inet address = 137.39.1.3
HIPBAR.RU.AC.ZA               inet address = 146.231.999.1
```

I look up the domain name ".za" and discover it stands for South Africa. This tells me that when I did this mapping (Feb. 1997), the Internet was in its infancy in

Botswana—no nameservers there. South Africa was doing all the nameserver work for Botswana.

Newbie note: A DNS nameserver is a computer program that stores data on the Domain Name System and provides that information to client software programs such as the nslookup program we are playing with today. It also stores information on how to find other computers. When various nameservers get to talking with each other, they eventually, usually within seconds, can figure out the routes to any one of the millions of computers on the Internet.

Next let's learn more about South Africa. Since we are still in the nslookup program, I command it to tell me what computers are nameservers for South Africa:

```
za.
Server:   southwestfoobar.com
Address:  198.59.999.2
Non-authoritative answer:
za        nameserver = FOOFLOWER.EE.FOO.BAR.za
za        nameserver = UCTHPX.fu.AC.za
za        nameserver = HIPBAR.RU.AC.za
za        nameserver = SLEET.PSG.COM
za        nameserver = FUBARRI.OZ.AU
za        nameserver = NS.EU.NET
za        nameserver = NS.UU.NET
za        nameserver = UUCP-GW-1.PA.DEC.COM
za        nameserver = FUPIES.FRD.AC.za
Authoritative answers can be found from:
FOOFLOWER.EE.FOO.BAR.za      inet address = 146.999.999.18
UCTHPX.fu.AC.za              inet address = 137.158.999.1
HIPBAR.RU.AC.za              inet address = 146.231.999.1
SLEET.PSG.COM                inet address = 147.28.999.34
FUBARRI.OZ.AU                inet address = 128.250.999.2
FUBARRI.OZ.AU                inet address = 128.250.999.21
NS.EU.NET                    inet address = 192.16.999.11
UUCP-GW-1.PA.DEC.COM         inet address = 204.123.999.18
UUCP-GW-1.PA.DEC.COM         inet address = 16.1.999.18
FUPIES.FRD.AC.za             inet address = 137.214.999.1
```

Newbie note: What does *inet address = 137.214.999.1* mean? That's the name of a computer on the Internet—in this case FUPIES.FRD.AC—in octal. Octal is like regular numbers except in base 8 rather than base 10. All computer names on the Internet must be changed into octal numbers so that other computers can understand them. Those number "9s" you see in numerical IP addresses in this book are there to disguise it so the truly clueless won't bother them by running port scanners against then.

Aha! Some of those nameservers are located outside South Africa. We see computers in Australia (.au) and the US (the .com domain).

So what can we do next? Presuming you are using the Unix nslookup, we exit the nslookup program with the command ^D. That's made by holding down the control key while hitting the small "d" key. It is *very important* to exit nslookup this way and not with ^C, even though ^C is a common way to stop programs in Unix.

Next, we take one of the nameservers in South Africa and use the whois command.

If you are using Windows, there are several ways to do a whois command. There are several whois programs you can install. Tidewater Systems has a program WsFinger, that also can run the whois command. It works by connecting to rs.internic.net's whois server. Or you can do it yourself without a whois program. Telnet to whois.internic.net and enter the command: whois HIPBAR.RU.AC.ZA.

Better yet, if you have a shell account, you will get identical results with this:

```
->whois HIPBAR.RU.AC.ZA
[No name] (HIPBAR)
   Hostname: HIPBAR.RU.AC.ZA
   Address: 146.231.999.1
   System: SUN running SUNOS
   Domain Server
   Record last updated on 24-Feb-92.
```

To see this host record with registered users, repeat the command with a star ('*') before the name; or, use '%' to show *just* the registered users.

The InterNIC Registration Services Host contains *only* Internet Information (Networks, ASN's, Domains, and POC's). Use the whois server at nic.ddn.mil for MILNET Information.

Figure 1. The whois server run by Internic. First aid for hackers stuck with Windows only. Enter the name of the Internet host you want to investigate after the prompt.

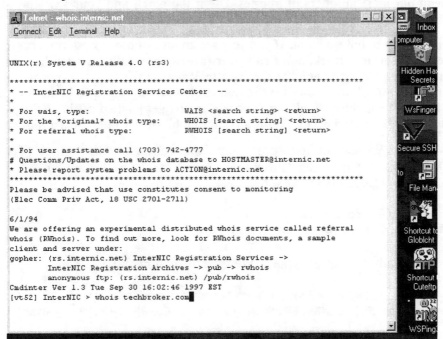

Kewl! This tells us what kind of computer it is—a Sun—and the operating system, Sun OS. However, the whois command often won't tell us nearly this much. But below we will explore other ways to learn this sort of stuff.

Now, just for variety, I use the whois command with the numerical address of one of the nameservers above. This doesn't always give back the text name, but sometimes it does. (Please understand that part of what this chapter is trying to show is that you can get many different results from using the same Internet mapping tools.) And, voila, we get:

```
-whois 146.999.999.18
[No name] (FOOFLOWER1)
   Hostname: FOOFLOWER.EE.FOO.BAR.ZA
   Address: 146.999.999.18
   System: HP-9000 running HP-UX
   Domain Server
   Record last updated on 14-Sep-94.
```

But all this is doing so far is just telling us info about who is a nameserver for whom. Just because a computer is a nameserver for another does not necessarily mean that one is directly linked to another. But nameserver relationships do help us get the general picture.

So how about directly mapping a route from my computer to South Africa? For that we will use the trace route command. In a Unix shell account it is traceroute; in Windows 95, tracert.

> **You can get punched in the nose warning: Traceroute is intended for use in network testing, measurement and management. It should be used primarily for manual fault isolation. Because of the load it could impose on the network, it is unwise to use traceroute from automated scripts which could cause that program to send out huge numbers of queries. Use it too much and your ISP may start asking you some sharp questions.**

> **You could go to jail warning: If you just got an idea of how to use traceroute for a denial of service attack, don't call your favorite journalist and tell him or her that you are plotting a denial of service attack against the ISPs that serve famous people like Bill Clinton! Don't write that exploit script. If you write it, don't use it. If you get caught we'll all laugh at you as you get hustled off in chains while your journalist friend gets a $250K advance on his or her book deal about you.**

In Windows 95 you run the tracert command from the DOS prompt. (To get to MS-DOS, click "Start," then "Programs," then "MS DOS Prompt.")

In some shell accounts we may first need to find traceroute:

```
->whereis traceroute
traceroute: /usr/local/bin/traceroute
```

Now we're ready to map in earnest. We give the command:

```
->/usr/local/bin/traceroute FOOFLOWER.EE.FOO.BAR.ZA
traceroute to FOOFLOWER.EE.FOO.BAR.ZA (146.999.999.18), 30 hops max,
40
```

```
byte packets
 1 sisko (198.59.999.1) 3 ms 4 ms 4 ms
 2 glory-cyberport.foo.westnet.net (204.999.999.33) 47 ms 8 ms 4 ms
 3 ENSS365.foo.ORG (129.999.1.3)  5 ms  10 ms  7 ms
 4 h4-0.cnss116.Albuquerque.t3.barbar.net (192.999.74.45) 17 ms 41
ms 28 ms
 5 f2.t112-0.Albuquerque.t3.barbar.net (999.222.112.221) 7 ms 6 ms 5
ms
 6 h14.t16-0.Los-Angeles.t3.barbar.net (999.223.17.9) 31 ms 39 ms
84 ms
 7 h14.t8-0.San-Francisco.t3.barbar.net (999.223.9.13) 67 ms 43
ms 68 ms
 8 enss220.t3.barbar.net (999.223.9.22) 73 ms 58 ms 54 ms
 9 fu-mae-w-F0/0.Sprintlink.net (198.32.999.11) 97 ms 319 ms 110 ms
10 fu-stk-1-H11/0-T3.Sprintlink.net (144.999.10.109) 313 ms 479 ms
473 ms
11 fu-stk-2-F/T.Sprintlink.net (198.999.999.2)  179 ms * *
12 fu-dc-7-H4/0-T3.Sprintlink.net (144.999.10.106) 164 ms * 176 ms
13 fu-dc-7-F/T.Sprintlink.net (198.999.0.1) 143 ms 129 ms 134 ms
14 gfu-dc-3-Fddi0/0.bar.net (204.59.999.197) 135 ms 152 ms 130 ms
15 204.59.999.66 (204.59.999.66) 583 ms 545 ms 565 ms
16 * * *
17 e0.csir00.fooey.net.za (155.999.249.1)  516 ms  436 ms  400 ms
18 s1.und00.fooey.net.za (155.999.70.1)  424 ms  485 ms  492 ms
19 e0.und01.fooey.net.za (155.999.190.2)  509 ms  530 ms  459 ms
20 s0.und02.fooey.net.za (155.999.82.2)  650 ms * 548 ms
21 Gw-Uninet1.CC.foo.bar.za (146.999.196.1)  881 ms  517 ms  478 ms
22 cisco-unp.foo.bar.za (146.999.128.8)  498 ms  545 ms *
23 IN.ee.foo.bar.za (146.999.999.18)  573 ms  585 ms  493 ms
```

What does all this stuff mean?

The number in front of each line is the number of hops since leaving the computer that has the shell account we are using.

The second entry is the name of the computer through which this route passes, first in text, and then (in parentheses) its numerical representation.

The numbers after that are the time in milliseconds it takes for each of three probe packets in a row to make that hop. When a * appears, the time for the hop timed out.

In the case of the options we have chosen on this traceroute, any time greater than 3 seconds causes a * to be printed out.

 Evil genius tip: Want to play traceroute like a Stradivarius violin? In a shell account give the command "man traceroute" to get a capsule summary of your options. You Windows only dudes will just have to suffer.

How about hop 16? It gave us no info whatsoever. That silent gateway may be the result of a bug in the 4.1, 4.2 or 4.3 BSD Unix network code. A computer running one of these operating systems sends an "unreachable" message. Or it could be something else. Sorry, I'm not enough of a genius yet to figure this one out for sure. Are we having phun yet?

Now this is getting interesting. We know that Fooflower is directly connected to at least one other computer, and that computer in turn is connected to cisco-unp.foo.bar.za. Let's learn a little something about this cisco-unp.foo.bar.za, okay?

First, we can guess from the name that is it a Cisco router. In fact, the first hop in this route is to a computer named "sisco," which is also a Cisco router. Since 85% of the routers in the world are Ciscos, that's a pretty safe bet. But we are hackers, so we aren't satisfied with guesses. Not only will we prove cisco-unp.foo.bar.za is a Cisco, we are also going to find out the model number, and a few other goodies.

First we use whois:

```
->whois cisco-unp.foo.bar.za
No match for "CISCO-UNP.FOO.BAR.ZA".
```

Huh? Traceroute tells us cisco-unp.foo.bar.za exists, but whois can't find it! Actually this is a common problem, especially trying to use whois on distant computers. What do we do next? If you are lucky, the whereis or find command on your computer will turn up another incredibly cool program: dig!

 Newbie note: Dig stands for "domain information groper." It does a lot of the same things as nslookup. But dig is a much older program, in many ways harder to use than nslookup. For details on dig, use the command from your shell account "man dig." Sorry, if you are bound and determined to only use Windows, I don't know where to find a dig program for your computer.

On my shell account I found I could run dig straight from the bash prompt:

```
->dig CISCO-UNP.FOO.BAR.ZA
; <> DiG 2.0 <> CISCO-UNP.FOO.BAR.ZA
;; res options: init recurs defnam dnsrch
;; got answer:
;; ->HEADER<- opcode: QUERY, status: NOERROR, id: 6
;; flags: qr aa rd ra; Ques: 1, Ans: 4, Auth: 5, Addit: 5
;; QUESTIONS:
;;      CISCO-UNP.FOO.BAR.ZA, type = A, class = IN

;; ANSWERS:
CISCO-UNP.FOO.BAR.ZA.    86400    A    146.999.248.1
CISCO-UNP.FOO.BAR.ZA.    86400    A    146.999.12.1
CISCO-UNP.FOO.BAR.ZA.    86400    A    146.999.60.1
CISCO-UNP.FOO.BAR.ZA.    86400    A    146.999.128.8

;; AUTHORITY RECORDS:
foo.bar.za.     86400    NS    Eagle.foo.bar.za.
foo.bar.za.     86400    NS    Shrike.foo.bar.za.
foo.bar.za.     86400    NS    ucthpx.fu.ac.za.
foo.bar.za.     86400    NS    hipbar.ru.ac.za.
foo.bar.za.     86400    NS    Sleet.psg.com.

;; ADDITIONAL RECORDS:
Eagle.foo.bar.za.       86400    A    146.999.128.15
Shrike.foo.bar.za.      86400    A    146.999.128.13
ucthpx.fu.ac.za.        86400    A    137.158.999.1
```

```
hipbar.ru.ac.za.          86400    A        146.231.999.1
Sleet.psg.com.            14400    A        147.28.999.34

;; Total query time: 516 msec
;; FROM: llama to SERVER: default—198.59.999.2
;; WHEN: Fri Jan 17 13:03:49 1997
;; MSG SIZE  sent: 37  rcvd: 305
```

Ahhh, nice. The first few lines, the ones preceded by the ;; marks, mostly tell what the default settings of the command are and what we asked it. The line "Ques: 1, Ans: 4, Auth: 5, Addit: 5" tells us how many items we'll get under each topic of questions, answers, authority records, and additional records. (You will get different numbers on that line from different queries.)

This "records" stuff refers to information stored under the domain name system.

Dig tells us that CLASS=IN, meaning CISCO-UNP.FOO.BAR.ZA is a domain name within the Internet. But we already knew that. The first *new* thing we learn is that four routers all share the same domain name. We can tell that because their numerical Internet numbers are different even though they all are named CISCO-UNP.FOO.BAR.ZA. Use dig enough and you'll someday see the reverse: several domain names can all belong to the same numerical address. If you use the dig command on each link in this route to FOOFLOWER.EE.FOO.BAR.ZA, you'll find a tremendous variation in whether the routers map to same or different domain names. As hackers, we want to get wise to all these variations in how domain names are associated with boxes. Are you reading this, GALF guys?

But we can still learn even more about CISCO-UNP.FOO.BAR.ZA. We go back to nslookup and run it in interactive mode:

```
->/usr/etc/nslookup
Default Server:  southwestfoobar.com
Address:  198.59.999.2
```

Now we are ready to go. Let's do something new with nslookup, a command that comes in really, really handy when we're playing vigilante and need to persecute a spammer or bust a child porn Web site or two. Here's how we can get the email address for the sysadmin of an Internet host computer.

```
->set type=soa
```

Then we enter the name of the computer about which we are curious. Note that we put a period after the end of the host name. It often helps to do this with nslookup:

```
>CISCO-UNP.FOO.BAR.ZA.
Server:  southwestfoobar.com
Address:  198.59.999.2
*** No start of authority zone information is available for
CISCO-UNP.FOO.BAR.ZA.
```

Now what do we do? Give up? No, we're hackers, right? So we enter just part of the domain name, again remembering to put a period at the end:

```
>foo.bar.za.
Server:  southwestfoobar.com
Address:  198.59.999.2
foo.bar.za        origin = Eagle.foo.bar.za
        mail addr = postmaster.foo.bar.za
        serial=199610255, refresh=10800, retry=3600,
expire=3000000, min=86400
Eagle.foo.bar.za inet address = 146.999.128.15
Shrike.foo.bar.za       inet address = 146.999.128.13
ucthpx.fu.ac.za         inet address = 137.158.999.1
hipbar.ru.ac.za  inet address = 146.231.999.1
Sleet.psg.com    inet address = 147.28.999.34
```

Bingo!!! We got the email address of a sysadmin whose domain includes that Cisco router, and the IP addresses of some other boxes he or she administers. But notice it doesn't list any of those routers which the sysadmin undoubtedly knows a thing or two about.

But we aren't done yet with cisco-unp.foo.bar.za (146.999.128.8). Of course we have a pretty good guess that it is a Cisco router. But why stop with a mere guess when we can port surf? So we fall back on our friend the telnet program and head for port 2001.

If you, poor thing, are following this lesson in Windows, get your telnet program going with a PPP session, and bring up the connection dialog box. Be sure to put the name of your suspected Cisco router in the "hostname" box and "2001" in the "port" box. Meanwhile, those of us with a shell account simply give this command:

```
->telnet 146.999.128.8 2001
Trying 146.999.128.8 ...
Connected to 146.999.128.8.
Escape character is '^]'.
C
*******************************************************
***  Welcome to the University of Fubar
***
***
***
*** Model : Cisco 4500 with ATM and 8 BRI ports          ***
***
***
*** Dimension Data Durban - 031-838333
***
***
***
*******************************************************
```

Whoopee! We know now that this is a Cisco model 4500 owned by the University of Fubar, and we even got a phone number for the sysadmin. From this we also can infer (using those numerical IP addresses that I foobarred) that this router handles a subnet which serves the U of Fubar and includes fooflower.

Newbie note: A subnet isn't quite the same thing a a local area network (LAN), although a subnet might all be located in one building group of buildings such as the University of Fubar. A subnet divides a larger network into several smaller ones, with each subnet usually connected to another by a router.

But how did I know to telnet to port 2001? It's in common use among routers as the administrative port. This information comes from the RFC (request for comments) that covers all commonly used port assignments. You can find a copy of this RFC at *http://ds2.internic.net/rfc/rfc1700.txt*. Read it and you'll be in for happy port surfing!

There are a bunch of ports commonly used by Cisco routers:

```
cisco-fna        130/tcp    cisco FNATIVE
cisco-tna        131/tcp    cisco TNATIVE
cisco-sys        132/tcp    cisco SYSMAINT
licensedaemon    1986/tcp   cisco license management
tr-rsrb-p1       1987/tcp   cisco RSRB Priority 1 port
tr-rsrb-p2       1988/tcp   cisco RSRB Priority 2 port
tr-rsrb-p3       1989/tcp   cisco RSRB Priority 3 port
stun-p1          1990/tcp   cisco STUN Priority 1 port
stun-p2          1991/tcp   cisco STUN Priority 2 port
stun-p3          1992/tcp   cisco STUN Priority 3 port
snmp-tcp-port    1993/tcp   cisco SNMP TCP port
stun-port        1994/tcp   cisco serial tunnel port
perf-port        1995/tcp   cisco perf port
tr-rsrb-port     1996/tcp   cisco Remote SRB port
gdp-port         1997/tcp   cisco Gateway Discovery Protocol
x25-svc-port     1998/tcp   cisco X.25 service (XOT)
tcp-id-port      1999/tcp   cisco identification port
```

For giggles, now let's telnet to the "normal" telnet port, which is 23. Since it is the "normal" port, the one you usually go to when you want to log in, we don't need to put the 23 after the host name:

```
->telnet 146.999.128.8
Trying 146.999.128.8 ...
Connected to 146.999.128.8.
Escape character is '^]'.
C
****************************************************************
***  Welcome to the University of Fubar
***
***
***
*** Model : Cisco 4500 with ATM and 8 BRI ports
***
***
***
*** Dimension Data Durban - 031-838333
***
****************************************************************
```

```
User Access Verification

Password:
```

This is interesting, no username requested, just a password. If I were the sysadmin, I'd make it a little harder to log in. But I resist the temptation to attempt an illegal break-in. Hmmm, what happens if we telnet to the finger port, which is 79:

```
->telnet 146.999.128.8 79
Trying 146.999.128.8 ...
Connected to 146.999.128.8.
Escape character is '^]'.
C
********************************************************************
***   Welcome to the University of Fubar
***
***
***
*** Model : Cisco 4500 with ATM and 8 BRI ports
***
***
***
*** Dimension Data Durban - 031-838333
***
***
***
********************************************************************
      Line       User        Host(s)              Idle Location
*   2 vty 0                   idle                   0
kitsbar.southwestfoobar.com
    BR0:2                     Sync PPP             00:00:00
    BR0:1                     Sync PPP             00:00:00
    BR1:2                     Sync PPP             00:00:00
    BR1:1                     Sync PPP             00:00:00
    BR2:2                     Sync PPP             00:00:01
    BR2:1                     Sync PPP             00:00:00
    BR5:1                     Sync PPP             00:00:00
Connection closed by foreign host.
```

Notice that finger lists the connection to the computer I was port surfing from: kitsbar. But no one else seems to be on line just now. What a great time to break in! If I were the sysadmin I would close the finger port so computer criminals wouldn't be able to learn so much.

Now let's try the obvious. Let's telnet to the login port of fooflower. I use the numerical address just for the heck of it:

```
-telnet 146.999.999.18
Trying 146.999.999.18 ...
Connected to 146.999.999.18.
Escape character is '^]'.
NetBSD/i386 (fooflower.ee.foo.bar.za) (ttyp0)
login:
```

Since we now know this is a university, that "ee" in the name of this computer probably means this is the electrical engineering (EE) department. And NetBSD is a freeware Unix that runs on a PC!

Getting this info makes me almost feel like I've been hanging out at the University of Fubar EE computer lab. Judging from their router, security is way lax, so there must not be any malicious hackers on campus. Alas, they must make do with cheap computers. Their login messages are friendly.

Let's finger and see who's logged in just now. Since I am already in the telnet program (I can tell by the prompt "telnet"), I go to fooflower using the "open" command:

```
>telnet open fooflower.ee.foo.bar.za 79
Trying 146.999.999.18 ...
telnet: connect: Connection refused
telnet quit
```

Since that didn't work, I exit telnet and try the finger program on my shell account computer:

```
->finger @fooflower.ee.foo.bar.za
[fooflower.ee.foo.bar.za]
finger: fooflower.ee.foo.bar.za: Connection refused
```

Sigh. It's hard to find open finger ports any more. Maybe I was wrong, maybe there are some malicious hackers on the U of Foobar campus. On the other hand, maybe someone in the EE department decided to follow the good security practice of closing the finger port because fooflower is, after all, connected to the Internet. Guess what, there are lots of bad dudes prowling the Internet.

What next? I have a goody for you Windows users! Surf over to *http://www.ip-switch.com* and look for a program called "What's Up." With luck, by the time you read this, they will still offer free evaluation copies.

What's Up is a network analysis tool that R.J. Gosselin used to research his doctoral computer science dissertation, "External threats to computer security in networked systems." Translated into plain English, that title means "How I cracked into every box in sight, only I got permission first from the owners of the computers, so I got a Ph.D. for it instead of a prison term."

Basically, if a computer has an IP address, you can find it with What's Up and map its relationship to other computers. Figure 2 shows a first step in this mapping process, and Figure 3 an example of a final result. Yes, believe it or not, this tool runs on Windows 95!

Evil Genius tip: Run nslookup again. Give these commands:
```
>set quertype=mx
Server: nic.foo.net (or whatever server your ISP uses).
Address: 198.53.999.6
>ls foo.net
```

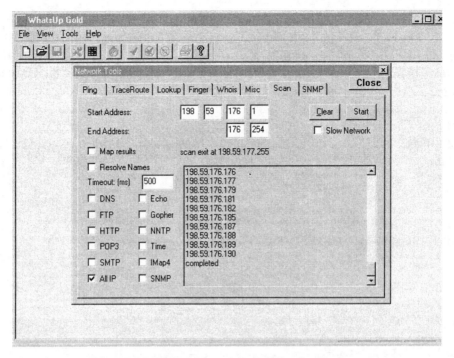

Figure 2. What's Up has just identified all the computers with Internet addresses within the range of 198.59.176.1 and 198.59.176.255.

Next, we check out the Internet backbone on the traceroute that led us to the University of Fubar. You can pretty much expect that links in the middle of a long traceroute will be big computers owned by the bigger companies that form the backbone of the Internet. We check out number 20 on the list:

```
->telnet 155.999.82.2 2001
Trying 155.999.82.2 ...
Connected to 155.999.82.2.
Escape character is '^]'.


                     Id: und02
              Authorised Users Only!
              - - - - - - - - - - - -

User Access Verification
Username:
```

We're out of friendly territory now. Since port 2001 works, it probably is another router. But look at the login sequence. It doesn't say "login." That makes me suspect this computer isn't running any kind of Unix. Or if it is, we first login to some other kind of thing, perhaps a firewall of some sort?

We go to the default telnet port and get an identical message and login sequence.

Now just maybe this backbone-type computer will tell us gobs of stuff about all the computers it is connected to. We try telneting to the netstat (network statistics) port, 15. This, if it happens to be open to the public, will tell us all about the computers that connect through it:

```
->telnet 155.999.82.2 15
Trying 155.999.82.2 ...
telnet: connect: Connection refused
```

Sigh. I give an example of the incredible wealth of information you can once in a blue moon get from netstat on a backbone computer in the chapter *Port Surf's Up*. But every day it gets harder to find a public netstat port. That's because the information netstat gives is so useful to the computer criminals who have ruined the Internet for the rest of us. In fact, port 15 is no longer reserved as the netstat port (as of 1994, according to the RFC). So you will find few boxes using it. But it's always worth a try!

 Evil Genius tip: want to know what port assignments your ISP uses? The file /etc/services on most machines will tell you this. How can you can read that information? Try this: First, change to the /etc/ directory, then command it to print it out to your screen with: "more services". Alas, just because your shell account has a list of port assignments doesn't mean they are actually in use.

F

igure 3: A fictitious example of a finished map of some poor victim company's computers, with, cough, cough, monitoring under way. You can tell this is fictitious because the IP address for the Hong Kong box is 127.0.0.1, which is the IP address that simply means "my own computer." Also, I'd get sued if I put a real victim network in this book!

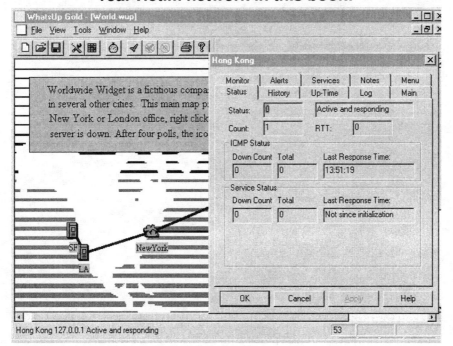

Recently, after surfing about two dozen somewhat randomly chosen netstat ports, the only answer I got other than "Connection refused" was:

```
-telnet ns.newfoobar.com 15
Trying 198.59.999.10 ...
Connected to ns.newfoobar.com.
Escape character is '^]'.
Yes, but will I see the easter bunny in skintight leather at an Iron
Maiden concert?
```

Now what about all those Sprintlink routers in that traceroute? That's a major Internet backbone based in the US provided by Sprint. Once upon a time you could study the topology of the Sprintlink backbone at *http://www.Sprintlink.net.* Alas, Sprintlink has quit doing that.

Sigh. The Internet is getting less friendly, but more secure. Some day when we're really ancient, say five years from now, we'll be telling people, "Why, I remember when we could port surf! Why, there used to be zillions of open ports and people could choose *any* password they wanted. Hmph! Today it's just firewalls and encrypted tunnels everywhere you look!" Explore while it is still easy, folks!

Section 3
Welcome to war!

Some people learn how to hack out of pure curiosity. Sadly enough, others learn to hack so they can raise hell. But maybe you are the kind of guy who wants to become a white hat on the frontier of cyberspace. Maybe you want your life to count, to become a hero on this new frontier.

If so, you came to the right place.

First, a quick technical note. To really make the best use of this section, you should have already learned how to use Unix.

Now for the serious talk. Before you plunge into the activities of this section, think about it carefully. Talk it over with your friends, teachers, and spiritual leaders. If you are under 18, talk this over with your parents. The problem is, there are dangerous people out in cyberspace. Whether you choose to fight the bad guys or succumb to the temptation to join them, you are asking for trouble.

From the humorous tone of this book you may think that hackers are no more than cute nerdz with attitude. Sure, lots of them are like me and many of the other people you have met in this book. We're full of laughter and high jinks. But others—people who have the nerve to call themselves hackers, but who are really just computer criminals—are serious bad news. Before you tangle with the bad guys, be they the people who make their living running spam empires, keyboard fascists who try to run people who they hate off the Internet, digital con artists, or just plain computer vandals, count up the cost. Are you prepared for the worst they can throw at you?

A book that will help you measure the cost of fighting cyberspace bad guys is *Information Warfare: Protecting your Personal Security in the Electronic Age,*[1] by Winn Schwartau. It will also give you additional self-defense strategies beyond those in this book.

Most important, Schwartau shares with us some of the ways the criminals he opposes have attacked him: massive credit card fraud, messing up and cutting off his phones and electrical power—even making the local 911 services direct a swarm of police and fire engines to his home—an act that could have cost the lives of the

---

1 Thunder's Mouth Press, New York, 2nd edition, 1996

people who needed to get to the hospital or protection from crime. Reading *Information Warfare* gives you a sense of just how callous and dangerous computer criminals can be.

If, despite this, you choose to join us on the front lines of cyberwar—bravo! "The condition upon which God has given liberty to man is eternal vigilance."—John Philpot Curran.

But don't come crying to me if it isn't all fun and jokes.

And if you ever see me whining about, sob, how horrid, just horrid it is to be pursued by computer criminals, tell me to shut up and remember that no one forced me to write this book. No one forced me to stand up to the bad guys.

"Those men and women are fortunate who are born at a time when a great struggle for human freedom is in progress."—Emmeline Pankhurst.

Section 3, Chapter 1
How to Break into Computers— or Keep the Bad Guys Out

One day a young fellow and I were chatting on AOL. He told me that he had typed in the URL "http://victim.computer.com/cgi-bin/phf?Qalias=x%0a/bin/cat%20/etc/passwd" on his AOL browser—and had gotten back an encrypted password file. From that file, running a simple program on Windows 95, he extracted quite a few passwords.

You can go to jail warning: in the US, even possession of those stolen passwords is illegal.

This is known as the "phf" exploit (guess why). For awhile in 1996-7, this exploit made a lot of computer vandals merry—and sysadmins mad as they rushed to fix that flaw.

In this chapter you will learn:
- How to break into a Unix computer that doesn't have a shadowed password file.
- Basics of several classes of attacks.
- Basic concept of how to move from an ordinary user account to superuser.
- Where to find archives of exploit programs that allow you to break into Unix and Windows NT computers.
- Where to find programs that scan prospective victims' ports and identify security weaknesses.
- How to keep the bad guys out.

This chapter will not tell you how to keep from getting caught. That's because there is no way to be absolutely certain you won't get caught. Wise up and only

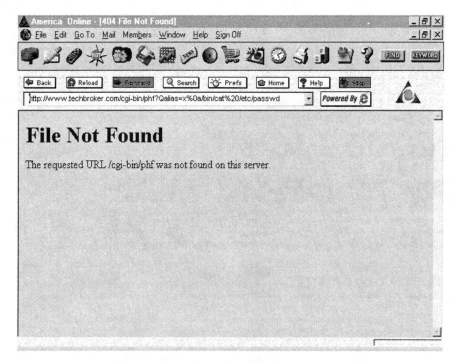

Figure 1: An AOL browser is using the phf exploit to try to get the password file from a Unix box. This is an attack against my own Web site, techbroker.com, which runs on an SGI Irix. I'm really glad this didn't work!

break into computers whose owners have given you permission to break in! That's how real hackers do it. The guys who break into computers without the owners' permission are merely crackers.

Another fellow told me "I actually was able to get . . . the password file of a Unix host . . . it couldn't have been any simpler. I merely used the tftp client to go retrieve /etc/passwd. I thought 'you have got to be kidding me, it can't be that easy.' I ran the file through crackerjack and called the (sysadmin) with his passwords—no, I did not use them."

> **You can go to jail warning:** We presume this fellow was good friends with the sysadmin—or else called him from a payphone and then ran like heck. It is illegal to crack other people's passwords without their permission, even if you are just doing it to volunteer help. If they want your help, they will give you permission first.

> **You can go to jail warning:** Almost everywhere on the planet, breaking into a computer is illegal. The only exceptions are breaking into your own computer, or breaking into a computer whose owner—not just some user on the system, but the owner—has given you permission to break in. It doesn't matter if you are just quietly sneaking around doing no harm. It doesn't matter if you make some stranger's computer better. You're still in trouble if you break in without permission. There, have I warned you enough?

You don't have to be a genius to break into computers. You can prove that to yourself today. Heck, there are so many ways to break into computers, I could write book after book showing ways to break in, and people would still discover new exploits faster than I could write them up.

What's the big deal over cracking, anyhow? If you are the one trying to keep vandals and criminals out of your computer, yes, it's a big deal. But why is it such a big deal for all these guys on AOL whose only interest is in breaking into some stranger's computer?

I've lost track of how many people have pleaded with me to teach them how to break into computers. I keep on getting email like this: "I bow to the supreme one . . . I've tried a lot of tricks. But none of them seem to get me root access." Worse yet, I get email like this from guys who did break in and messed up: "Hi, Carolyn, sorry, but I'm on a rush. As I was trying to break into a UNIX system, I really f***ed up the finger port, and the login process. What can I do to fix that?"

Maybe these d00dz are so hot to break into computers because if you ask just about anyone at a grocery store checkout line what a hacker is, he or she will say "a criminal who breaks into computers."

Yes, there are plenty of news stories which make it seem like the only thing a hacker does is break into computers. But there also is some truth to the public view. An obsession with illegally breaking into computers is now common in the hacker world.

So if you are determined to become yet another of those guys who absolutely must break into computers, read on. In this chapter you can learn how to become a genuine computer cracker and make everyone quake in his or her boots or slippers or whatever footgear they are wearing lately.

"But, but," I can hear some readers saying. "This book is for legal hacking. Sez right here in the introduction."

Welcome to reality, Bub. Hackers fib sometimes.

Wait, I'm kidding, there are legal, honorable ways to break into computers:

1) Break into your own.
2) Get a friend to give you permission to break in. Warning! If your friend tells you it's okay to try to break into the Internet Service Provider he or she uses, no good! Only the owner of a computer, not just ordinary users, can legally give you permission to crack.
3) Sometimes companies hold cracking contests. They may even offer cash prizes.
4) Occasionally hackers will seek to prove their skill at defense by offering to let the public attack their computers. Oblige these guys by testing your skills against them.
5) Offer to work for free at your local ISP. They will probably give you superuser powers as part of the job. If you are in high school, ask your computer lab teacher to get you an internship at an ISP. Then offer to see if there are ways bad guys could break in (penetration testing). This way you also get to find out what it's like being on the receiving end of all these d00dz who try to break in.
6) Better yet, get a paying job with an ISP.
7) Persuade your computer teacher to give you permission to try to break in to your school computers.

8) Persuade companies to pay you to try to break in. You can make lots of money at this, but only if you not only know how to break into computers but also have a good reputation and don't run one of those silly hacker Web pages with evil organ music and naughty words and flaming skulls and stuff.

Then there is the gray area. You will hear many hackers say that it is OK to break into any computer if you do no harm and especially if you help make it better.

This ethical principle first arose back in the late 60s and early 70s. Back then there weren't many hackers, and computers were rare. We generally were meek, harmless people, collegial, possessing ARPAnet accounts so we could do good citizen things like design nuclear weapons. So if someone broke into a computer, it was probably just Joe the plutonium trigger guy down the corridor at Los Alamos and we all knew he was just a wild and crazy but basically decent guy having fun. No sweat.

But it isn't like that any more. The average corporation takes security as seriously as a nuclear weapons lab. Mess with them and you may become really sorry.

For example, at a panel I ran at the Def Con V hackers' conference, a fellow told us he had broken into a computer—and made it better. "Telnet didn't work right. I fixed it. I fixed several things."

His reward? Handcuffs and a trip to the police station. Now he has a criminal record and will have a hard time getting a good paying job administering computers. He'll probably never get one of those $200,000 per year salaries really good—and respectable, and safe—hackers make from all those companies that will pay you to test their security by trying to break into their computers.

> **You can go to jail warning: Don't find out the hard way. If you want to fix someone else's computer, get permission first. If they don't want you to fix it, that's their problem. Fxing a computer without permission has to be the stupidest reason I ever heard of to go to jail.**

So the point of this rant is to convince you to only try out what you learn in this chapter on computers that are legal for you to attack. Or else.

If you want a list of the latest computers that are legal for anyone to try to break into, check out the Happy Hacker official Web site at *http://www.happyhacker.org*. If you don't find us there—who knows, maybe a hacker war will be raging at the time—do a Web search on "Happy Hacker" or email me at hacker@techbroker.com to locate our home in exile.

But how do you know whether any announcement of a computer break-in welcome mat is legitimate? How do you know the Happy Hacker Web site isn't just fooling thousands of hackers into attacking these places? It would be a nasty trick for some bad guy to hack our Web site and tell you it's okay to break into fbi.gov.

Here's one way to check the truth of these invitations. Get the domain name of the target computer, for example "victim.computer.com." Then add "root@" to the domain name, for example root@victim.computer.com. Email to this address should reach the administrator of that computer (if its a Unix computer). Ask "root" if we were fibbing about his offer. If he says we made it up, that victim.computer.com doesn't want you to try to break in, tell him he's just chicken, that if he was a real man he'd be happy to have thousands of hackers running Satan against his box. (Just kidding.)

There are an amazing number of ways to break into computers. Of course most of them only work on a few computers each. So the trick is to either find a computer that your attack will work on, or else find an attack that will work on the computer you want to break into.

> **You can go to jail warning:** The approach of taking an exploit, like the phf attack, and trying it on lots and lots of computers until you get a password file, is stupid, lazy and illegal. To keep out of trouble, take the opposite approach and research and try out all the exploits you can find on a computer that you have permission to attack.

Password Cracking

We began this chapter with two ways to get a password file from a computer. Of course the password file will be encrypted. But if your target computer doesn't run a program to prevent people from picking easy passwords, it is easy to crack many of them.

Let's say you have managed to get an encrypted password file. How do you crack it (extract the passwords)? First, you need to determine what kind of operating system is running on the computer from which you got your password file. You can't extract Unix password using a Windows NT cracker, or vice versa.

An example of one of the many programs that can crack poorly chosen passwords is Unix Password Cracker by Scooter Corp. It is available at *ftp://ftp.info.bishkek.su/UNIX/crack-2a/crack-2a.tgz* or *http://iukr.bishkek.su/crack/index.html*.

A good tutorial on some of the issues of cracking Windows NT passwords may be found at *http://ntbugtraq.com*.

The most highly acclaimed password cracker for Windows NT is L0phtcrack. It is available for free from *http://www.L0pht.com* (that's a ZERO after the 'L', not an 'o'). It comes with source so you can build it on just about any platform. Authors are mudge@l0pht.com and weld@l0pht.com.

But what if a password file is shadowed? A good systems administrator will hide the shadowed password file so well that even users on the machine that holds them can't easily obtain the file.

 Newbie note: A shadowed password file is one in which the encrypted passwords are replaced with "*"s. The actual encrypted passwords are hidden in a different file and matched with the user names during the login sequence.

The simplest way to get a shadowed password file is to steal a backup tape from your victim. This is one reason that most computer break-ins are committed by insiders.

> **You can go to jail warning:** Of course theft of a backup tape is illegal as heck. We're talking burglary here.

But often it is easy to get the entire password file of a computer or even an entire LAN remotely from across the Internet. Why should this be so? Think about what happens when you log in. Even before the computer knows who you are, you must be able to command it to compare your user name and password with its password file.

What the computer does is perform its encryption operation on the password you enter and then compare it with the encrypted entries in the password file. So the entire world must have access somehow to this encrypted password file. You job as the would-be cracker is to figure out the name of this file and then get your target computer to deliver it to you.

A tutorial on how to do this, which was published in the ezine K.R.A.C.K (produced by od^pheak <butler@tir.com>), follows. Comments in brackets have been added by me to the K.R.A.C.K. text.

Strategy For Getting Root With a Shadowed passwd

Step #1: anonymous ftp into the server get passwd [This step will almost never work, but even the simplest attack may be worth a try.]

Step #2: To defeat password shadowing on many (but not all) systems, write a program that uses successive calls to getpwent() to obtain the password file. Example:

```
#include <pwd.h>
main()
{
  struct passwd *p;
  while(p=3Dgetpwent())
    printf("%s:%s:%d:%d:%s:%s:%s\n", p-pw_name,
      p-pw_passwd,
      p-pw_uid,
      p-pw_gid,
      p-pw_gecos,
      p-pw_dir,
      p-pw_shell);
}
```

Or u can look for the unshadowed file . . .

The following is a list of likely places to find the unshadowed backup is available from the *Hack FAQ* written by Voyager.

Unix Version	Path	needed	Token
AIX 3	/etc/security/passwd		!
or	/tcb/auth/files/		
	<first letter of username>/<username>		#
A/UX 3.0s	/tcb/files/auth/?/		*
BSD4.3-Reno	/etc/master.passwd		*
ConvexOS 10	/etc/shadpw		*
ConvexOS 11	/etc/shadow		*
DG/UX	/etc/tcb/aa/user/		*
EP/IX	/etc/shadow		x
HP-UX	/.secure/etc/passwd		*
IRIX 5	/etc/shadow		x
Linux 1.1	/etc/shadow		*
OSF/1	/etc/passwd[.dir|.pag]		*
SCO Unix #.2.x	/tcb/auth/files/<first letter		*
	of username>/<username>		
SunOS4.1+c2	/etc/security/passwd.adjunct =##username		
SunOS 5.0	/etc/shadow		
	<optional NIS+ private secure		
	maps/tables/whatever>		
System V Release 4.0	/etc/shadow		x
System V Release 4.2	/etc/security/* database		
Ultrix 4	/etc/auth[.dir|.pag]		*
UNICOS	/etc/udb		=20

Step #3: crack it

Even if you crack some passwords, you will still need to correlate passwords with user names. One way to do this is to get a list of users by fingering your target computer (see the chapter on fingering for details). The vrfy and expn commands in sendmail are another way to get user names (see the chapter on forging email for details). A good systems administrator will turn off both the finger daemon and the sendmail vrfy and expn commands to make it harder for outsiders to break into their computers.

If finger and the sendmail vrfy and expn commands are disabled, there is yet another way to get user names. Normally the part of a person's email that comes before the "@" will also be a user name.

Social Engineering

Another simple attack is to social engineer your way in. This generally involves lying. Here's an example of how not to social engineer. An honest-to-gosh true example. Only the name of the perpetrator has been changed.

Read Newfpyr's masterful turning of the tables on a hacker . . . Certainly one of the best Absurd IMs we've EVER received! Newfpyr's comments are in brackets throughout.

    Zzzzbu451: Hello from America Online! I'm sorry to inform you that there has been an error in the I/O section of your account database, and this server's password information has been temporarily destroyed. We need you, the AOL user, to hit reply and type in your password. Thank you for your help.

Newfpyr: Hello! This is Server Manager #563. I'm sorry to hear that your server has lost the password info. I mean, this has been happening too much lately. We have developed some solutions to this problem. Have you got the mail sent out to all server managers?

Zzzzbu451: no

NewfPyr: Really? Ouch. There's been some problems with the server mailer lately. Oh, well. Here's a solution to this problem: try connecting your backup database to your main I/O port, then accessing the system restart.

Zzzzbu451: no i still need passwords

NewfPyr: I see. Do you want me to send you the list of all the passwords of all the screen names of your server?

Zzzzbu451: ya i want that

NewfPyr: Let me get the server manager to send it . . .

NewfPyr: He says I need your server manager password. Could you please type it in?

Zzzzbu451: i dont have one

NewfPyr: What do you mean? That's the first thing every manager gets!

Zzzzbu451: it got deleted

NewfPyr: Wow! You must be having a lot of trouble. Let me find out what server you're using . . . [Note: I checked his profile. It said he was from Springfield, Mass.]

NewfPyr: Okay, your number has been tracked to an area in Springfield, Mass.

Zzzzbu451: how did u know?!!!?!?!!?!?!?!?!??!!

NewfPyr: I used Server Tracker 5.0 . Don't you have it?

Zzzzbu451: do you know my address!?!?!?!!?!?

NewfPyr: Of course not.

Zzzzbu451: good

NewfPyr: I only know the number you're calling AOL from, which is from your server, right?

Zzzzbu451: yes

NewfPyr: Good. Okay, now that we have your number, we have your address, and we are sending a repair team over there.

Zzzzbu451: nonononono dont stop them now

NewfPyr: Why? Isn't your server down?

Zzzzbu451: nonono its working now

NewfPyr: They're still coming, just in case.

Zzzzbu451: STOP THEM NOW

NewfPyr: I can't break AOL Policy.

Zzzzbu451: POEPLE ARE COMING TO MY HOUSE?!?!?!?!??

NewfPyr: No! To your server. You know, where you're calling AOL from.

Zzzzbu451: im calling from my house

NewfPyr: But you said you where calling from the server!

Zzzzbu451: i lied im not reely a server guy

NewfPyr: But you said you were!

Zzzzbu451: i lied i trying to get passwords please make them stop

NewfPyr: Okay. The repair team isn't coming anymore.

Zzzzbu451: good

NewfPyr: But a team of FBI agents is.

Zzzzbu451: NONONONO

Zzzzbu451: im sorry

Zzzzbu451: ill never do it again please make them not come

Zzzzbu451: PLEASE IL STOP ASKING FOR PASSWORDS FOREVER PLEASE MAKE THEM STOP!!

NewfPyr: I'm sorry, I can't do that. They should be at your house in 5 minutes.

Zzzzbu451: IM SORRY IL DO ANYTHING PLEASE I DONT WANT THEM TO HURT ME

Zzzzbu451: PLEASE

Zzzzbu451: PLEEEEEEEEEEEEEEAAAAAAAAASSSSSSSSE

NewfPyr: They won't hurt you! You'll probably only spend a year of prison.

Zzzzbu451: no IM ONLY A KID

NewfPyr: You are? That makes it different. You won't go to prison for a year.

Zzzzbu451: i thout so

NewfPyr: You'll go for two years

Zzzzbu451: No! IM SORRY

Zzzzbu451: PLEASE MAKE THEM STOP

Zzzzbu451: PLEASE

[I thought this was enough. He was probably wetting his pants.]

NewfPyr: Since this was a first time offense, I think I can drop charges.

Zzzzbu451: yea

Zzzzbu451: thankyouthankyouthankyou

NewfPyr: The FBI agents have been withdrawn. If you ever do it again, we'll bump you off.

Zzzzbu451: i wont im sorry goodbye

[He promptly signed off.]

One of the RARE RARE occasions that we've actually felt sorry for the hacker. SEVENTY FIVE TOKENS to you, NewfPyr! We're STILL laughing—thanks a lot!

Submitted by: Fran C. M. T. @ aol.com

(Want more of this humor in a jugular vein? Check out *http://www.netforward.com/poboxes/?ablang*)

Trumpet Winsock Trick

Let's look at yet another easy but old break-in technique. If you want to get a password on a computer that you know is being accessed remotely by someone using Windows 3.X, and if it is using an old version of Trumpet Winsock, and if you can get physical access to that Windows box, there is a super easy way to uncover the password.

Open the file named trumpwsk.ini, and look for a line that begins $password=. Cut out the bunch of stuff following that, which is the encrypted password. Guess what, you don't have to crack this password. Just place the encrypted password after ppp-username= . Then run tcpman.exe, go to File PPP Options and there in plain text is sitting the user's password!

Trojan Horse

Maybe you are ready to try the Trojan Horse. This is a type of attack wherein a program that appears to be innocuous has been altered to instead attack a computer.

Newbie note: Does this chapter tempt you to run out to a bunch of hacker Web sites and download—and run—those programs they say can break into computers? Programs with names like "Root Kit"? Think Trojan. That nifty program might be designed to wipe out your hard disk instead . . . or start up your online banking program and transfer money.

For example, in a Unix shell account you might put a Trojan in your home directory named "ls." Then you tell tech support that there is something funny going on in your home directory. If the tech support guy is sufficiently clueless, he may go into you account while he has root permission. He then gives the command "ls" to see what's there. But, according to Damien Sorder, "This will only work depending on his 'PATH' statement for his shell. If he searches '.' before '/bin', then it will work. Else, it won't."

Presuming the sysadmin has been this careless, and if your Trojan is well written, it will call the real ls program to display your file info—while also spawning a root shell for your very own use!

Newbie note: if you can get into a root shell you can do anything—*anything*—to your victim computer. Alas, this means it is surprisingly easy to screw up a Unix system while operating as root. A good systems administrator will give him or herself root privileges only when absolutely necessary to perform a task. Trojans are only one of the many reasons for this caution. Before you invite your friends to hack your box, be prepared for anything, and I mean *anything*, to get messed up even by the most well-meaning of friends.

Sniffe
rs

Another attack is to install a sniffer program on an Internet host and grab passwords. What this means is any time you want to log into a computer from another computer by using telnet, or download email from a POP server, your password is at the mercy of any sniffer program that may be installed on any computer through which your password travels.

However, to set up a sniffer you must be superuser on the computer where it is installed. So this attack is clearly not for the beginner.

But if you are trying to protect a computer against crackers, you will want to learn how to foil sniffers. To get an idea of how many computers "see" your password when you telnet into your remote account, give the command (on a Unix system) of "traceroute my.computer" (it's "tracert" in Windows 95) where you substitute the name of the computer you were planning to log in on for the "my.computer."

Sometimes you may discover that when you telnet from one computer to another even within the city you live in, you may go through a dozen or more computers! For example, when I trace a route from an Albuquerque AOL session to my favorite Linux box in Albuquerque, I get:

```
C:\WINDOWS>tracert fubar.com
Tracing route to fubar.com [208.128.xx.61] over a maximum of 30 hops:
 1  322 ms  328 ms  329 ms  ipt-xx.proxy.aol.com [999.163.205.95]
 2  467 ms  329 ms  329 ms  tot-xx-r5.proxy.aol.com [999.163.205.126]
 3  467 ms  323 ms  328 ms  f4-xx.t60-4.Reston.t3.ans.net [999.25.134.69]
 4  467 ms  329 ms  493 ms  h10-xx.t56-1.Washington.t3.ans.net [14.23.57.25]
 5  469 ms  382 ms  329 ms  140.999.56.70
 6  426 ms  548 ms  437 ms  coxxx.Memphis.mci.net [999.70.125.1]
 7  399 ms  448 ms  461 ms  coxxx-hssi-2.Houston.mci.net [999.70.1.169]
 8  400 ms  466 ms  512 ms  border7-xxx-0.Houston.mci.net [999.70.191.51]
 9  495 ms  493 ms  492 ms  american-comm-xxx.Houston.mci.net [999.70.194.86]
10  522 ms  989 ms  490 ms  webdownlink.foobar.net [28.128.37.98]
11  468 ms  493 ms  491 ms  208.128.999.33
12  551 ms  491 ms  492 ms  fubar.com [208.128.999.61]
```

If someone were to put a sniffer on any computer on that route, they could get my password! Now do you want to go telneting around from one of your accounts to another?

A solution to this problem is to use Secure Shell, which runs on both Unix and Windows operating systems. This is a program you can get for a one month free trial from F- Secure (http://www.datafellows.com). According to the promotional literature, "Ssh (Secure Shell) is a program to log into another computer over a network, to execute commands in a remote machine, and to move files from one machine to another. It provides strong authentication and secure communications over insecure channels."

You must use the RSA authentication rather than "password" for ssh to protect your password. Better yet, use Kerberos.

Advanced Techniques

To be honest, I'm not afraid to give out details on password cracking and social engineering because they only work with poorly defended systems. The majority of computers are much harder to crack. I'm presuming you have too much pride to stoop to using the phf exploit or tricking people to give you their passwords like that AOL guy.

But there are many—way too many—additional ways to break into a computer. Following are some suggestions on how to learn these techniques.

1. Learn as much as you can about the computer you have targeted.

Find out what operating system it runs; whether it is on a local area network; and what programs it is running. Of special importance are the ports that are open and the daemons running on them.

For example, if you can get physical access to the computer, you can always get control of it one way or another. See the chapter on breaking into Windows computers for many examples. What this means, of course, is that if you have something on your computer you absolutely, positively don't want anyone to read, you had better encrypt it with RSA (the algorithm used by Secure Shell and some versions of PGP). Then you should hope no one discovers a fast way to factor numbers (the mathematical Achilles Heel of RSA.)

If you can't get physical access, your next best opportunity arises if you can get on the same LAN. In fact, the vast majority of computer break-ins are done by people who are employees of the company that is running the LAN on which the victim computer is attached, or who have accounts on the ISP they attack. The most common mistake of computer security professionals is to set up a firewall against the outside world while leaving their LAN wide open to insider attack. Use kerberos to protect your LAN traffic!

Important note: if you have even one Windows 95 box on your LAN, you can't even begin to pretend you have a secure network. That is in part because it will run in DOS mode, which allows any user to read, write and delete files. The other problem is that Win95 sends its LAN passwords in a form that is trivially easy to crack.

If the computer you have targeted is on the Internet, your next step would be to determine how it is connected to the Internet. The most important issue here is what TCP/IP ports are open and what daemons run on these ports.

For a complete list of commonly used TCP/IP ports, see RFC 1700. One place you can look this up is *http://ds2.internic.net/rfc/rfc1700.txt*.

2. Become an expert on the operating system of the computer you plan to crack.

Sure, lots of people who are ignorant about operating systems break into computers by using canned programs against pitifully vulnerable boxes. As one teen hacker told me after returning from the Def Con V hackers' convention, "Many of the guys there didn't even know the cat command!"

Evil genius tip: Figure out how to cat port 19 into the terminal your friend is using. He'd better have a sense of humor, though, or you could get punched in the nose. Don't want port 19 catted into your terminal? Turn off messaging.

Anyone can break into some computer somewhere if they have no pride or ethics. We assume you are better than that. If the break-in is so easy you can do it without having a clue what cat can do, you aren't a hacker. You're just a computer vandal.

3. Study the ways other people have broken into a computer with that operating system and software.

Here are the best places to get exploits: Bugtraq archives: *http://www.net-space.org/lsv-archive/bugtraq.html*. To subscribe to Bugtraq, email listserv@netspace.org with message "subscribe bugtraq" NT Bugtraq archives *http://www.ntbugtraq.com* To subscribe to NT Bugtraq, send a message to list-serv@ntadvice.com with "subscribe ntbugtraq firstname lastname."

You will discover, however, that the vast majority of these exploits work to gain control over a computer only if you are already inside with an ordinary user account.

4. Use a port scanner

A cheap and easy partial shortcut to the arduous process of exploring the computer you have targeted is to run a program that scans its ports, finds out what daemons are running on each port, and then may give you information on break-in techniques known to exist for those daemons.

Satan is a good one, and absolutely free. You can download it from *ftp://ftp.fc.net/pub/defcon/SATAN/* or a bazillion other hacker ftp sites.

Another great port scanner is Internet Security Scanner. It is offered by Internet Security Systems of Norcross, Georgia USA, 1-800-776-2362. This tool costs lots of money, but is the security scanner of choice of the people who really, seriously want to keep hackers out by finding out if they can break in. You can reach ISS at *http://www.iss.net/*.

Internet Security Systems also offers some freebie programs. The "Localhost" Internet Scanner SAFEsuite is set to only run a security scan on the Unix computer on which it is installed (hack your own box!) You can get it from *http://www.blanket.com/iss.html*. You may still be able to get a free beta copy of their scanner for Win NT at *http://www.iss.net*.

In theory, ISS programs are set so you can only use them to probe computer networks that you own. However, a few months ago I got a credible report that an Internet backbone company accidentally shut down an ISP in El Paso with an ISS automated syn flood attack that it had meant to only test on its own computers.

If you want to get a port scanner from a quiet little place, try out *http://204.188.52.99*. This offers the Asmodeus Network Security Scanner for Windows NT 4.0.

Most port scanners only run under Unix or Windows NT. If you want a darn good port scanner that runs under Windows 95, you can get "What's Up" from *http://www.ipswitch.com*.

You can get punched in the nose warning: In most places it is legal to scan the ports of other people's computers. Nevertheless, if you run Satan or any other port scanner against computers that you don't have permission to break into, you may get kicked off of your ISP.

For example, recently an Irish hacker was running "security audits" of the Emerald Island's ISPs. He was probably doing this in all sincerity. He emailed each of his targets a list of the vulnerabilities he found. But when this freelance security auditor probed the ISP owned by one of my friends, my friend got that hacker kicked off his ISP.

"But why give him a hard time for just doing security scans? He may have woken up an administrator or two," I asked my friend.

"For the same reason they scramble an F-16 for a bogie," he replied.

The way I handle the problem of getting people mad when I port scan is to do it by hand using a telnet program. Several chapters in this book show examples of port scanning by hand. This has the advantage that most systems administrators assume you are merely curious.

You may laugh yourself silly warning: If you port scan by hand against certain computers you may run into some prank daemons installed on weird high port numbers.

However, some computers have a daemon set up so that every time you scan even one port, it automatically sends an email to the systems administrator of your ISP complaining that you tried to break in—and another email to you telling you to turn yourself in!

 Evil Genius Tip: The solution to this is to use IP spoofing to hide who you are when you port scan.

5. Find exploit programs

Now that you know what vulnerable programs are running on your target computer, next you need to decide what program you use to break in.

But aren't hackers brilliant geniuses that discover new ways to break into computers? Yes, some are. But the average hacker relies on programs other hackers have written to do their deeds. That's why, in the book *Takedown*, some hacker (maybe Kevin Mitnick, maybe not) broke into Tsutomu Shimomura's computer to steal a program to turn an Oki cell phone into a scanner that could eavesdrop on other people's cell phone calls.

This is where those zillions of hacker web pages come into play. Do a web search for "hacker" and "haxor" and "h4ck3r" etc. You can spend months downloading all those programs with promising names like "IP spoofer."

Unfortunately, you may be in for an ugly surprise or two. This may come as a total shock to you, but some of the people who write programs that are used to break into computers are not exactly Eagle Scouts. Yes, once again I am harping on the topic of Trojans.

For example, the other day a fellow wrote to me "I discovered a person has been looting my www dir, where I upload stuff for friends so I am gonna leave a nice little surprise for him in a very cool looking program (if you know what I mean)."

One way I keep people who try to intercept my email on their toes is to send out Trojans as attached files. Execute my philez at your own risk, snooper d00dz!

6. Get that exploit to run

Let's say you download a program that promises to exploit that security hole you just found with a Satan scan. Let's say you aren't going to destroy all your files from some Trojan hidden in that program. Your next task may be to get this exploit program to compile and run.

Most computer break-in programs run on Unix. Alas, there are many different flavors of Unix. For each flavor of Unix you can mix or match several different shells. (If none of this makes sense to you, see the chapter on how to get a good shell account.) The problem is that a program written to run in, for example, the csh shell on Solaris Unix may not run from the bash shell on Slackware Linux or the tcsh shell on Irix, etc. Even if you have two computers with the same flavor of Unix running the same shell, if they are configured differently, your compiled exploit may not run. Or a library routine may be missing that you will have to hunt down.

It is also possible that the guy who wrote that exploit you plan to use may have a conscience. He or she may have figured that most people would want to use it maliciously. So the author of that code made a few little teeny weeny changes, for example commenting out some lines. So Mr./Ms. Tender Conscience can feel that only people who know how to program will be able to use that exploit software. And as we all know, computer programmers would never, ever do something mean and horrible to someone else's computer.

So this brings us to the next thing you should know in order to break into computers.

7. Programmers break in better

Learn how to program! Even if you use other peoples' exploit programs, you may need to tweak a thing or two to get them to run. The two most common languages for exploit programs are probably C and Perl. Then you can pick up programs that come with source code rather than being already compiled, so that if they don't run you have a chance of fixing them.

 Newbie note: If you can't get that program you just downloaded to run, it may be that it is designed to run on the Unix operating system, but you are running Windows. A good tipoff that this may be your problem is a file name that ends with ".gz".

 Newbie note: A compiled program is ready to run. Source code is the program before it has been compiled. You can't read or alter the commands in a compiled program. But you can read and change the commands in source code. Okay, okay, all you nitpickers, some programming languages can be run without being compiled, for example Basic and perl. But most exploits need compiled versions to actually run.

So, now that we have gotten to the end of this section, are you planning to be a good guy or a bad guy with this information?

Someone who thinks it is phun to break into poorly defended computers run by dunces is eventually going to get into really stupid kinds of trouble. However, if you manage to break into a computer that is well managed, and that you have permission to test, you are on your way to a high paying career in computer security.

You can go to jail warning: If you get busted for breaking into a computer, you are in trouble big time. Even if you say you did no harm. Even if you say you made the computer better while you were prowling around in it. And your chances of becoming a computer security professional drop almost to zero. And—do you have any idea of how expensive lawyers are?

I haven't even hinted in this chapter at how to keep from getting caught. It is very hard to cover your tracks when breaking into a computer. Worse yet, if the guys who want to throw you in jail want you badly enough, they can bring into play technologies that will defeat even the most brilliant hacker. Did you know that erased Unix files actually can be recovered—even if they have been overwritten many times?

Besides, those crackers who go searching for vulnerable computers and breaking into them are like Lounge Lizard Larry going into a bar and picking up the drunkest, most obnoxious gal (or guy) in the place. Uncool. Gross.

Super duper hacker Rogue Agent argues "I think your silly campaign to make hackers stop breaking the law by calling it uncool has as much chance of success as Nancy Reagan's 'Just say no to drugs' idea."

Well, pooh on Rogue Agent. Sure, he's right that some computer criminals don't give a darn whether people are laughing at them. There also are criminals on Wall Street and running dictatorships who don't care who they hurt or whether people laugh at them, all they want is power or money or the thrill of war.

But even Napoleon, the French ruler whose wars slaughtered millions, admitted "The pen is mightier than the sword." So I'm going to continue to write stuff that makes fun of computer criminals.

The reason I just showed you the basics of how to break into computers is that I believe that you are better than some AOL code kiddie using a Web browser to filch passwords. You want more out of life than to be a computer vandal. You want to learn about cracking so you can protect computers from the Lounge Lizard Larrys— and the serious computer criminals and terrorists of the computer scene. You'd rather become a high paid computer security consultant than the "girlfriend" cell mate of a guy named Spike.

How to Keep the Bad Guys Out

Alas, there will always be those who want to break into computers. Even if we are all laughing at them.

Some are merely polite cybertourists. Back in the good old days, most crackers were careful not to do any harm. But today many crackers intend vandalism, theft and violation of people's freedoms. So you have to take any intrusion seriously.

If you run a proprietary network of some sort, you are free to employ security techniques which are well beyond the scope of this chapter. But if you are running an ISP, you have a serious problem. Because you must be easily reached by the general public, you can't use one-time passwords, firewalls that reject packets from just about anywhere, and more. All your attacker has to do is buy an account, telnet in from a spoofed IP address or test shell account or another hacked account, and from there it is easy to exploit some buffer overflow or another to get root.

The saddest defense of all is to quit offering shell accounts. But let's face it, if you want security for your ISP, close those shell accounts.

Some ISPs offer bastardized shell accounts. They disable many commands and alias lots of DOS commands to their Unix counterparts. They might only offer the bash shell so that the user would have to customize most cracker exploits. But this is only effective against newbie code kiddies.

A more sophisticated approach is to patrol userspace for suspicious executables, looking for hidden files buried deep in directory space or given names of innocuous programs such as Pine. Wise sysadmins will also monitor ongoing jobs for suspicious processes. They will work as root only when it is absolutely necessary. They will enable logging and pipe logs elsewhere to guard against deletion or editing by intruders.

Judging from my friendly (honest!) explorations, there are also a number of really easy precautions. Yet few of these are used today by ISPs.

1) **Ports.** Shut down all ports except those that are absolutely essential. That especially means finger! Why give away all that info to outsiders?

2) **Exploits.** Subscribe to the Bugtraq (for Unix) and NT Bugtraq (Windows NT) mailing lists and pore through their archives. (See above for contact info.) You will get security alerts days, weeks, or months ahead of CERT announcements. You'll get lots more details, too. These lists tell you exactly how each exploit works and what the fix is. This way you can test your system to make sure you correctly installed the patches.

3) **Telnet.** Shut down port 23. Make your customers login to their shell accounts through 22 using the Secure Shell RSA encrypted tunnel using RSA login. The Datafellows Unix, Windows and Mac clients are as easy to use as any other telnet client I have tried, and so efficient that I don't notice the lag caused by processing RSA. You can get both server and client programs at http://Datafellows.com. Maybe they will give you a good deal on a bulk buy for your customers? Think of how much you'll save on tech support by no longer having to deal with hackers who break in using sniffed passwords.

4) **POP accounts.** Over a PPP connection, only let your users download email via APOP protocol. This will keep POP account passwords from being sniffed. Eudora Pro offers APOP.

5) **Passwords.** Insist on separate passwords for POP, shell and PPP accounts. Run one of those programs that won't allow a user to choose an easy-to-crack password. Give your users easy instructions on how to change passwords, and set expiration times.

6) **Mail forwarding.** Why should total strangers who may well be spammers burden your mail server by forging junk? You can set sendmail, smail and qmail to refuse outside users. Be especially sure to disable that pesky sendmail "%" test feature, the one that lets you email joe%myhost.com@otherhost.com so the mail goes first to otherhost.com and then forwards it to joe@myhost.com. This is more than just good Internet hygiene. Leaving your mail server free to be raped may win you a visit by a major spammer someday, followed by attacks by vigilantes who punish ISPs that pipe spam.

These tips are only the beginnings of how to deal with crackers. But they ought to make fast work of blockading anyone whose knowledge of hacking comes mostly from this book.

Happy Hacking! But no Cyber-Lounge Lizard Larrys, please!

Section 3, Chapter 2
How to Fight Spam

Want to join the war against spam?

Just what is spam, anyhow? The Hormel company sells a lunch meat called "Spam." But when we talk about Internet spam, we are thinking of the Monty Python song, "Spam spam spam spam, spam spam spam spam, lovely spam, wonderful spam . . ."

Do you hate it when your favorite Usenet news groups get hit with gazillions of 900 number sex ads and Make Money Fast pyramid schemes, all with the appeal of mystery lunch meat? If so, welcome to the club! I hate spam, too.

In this chapter you will learn:
- how spammers do the deed
- why spam is a serious menace to the Internet
- why outlawing spam won't solve the problem
- how to identify the culprits
- the ordinary citizen way to fight spam
- why fighting spam the hacker way may be dangerous to you
- the hacker way to fight spam—legally
- what sysadmins can do to fight spam
- how ISP owners can fight spam
- the hacker way to fight spam—illegally

It was in April of 1994 that the Arizona law firm of Canter & Siegel invented spam. They used an automated script to post to almost all Usenet newsgroups their advertisements promising to help immigrants get the "green cards" needed to hold US jobs. The law firm even posted to some moderated groups by forging the authorization codes in the headers. Classic hacker technique!

So many Usenet readers were incensed at this violation of netiquette that their protest email crashed the mail server of the PSInet, which the law firm had used to post its spam.

PSInet made Canter and Siegel sign an agreement to never spam again. The firm broke the agreement; PSI closed its accounts. Yet soon Canter and Siegel turned up elsewhere, spamming again. They had set the pattern for spam. Hack, hit, run, hide, get mail bombed, hack and spam again. The firm's owners, Martha Siegel and Laurence Canter, even wrote a book on how to make money spamming the Internet.

Soon Usenet was flooded by junk! Spam email also flooded into our mailboxes. Software bots patrolled Usenet stealing addresses to feed into email forgery programs. "Amazing Free Offer!!!!" "Make Money Fast!!!!"

Jeff Slayton of Albuquerque, NM, was the first Spam King, the first to become widely known for selling the software that would enable anybody with a Windows computer to do industrial grade, hacker quality spamming. He had begun by doing the spamming himself. But after heavy harassment by vigilantes, in the fall of 1995 he sent out a surrender message which got us to leave him alone.

But Slayton was, in his own words, "a programmer with attitude." He had merely gone underground to work on his Lightningbolt program. In 1996 he resurfaced sending out mass emailings advertising Lightningbolt for its power to troll "both accessible systems and newsgroups for addresses. The newsgroup scanner uses a control file for groups to troll and a second control file for which key words to look for in the newsgroups . . . in the background . . . while you are logged off, 24 hours a day, 7 days a week until you stop it."

Slayton was only one of the "programmers with attitude" who sprang up to serve the teeming masses yearning to make money fast. The reason we haven't gotten totally buried in this email is that we fight it.

Do you want to get in on our shadow war against spammers? Using the knowledge you have gained from the chapters on how to decipher headers, forge email and map the Internet, you now have the knowledge it takes to fight—using legal, honorable tactics—alongside the best.

Warning: some people don't like it when we fight spammers. They say it's a matter of freedom of speech, that if we want freedom of speech for ourselves, we should uphold it for spammers, too. Sanford Wallace, head of giant spam factory Cyber Promotions, Inc., is always crying to the press that hackers pick on him, attacking his freedom of speech.

But either we fight spammers without mercy (yet within the law), or they will destroy the Internet.

Some people will laugh at this. Sure, spammers are obnoxious. But destroy the Internet?

How Spammers Do the Deed

To see why spammers are such bad news, we need to understand their tactics.

You can get punched in the nose warning: If people reading this book use the information below to write a spam program and sell it to the teeming masses yearning to make money fast, I will personally punch them out.

Lightningbolt is an example of how spammers get your email address. The other half of the spam equation is to run a program to send out spam. A typical program will telnet to port 25 on a computer where the spammer doesn't have an account. This program (heck, a few lines of perl code will do it) puts in one "rcpt to:" after another, each followed by one each from a list of thousands of email addresses. Then it gives just one data command, which inserts phony headers followed by the spam message itself, and logs off. It may do some extra bells and whistles like specifying that it be routed through a certain path through the Internet.

Then that computer on which the spammer just forged email has to spend a long time putting that data into each email it sends out from that long list of rcpt to: commands. Meanwhile, the spammer program can move on to another victim computer and forge yet another message to hundreds or thousands of people.

So the spammer has gotten large numbers of computers to work hard at sending and forwarding spam to its final destination. As you know from the chapter on how to map the Internet, an email message may have to be relayed through two dozen or more computers to reach its destination. Every one of these intermediary computers must receive, temporarily store, and then forward that message.

Thus one relatively short forging session at one computer can balloon into thousands of busy computers.

By contrast, the culprit's computer and its connection to the Internet hardly did any work at all, and cost almost nothing. So anyone with a spam program and Internet access can pump out hundreds of thousands or even millions of emails every week, almost for free. Other people end up paying most of the cost of the mailing.

Why Is Spam a Serious Menace to the Internet?

Because spam is cheap and easy to send, if we were to quit fighting it, you would open your email account to find ten thousand messages from hungry spammers. Maybe a million. Usenet, too, would be buried under spam.

Why can't we just ignore all this spam? Filter it out?

Some people say that with Usenet all you need is a reader with a killfile. For email, if your ISP has a Unix mail server, you can use the free procmail program to sort out and throw away junk. On AOL you can easily set up email filters.

But if you reject spam at your email box, does that mean it just disappears? No!

In the case of Usenet, spam fills up hard disks on news servers and makes it take a long time for your newsreader to sort and kill the 3,017 messages in alt.hack saying "Ivan Blow is a dirty stukach pervert." (Yes, some people send out spam not for money but because they are pure cussed.)

Even the killfile won't save you from facing a vast sea of spam, either. That's because the culprit probably forged those 3,017 posts. He'll forge the next 4,876 spams under a different email address. And the next ten thousand under yet a new one. You can't often killfile him in advance of his next spam because his apparent email address will be different every time.

In the case of email spam, you have almost the same problem as with Usenet. You usually are fighting forged messages. That stuff comes pouring into the computer on which you have an email account, filling up disk space and using up CPU time as the computer sorts it, rejects junk, and perhaps bounces it back hoping against hope to return it to the culprit. So when you reject spam email instead of deleting it, your ISP still is being burdened by the bad guys.

That flood of Usenet and email spam also chokes the communications links of the Internet. Too much spam could, for example, force your ISP to replace its T1 communications link with a T3.

Guess who ends up paying for all this extra disk space, computing power and communications bandwidth that spammers soak up? Us users! The spammer sends at almost no cost and we, in one way or another, must pay to receive.

We could stamp out almost all spam if the administrators of every single computer hooked up to the Internet were to disable mail forwarding or use of the mail servers by people who don't have accounts on their computers. This makes it almost impossible to forge email. But my most recent sample of commercial ISPs shows that many of them still allow any idiot to forge email.

Why Not Make Spamming a Crime?

There ought to be a law, right? In fact, as of this writing, laws are being considered to ban spam. But how well do you think these laws will work? This is the Internet. Ban spam in the US, in Europe, in Asia, South America, Australia, Africa, and it will keep on moving, running, hiding. As long as there is any corner in the world a spammer can hide, spam we will get. Do you think we could extradite Sanford Wallace, who runs the biggest spam company in the world, from Somalia?

A world government powerful enough to stamp out spam everywhere is not in the works. Maybe that is a Good Thing.

If we are going to put spammers out of action, the first step is to figure out who they are. As we learned in the chapter on how to decipher headers, this is a group effort. We have to first figure out on what computer the spammer did his or her deed, then alert its sysadmin to check the logs of who was making spam that time. We give examples below.

How to Mess Up Spammers the Ordinary Citizen Way

Even if you are already a brilliant hacker, there are lots of spam fighting tools available that anyone can and perhaps ought to use, even if they don't know how to identify the culprits.

The simplest defense is to keep from getting on spam lists in the first place. I do this by having my own domain name. Why does this work? Mass mail programs work best by sending spam to lots of user names sorted by the ISP or online service they use. So a typical spammer mailing might first send 5 million mails to all its America Online addresses, half a million to Compuserve, and so on. When they get down to email addresses which only have one user per domain, the time it takes to mail them out soars because the computer on which spam is being forged has to hunt up the routing information for each domain name.

Your second defense is to be careful when posting to Usenet. As we saw with Thunderbolt, Usenet is constantly being combed by programs that work around the clock taking email addresses from newsgroup posts.

Your defense is to set your newsgroup reader so that it falsifies your email address in the header. For example, you could post as joe_blow@DIE_SPAMMER.com. Then in your signature you could tell people your real email address. Of course this means you need an email/newsreader program that allows you to put in a return address other than your real one.

The most important spam defense is to alert the support staff on your ISP by forwarding spam to them. If you have a good ISP, its sysadmins will be eager to block spam and glad for polite reports from you.

But perhaps your ISP isn't real helpful. For example, America Online, which I use and love (along with several other ISPs) is overwhelmed with spam. Or perhaps you want to do more than just block spam coming into your ISP. Perhaps you want to stamp out spam at its source.

Your next step is to read two Usenet news groups, news.admin.net-abuse.usenet and news.admin.net-abuse.email. On these groups you can meet and make friends with some of the most powerful spam fighters in the world. You will get the latest news on the tides of this shadow war, and find out where your help may be most needed. Oftentimes just reporting spam to these news groups will be enough to send several brilliant computer scientists (aka hackers) after the culprit.

The Coalition Against Unsolicited Commercial Email (*http://www.cauce.org*) is another resource you can use. Their approach is to make spamming against the law in the US. So if lobbying Congress is your thing, this is a good group to join. For a review of the legal issues of spam, see *http://server.Berkeley.EDU/BTLJ/articles/11-2/carroll.html.*

A place to get spam tracking tools is *http://kryten.eng.monash.edu.au/gspam.html.*

Another possibility is *http://spam.abuse.net/*. It offers you automated spam reporting software. It tells you over and over again to be ever so ever so nice to the people you suspect may be the culprits. I suspect this may be a spammer front designed to trick the users into wasting their protests because it encourages the reader to be, yes, ineffectual. I do not recommend this site.

Many times spam is used to commit fraud. If you find fraudulent spam which has been sent from the US, print the message out, add a cover letter saying why you believe it is fraudulent, and mail it to:

Federal Trade Commission
6th Street and Pennsylvania Ave NW
Washington, DC 20580

The FTC is reputed to pay more attention to snail mail messages than material received over the Internet. But if you are determined to save the postage, you may also report fraudulent spam to the FCC through: *http://www.junkemail.org/scam-spam/.*

If you get spam that is clearly a crime, for example a solicitation to sell kiddie porn, in the US the Federal Bureau of Investigation handles this. To get the location and phone number of your nearest FBI field office, see *http://www.fbi.gov/fo/fo.htm.* The FBI is short on computer crime experts. If you have enough hacker skills to track this kind of criminal spam to its source, you can help bust a child abuser and rescue their little victims.

For help from the best uberhackers on the planet at tracking down kiddie porn criminals, contact Ethical Hackers Against Pedophilia, ehap@mail.hackers.com, http://www.hackers.com/ehap. They have a great record of refusing to be tricked by malicious people who try to trick hackers into thinking innocent people are kiddie porn peddlers.

Or, you can take spammers to court. You may even be able to do this for free. In the US, go to *http://www.attorneygeneral.gov/Consumer/cmplnt.html* to get the form you need fill out to haul spammers into court. Want to know with whom you should file your spam complaint? *http://www.eskimo.com/~brucem/tug.htm* has a list of US Attorney Generals.

Oftentimes spam email gives you a postal mail address (snail mail, not email). You can have *lots* of fun with this. Greg Bulmash, my first spam-fighter ally, offers the following letter as an example of how to zing a culprit.

```
Dear Advertiser,

The address to which you sent your unsolicited advertisement for
"Search Engine Secrets" has no link from my listing on Yahoo. In
fact, there has been no link to it on my web site for well over three
months and when it did exist, many other addresses were much more
prominent.

What does this mean? It means you gathered it from elsewhere and it
had nothing to do with my Yahoo listing.

Doesn't all this lying and deception keep you awake at night,
wondering about how you are jeopardizing your immortal soul? Have
you become so lustful for cash that you have lost all honor, all
ethics, all morality, and given yourself over to Satan?

I have no need to tell you to "go to Hell" for spamming me. You are
already paving yourself a gilded path to those nether-regions. Get
thee to a house of God, renounce your deceptive ways, and repent for
your sins. If the lust for money is the root of all evil, your garden
is flourishing. Save yourself now, before you are lost.
```

Let's analyze this letter to see how it works. Notice how Bulmash first casually reveals that he did a little hacker research. This makes spammers squirm, because they will worry about what else Bulmash may know but not be telling.

Bulmash also is polite. A person who emails obscenities to a spammer sounds like an adolescent, someone who can easily be ignored. Think about it. Who would be more frightening to you? A bunch of grown men wearing business suits and slightly twisted smiles show up on your door to tell you they know a great deal about you and ask you politely to mend your ways? Or little kids throwing tomatoes at you? Bulmash's email, which combines the hint of hacker talent with politeness, is the equivalent of polite, yet faintly sneering, men in suits.

To see more of the incomparable Bulmash, check out *http://bulmash.com/*. This Web site is so cool, it has been featured in both *People* and *Us* magazines. Greg's forte is his "Washed-Update," in which he uses his detective powers for humorous write-ups on what has happened to celebrities that have fallen into obscurity. Bulmash has also contributed to the *Happy Hacker Digest*. Way to go, Greg!

Fight Spam at your own Risk

It's really tempting, isn't it, to use our hacking knowledge to blow spammers' computers to kingdom come. But that's like using an atomic bomb to kill an ant. Besides, oftentimes hackers end up attacking the wrong computers. Why risk going to jail, especially for accidentally hitting an innocent victim, when there are legal ways to keep the vermin of the Internet on the run?

But before you decide to stand out from the crowd in your spam warfare, first consider whether you are ready to face the possible consequences. Even if your hacking attacks are legal, you may get sued—as America OnLine and others have learned.

For example, one fellow posted a list of spammer sites on the Internet so systems administrators could block them at their routers. He had to take down his Web page when spammers hit him with a barrage of lawsuits. Other spammers will fight back by email bombing you.

According to Les Addison, chief engineer for the Apex Global Internet Services backbone provider, some spammers have sent out as many as 20 million spam messages with a forged return address that belonged to their opponent. This spam has even included the home address and phone number of the victim.

 Newbie note: An Internet backbone provider doesn't normally give out accounts to individuals, but rather connects entire Internet service providers (ISPs) and online services to the Internet. A backbone provider has super high speed links and often uses satellites to carry Internet traffic.

If a spammer attacks you like this, you can expect that the bounced bad addresses alone will crash the mail server of your online service provider or ISP. You also will get death threats and perhaps worse from clueless people who think they are fighting spam.

Remember. Spammers are often hackers of the most brutal and greedy sort. Get them mad and there is no telling what they will do. They will also try to trick you into attacking other spam fighters. You have to be crafty and courageous to get deep into this battle.

But, heck, I'm an old lady and I don't give a darn if they get mad at me. If you feel the same way, go for it!

How to Fight Spam the Hacker Way—Legally

If you do choose to face the wrath of the spam empire, your next step will be to figure out the identity of your target. Often you won't be able to learn this while working alone. But you can work with people you've met in the net abuse news groups and with the systems administrators of computers on which spam has been forged—or even just forwarded—to cut the bad guys off from the Internet!

In fighting spam, the most important thing to remember is that the Internet is voluntary. No one has a right to force an online service, ISP or Internet backbone provider to connect him or her to the Internet. Even Cyberpromo's Sanford Wallace has only been able to get the courts to briefly force anyone to let his company use the Internet. Our objective as hackers is to find out where these guys keep on sneaking back on, and help block them from the Internet.

First, let us consider how to read headers of Usenet posts. (For email headers, see the chapter on how to read headers.) The header is something that shows the route that email or Usenet posts take to get into your computer. The header gives the names of Internet host computers that have been used in the creation and transmission of a message.

When something has been forged, however, the computer names may be fake. Or a skilled forger may use the names of real hosts that weren't actually used to transmit the newsgroup post. But there are ways for you to tell whether a host listed in the header is real, often by emailing each site listed in the header.

The reason you will contact the sysadmin is because that person can review log files to see what kind of mischief the spammer committed. If the log files show that a user at that site committed the spam, bam, his account is history. If the spammer forged it from the outside, the sysadmin will hopefully set up the mail port to reject forging and forwarding of email.

Here is an example of forged Usenet spam. I got it from a really good place to spot spam, alt.personals. It is not nearly as well policed by anti-spam vigilantes as, say, rec.aviation.military. (People spam fighter pilots at their own risk! I should know because I'm married to one of them.)

So here is an example of spam, as shown with the Unix-based Usenet reader, tin.

```
Thu, 22 Aug 1996 23:01:56    alt.personals        Thread 134 of   450
Lines 110   >>FREE INSTANT COMPATIBILITY CHECK FOR SEL  No responses
ppgc@fozemail.com.au        glennys e clarke at Fozemail Pty Ltd
- Australia
CLICK HERE FOR YOUR FREE INSTANT COMPATIBILITY CHECK!
http://www.foobie-partners.com.au
WHY SELECTIVE SINGLES CHOOSE US
At Foobie Partners (Newcastle) International we are private and
confidential.  We introduce ladies and gentlemen for friendship and
marriage.  With over 15 years experience, Foobie Partners is one of
the Internet's largest, most successful relationship consultants.
```

Our first approach should be to send a copy back to the spammer's email address. Heck, you never know, it may not be forged.

On a popular group like alt.personals, if only one in a hundred readers throws spam back into the poster's face, that's an avalanche of mail. Even if the owners of the ISP where the spammer has an account thinks it is a good idea to make money by hosting spammers, this avalanche may give them second thoughts. If they get enough protest mail, they probably will give spammers the boot.

But to prevent this, today most spammers use fake email addresses.

To find out whether the email address is phony, I email a copy of the Foobie Partners spam to the return address. But as usual it bounces with a bad address message.

Next I go to the advertised Web page. It has an email address for this outfit, perfect.partners@hunterfu.net.au.

We could stop right here and spend an hour or two on a Unix box with a T3 connection emailing stuff with 5 MB attachments to perfect.partners@hunterfu.net.au. This would definitely crash the culprit's mail server. This is what a computer criminal would do, with no concern for whether the ISP Hunterfu.net.au even is aware that it is hosting a spammer.

> **You can go to jail warning: Sending a lot of large email attachments to one address, or thousands of short email messages, is mailbombing. This is a way to get into big trouble. According to computer security expert Ira Winkler (author of the book *Corporate Espionage*), "It is illegal to mail bomb a spam. If it can be shown that you maliciously caused a financial loss, which would include causing hours of work to recover from a spamming, you are criminally liable. If a system is not configured properly, and has the mail directory on the system drive, you can take out the whole system. That makes it even more criminal."**

Plus which, most mail bombers don't know how to find a computer with a mail server open that isn't running ident— and I'm not telling! Forge email on a server running ident and you can easily get caught.

Wanting to be a good guy, I simply emailed one copy of that spam back to Foobie Partners. I also copied this letter to root@hunterfu.net.au, webmaster@hunterfu.net.au, postmaster@hunterfu.net.au and abuse@hunterfu.net.au.

This might seem like a wimpy retaliation. (We will shortly learn how to do much more.) But I knew that even just sending one email message to Foobie Partners and four to sysadmins at their ISP could become part of a tidal wave of protest that gets them kicked off. Heck, most ISPs will kick a spammer off after the first complaint.

This kind of protest works. Heck, did anyone ever see another Foobie Partners spam?

Dale Amon, owner and technical director of The Genesis Access Project, which is the largest and oldest ISP in Northern Ireland, tells us "One doesn't have to call for a 'mail bomb.' It just happens. Whenever I see spam, I automatically send one copy of their message back to them. I figure that thousands of others are doing the same. If they (the spammers) hide their return address, I find it and post it (to news.admin.net-abuse.usenet or news.admin.net-abuse.email) . . . I have no compunctions and no guilt over it."

What if your initial protest fails? What if you need to protest more strongly, yet still legally? For this we need to find not just who hosts their website but also the computer from where Foobie Partners spammed Usenet. Reading news group headers and testing is similar to how we figure out email headers.

Since my newsreader isn't set up to show full headers, I use the newsreader option to email out copies of this post to send one to my shell account. It arrives a few moments later. I open it in the email program Pine and view the full header:

```
Path:
sloth.southwestfooport.com!news.foohorse.com!news.foostateu.ed
u!vixen.cso.uiuc.edu!news.stealth.net!nntp04.primenet.com!nntp
.primenet.com!gatech!nntp0.foospring.com!news.foospring.com!uu
net!in2.uu.net!Fozemail!Fozemail-In!news
From: glennys e clarke gc@fozemail.com.au
NNTP-Posting-Host: 203.15.166.999
Mime-Version: 1.0
Content-Type: text/plain
Content-Transfer-Encoding: 7bit
X-Mailer: Mozilla 1.22 (Windows; I; 16bit)
```

The first item in this header is definitely genuine: sloth.southwestfooport.com. It's the computer my ISP uses to host news groups. It was the last link in the chain of computers that unwittingly passed this Usenet spam around the world.

Newbie Note: Internet host computers all have names which double as their Net addresses. "Sloth" is the name of one of the computers owned by the company which has the "domain name" southwestfooport.com. So "sloth" is kind of like the news server computer's first name, and "southwestfooport.com" the second name. "Sloth" is also kind of like the street address, and "southwestfooport.com" kind of like the city, state and zip code. "Southwestfooport.com" is the domain name owned by Southwest Fooport. All host computers also have numerical versions of their names, e.g. 203.15.166.999. Those "!'s" (pronounced "bangs") separate the names of the hosts in the path that this Usenet post traveled to get to your computer. A bang path should mean this news post was transmitted using UUCP protocol.

Let's next do the obvious. The header says this post was composed on the host 203.15.166.999. So we telnet to its nntp (news) server, which is port 119:

```
telnet 203.15.166.999 119
```

We get back:

```
Trying 203.15.166.999 ...
telnet: connect: Connection refused
```

This looks a lot like a phony item in the header. If this really was a computer that handles news groups, it should have a nntp port that accepts visitors. It might only accept a visitor for the split second it takes to see that I am not authorized to use it. But in this case it refuses any connection whatever.

There is another explanation: there may be a firewall on this computer that filters out packets from anyone but authorized users. But this is not likely in an ISP that would be serving a spammer dating service. This kind of firewall is more commonly used to connect an internal company computer network with the Internet.

Next I try to email postmaster@203.15.166.999 with a copy of the spam. But I get back:

```
Date: Wed, 28 Aug 1996 21:58:13 -0600
From: Mail Delivery Subsystem AILER-DAEMON@techbroker.com
To: cmeinel@techbroker.com
Subject: Returned mail: Host unknown (Name server:
203.15.166.999: host not found)

The original message was received at Wed, 28 Aug 1996 21:58:06 -0600
from cmeinel@localhost
   ——-The following addresses had delivery problems——-
postmaster@203.15.166.999   (unrecoverable error)
   ——-Transcript of session follows——-
501 postmaster@203.15.166.999...   550 Host unknown (Name
server: 203.15.166.999: host not found)
        (snip)
```

Because this undeliverable mail message says the host is unknown, now we know for sure this nntp item in the header was forged.

Next we check the second item in the header. Because it starts with the word "news," I figure it must be a computer that hosts news groups, too. So I check out its nntp port:

```
telnet news.foohorse.com nntp
Trying 999.145.167.4 ...
Connected to boxcar.foohorse.com.
Escape character is '^]'.
502 You have no permission to talk.  Goodbye.
Connection closed by foreign host
```

Hurrah! We now know that this part of the header is a real news server. Oh, yes, we have also just learned the name/address of the computer foohorse.com uses to handle the news groups: "boxcar." I try the next item in the path:

```
telnet news.foostateu.edu nntp
Trying 128.999.220.25 ...
Connected to pith.foostateu.edu.
Escape character is '^]'.
502 You have no permission to talk.  Goodbye.
Connection closed by foreign host.
```

This one is a valid news server, too. Now let's jump to the last item in the header: in2.uu.net:

```
telnet in2.uu.net nntp
in2.uu.net: unknown host
```

Now this might mean that this is forged. But another explanation is that it is an Internet backbone computer. Those oftentimes give "unknown host messages." Let's check the domain name next:

```
whois uu.net
```

The result is:

```
UUNET Technologies, Inc. (UU-DOM)
   3060 Williams Drive Ste 601
   Fairfax, VA 22031
   USA

   Domain Name: UU.NET

   Administrative Contact, Technical Contact, Zone Contact:
      UUNET, AlterNet [Technical Support]   (OA12)
help@UUNET.UU.NET
      +1 (800) 900-0241
   Billing Contact:
      Payable, Accounts  (PA10-ORG)   ap@UU.NET
      (703) 206-5600
Fax: (703) 641-7702

   Record last updated on 23-Jul-96.
   Record created on 20-May-87.
   Domain servers in listed order:

   NS.UU.NET                    137.39.1.3
   UUCP-GW-1.PA.DEC.COM         16.1.0.18 999.123.2.18
   UUCP-GW-2.PA.DEC.COM         16.1.0.19
   NS.EU.NET                    192.16.202.11


The InterNIC Registration Services Host contains ONLY Internet
Information (Networks, ASN's, Domains, and POC's).
Please use the whois server at nic.ddn.mil for MILNET
Information.
```

So uu.net is a real domain. Not only that—my, my, my. UUNET had been infamous for being soft on ISPs that host spammers. But that changed after a number of other Internet backbones briefly cut off UUNET for allowing too much spam to go through. Remember, your legal, polite complaints can motivate not only your ISP but even your ISP's backbone provider to cut off spammers. And it's all legal. Never, never underestimate the power of informed, legal protest.

The interesting thing here is that we have come across an Internet backbone. This makes me wonder whether the next item above UUNET might be the actual news server on which this message was forged, contacted via telnet over UUNET? So we next try:

```
telnet news.foospring.com nntp
Trying 999.999.128.185 ...
```

```
Connected to news.foospring.com.
Escape character is '^]'.
502 You are not in my access file.  Goodbye.
Connection closed by foreign host.
```

Interesting. I don't get a specific host name for the nntp port. What does this mean? Well, there's a way to try. Let's telnet to the port that gives the login sequence. That's port 23, but telnet automatically goes to 23 unless we tell it otherwise:

```
telnet news.foospring.com
```

Now this is phun!

```
Trying 999.999.128.166 ...
telnet: connect to address 999.999.128.166: Connection refused
Trying 999.999.128.167 ...
telnet: connect to address 999.999.128.167: Connection refused
Trying 999.999.128.168 ...
telnet: connect to address 999.999.128.168: Connection refused
Trying 999.999.128.182 ...
telnet: connect to address 999.999.128.182: Connection refused
Trying 999.999.128.185 ...
telnet: connect: Connection refused
```

Notice how many host computers are tried out by telnet on this command! I'm guessing that they all must all specialize in being news servers, since none of them handles ordinary telnet logins. Note, too, that one domain name, news.foospring.com, represents four different computers, each with its own numerical IP address.

This looks like another candidate for the origin of the spam. Even though none of these, or any other of the news servers in this header will let outsiders use them, the culprit could easily have gotten an account at Foospring and telneted in from Australia.

Let's next do a whois command on the domain name:

```
whois foospring.com
```

We get:

```
Foospring Enterprises, Inc. (FOOSPRING-DOM)
   1430 West Footree Street NE
   Suite 400
   Atlanta, GA 30309
   USA
```
   (contact information snipped)
```
   Record last updated on 27-Mar-96.
   Record created on 21-Apr-94.

   Domain servers in listed order:

   CARNAC.FOOSPRING.COM          999.999.128.95
```

```
HENRI.FOOSPRING.COM          999.999.128.3
```

I'd say that Foospring could well be the ISP from which this post was forged. The reason is that this part of the header looks genuine, and offers lots of computers on which to forge a post. A letter to the technical contact at hostmaster@foospring.com with a copy of this post may get a result. How about also emailing them a more vigorous protest? Hmmm, maybe a 5 MB gif of mating hippos? Even if it is illegal?

But systems administrator Terry McIntyre cautions me, "One needn't toss megabyte files back (unless, of course, one is helpfully mailing a copy of the offending piece back, just so that the poster knows what the trouble was.)

"The Law of Large Numbers of Offendees works to your advantage. Spammer sends one post to 'reach out and touch' thousands of potential customers.

"Thousands of Spammees send back oh-so-polite notes about the improper behavior of the Spammer. Most Spammers (or ISPs hosting spammers) get the point fairly quickly.

"One note—one wrong thing to do is to post to the newsgroup or list about the inappropriateness of any previous post. Always, always, use private email to make such complaints. Otherwise, the newbie inadvertently amplifies the noise level for the readers of the newsgroup or email list."

There is another reason not to do something drastic to Foospring. That ISP is probably totally unaware that it is being used by spammers to forge Usenet posts. Or—wow, I may even be wrong in deducing this post was forged at Foospring. If we assume Foospring is guilty and attack without warning, we may hurt the innocent.

The bottom line is that if you really want to pull the plug on this spammer, send a polite note including the Usenet post with headers intact to the technical contact and/or postmaster at each and every of the valid links we found in this spam header. Chances are that they will thank you for your sleuthing and block the bad guys at their routers.

To get an idea of how happy some ISPs are when you alert them to spam, here's an example of an email I got from Netcom about one I helped them to track down.

```
From: Netcom Abuse Department abuse@netcom.com
Reply-To: abuse@netcom.com
Subject: Thank you for your report


Thank you for your report.  We have informed this user of our
policies, and have taken appropriate action, up to, and including
cancellation of the account, depending on the particular incident.
If they continue to break Netcom policies we will take further action.
The following issues have been dealt with:
        santigo@ix.netcom.com
        date-net@ix.netcom.com
        jhatem@ix.netcom.com
        kkooim@ix.netcom.com
(about 20 more addresses snipped)
Sorry for the length of the list.

Spencer
Abuse Investigator
```

Next let's look at an example of email spam. I have an AOL account which is an amazing spam magnet. I almost never get spam at any of my techbroker.com email addresses, but at least in 1997, the minute you signed up with AOL you would start getting several spams per day, often of the filthiest sort.

AOL tells its users to forward all unwanted spam to the address "tosspam." But often that mailbox is too full and bounces the complaints. Although AOL has gone so far in fighting spam as to sue Sanford Wallace himself, most spammers have discovered AOL is still fat pickings. Sigh.

Here's some spam that just came in on AOL:

```
Subj:    FREE 5 MINUTE PREVIEW
Date:    97-09-28 16:18:34 EDT
From:    fstarzx@aol.com
Reply-to:      xxx1try69@aol.com
To:      xxx1try69@aol.com

< 5 FREE MINUTES >
We have beautiful models waiting to fulfill your Wildest Fantasies.
With our 5 FREE MINUTES GAURANTEED with NO obligation.
See our models LIVE on your computer screen,check it out
FREE.... 24 hrs a day, 7 days a week.
  - CLICK HERE
%************************************************************
********* *%
———————————Headers————————————
Received:    from      mrin76.mail.aol.com    (mrin76.mail.aol.com
[152.163.116.114])
by air14.mail.aol.com (v33) with SMTP; Sun, 28 Sep 1997 16:18:33
-0400
Received:    from    mrin76.mx.aol.com    (sdn-ts-002miwarrP01.dial-
sprint.net
[206.133.110.36])
        by mrin76.mail.aol.com (8.5.5/8.8.5/AOL-4.0.0)
        with SMTP id QAA02332;
        Sun, 28 Sep 1997 16:16:52 -0400 (EDT)
From: fstarzx@aol.com
Received: from xxx1try69@aol.com by xxx1try69@aol.com (8.8.5/8.6.5)
with
SMTP id GAA02329 for <xxx1try69@aol.com>; Sun, 28 Sep 1997 16:16:01
-0600
(EST)
Date: Sun, 28 Sep 97 16:16:01 EST
To: xxx1try69@aol.com
Subject: FREE 5 MINUTE PREVIEW
Message-ID: %478612534@mail1.mail-promo.com
Reply-To: xxx1try69@aol.com
X-UIDL: 521452365258747211525485214523663
Comments: Authenticated sender is <xxx1try69@aol.com>
```

The first thing we try is to "click here." As in the case of Foobie Partners, with spam you best bet is usually to first check any associated Web site, which will tell us lots more much faster than dissecting what is obviously a forged header. If you get spam like this and read it in a browser such as Netscape, IE or the AOL browser, it will take you right to the Web. So we follow the link to http://209.14.999.210/bashar/.

(In case you are wondering, this is a typical el cheapo porno site. Words are misspelled. A perfunctory notice asks minors to pretty please browse no further.)

Our first step is to figure out who or what company owns Internet host 209.14.999.210. It could be that the owner has no idea that a spammer is operating a Web site there. Most Web server owners don't care much whether their customers put dirty pictures on their computer. But spam—that's a matter of life or death. So unless the owner of 209.14.999.210 is also a spammer or chooses to make money off spammers, you can usually shut down this kind of site.

Our first approach is to run nslookup. But this is the response we get:

```
mack:/home3/user/cpm # bash
bash$ nslookup 209.14.999.210
Server:  mack.fubar.com
Address:  999.59.162.1

*** Request to mack.fubar.com timed-out
```

This means nslookup couldn't find this computer on the nameserver it used. So our next task is to find a computer that might know something about 209.14.999.210. We use trusty old traceroute to find out the sequence of computers through which my computer had to go in order to view this porno site.

```
bash$ traceroute 209.14.999.210
traceroute to 209.14.999.210 (209.14.999.210), 30 hops max, 40 byte packets
 1  FUBAR-gwy.fubar.com (999.59.162.254)  3 ms  4 ms  2 ms
 2  lawr-engint.link.foomexico.org (999.134.77.999)  14 ms  5 ms  4 ms
 3  enss365.foomexico.org (129.121.1.3) 15 ms (ttl=252!) 8 ms (ttl=252!)
12 ms (ttl=252!)
 4  h4-0.cnss116.Albuquerque.t3.ans.net (192.103.74.45)  10 ms (ttl=251!)
10 ms (ttl=251!) 12 ms (ttl=251!)
 5  f2-1.t112-0.Albuquerque.t3.ans.net (140.222.112.221)  7 ms (ttl=250!)
11 ms (ttl=250!)  14 ms (ttl=250!)
 6  h14-1.t16-0.Los-Angeles.t3.ans.net (140.999.17.9)  41 ms (ttl=249!)  30
ms (ttl=249!)  30 ms (ttl=249!)
 7  h14-1.t8-0.San-Francisco.t3.ans.net (140.999.9.13)  38 ms (ttl=248!)
37 ms (ttl=248!)  44 ms (ttl=248!)
 8  999.32.128.65 (999.32.128.65)  137 ms (ttl=247!)  116 ms (ttl=247!)  39
ms (ttl=247!)
 9  999.32.128.226 (999.32.128.226)  44 ms (ttl=246!)  45 ms (ttl=246!)  47
ms (ttl=246!)
10  pb-nap.agis.net (999.32.128.19)  176 ms (ttl=250!)  302 ms (ttl=250!)
109 ms (ttl=250!)
11  ga002.santaclara4.agis.net (206.84.226.241)  292 ms  193 ms  208 ms
12  ga008.chicago3.agis.net (206.84.226.222)  175 ms  191 ms  176 ms
13  a0.1010.dearborn2.agis.net (205.254.999.238)  170 ms  152 ms  147 ms
14  205.137.51.999 (205.137.51.999)  168 ms  163 ms  160 ms
15  209.14.999.210 (209.14.999.210)  153 ms (ttl=50!)  207 ms (ttl=50!)
205 ms (ttl=50!)
```

I next look more closely at 209.14.999.210 using nslookup again, but this time on steroids. What I need to do is find a DNS server for nslookup that has info on this spam site. So I run nslookup again, but this time try to use the second to last computer in that traceroute as the DNS server.

```
Default Server:  mack.fubar.com
Address:  999.59.162.1
 server=205.137.51.999
Server:  mack.fubar.com
Address:  999.59.162.1
*** mack.fubar.com can't find server=205.137.51.999: Non- existent
host/domain
```

Oh, oh, I was getting overconfident there. Because traceroute, to my knowledge, does not show forged IP addresses, I figure those must be for real. Hmmm, how about using the second to last IP address on that traceroute.

```
Server:  mack.fubar.com
Address:  999.59.162.1

*** mack.fubar.com can't find server=205.254.999.238: Non- existent
host/domain
```

This is frustrating. I decide to try whois. Sometimes you can get better results on a whois query by telneting to whois.internic.net. But in this case I also get a message that the server cannot be found.

Nslookup and dig also don't find either of these IP addresses. Hmm, I'm beginning to wonder if we have stumbled across one of those megaspammer networks. But hang in there, we'll find someone who cares enough to cut these guys off yet. But the higher up we go in that traceroute, the bigger the chunk of rogue Internet we are fighting.

Hmm, let's take a look at the name associated with the hosts numbered 10 through 13 on that traceroute. They all have "agis" in them. Wait, I know who those guys are. AGIS is the Internet backbone that was famous for making its money from the biggest spammers in the world. I just got this spam from them Sept. 28. But only six days earlier AGIS had announced that it had just cut off Cyber Promotions, Quantum Communications and NancyNet, the triumvirate of junk email.

Well, AGIS obviously hasn't booted all its spammers. Although it had a reputation for ignoring spam complaints, I decide to figure out how to email them. Hmmm, about 5,000 emails each with a 5 MB attached image file of mating hippos? Oh, but that would be an illegal mail bombing. I will just send them a polite note. But where do I send it?

First I try asking Netscape 4.0 to look up http://agis.net. It automatically also checks http://www.agis.net, but says "the server may be down or not responding." It later turned out that this was the right Web address. But at the time AGIS was under heavy attack by computer criminals who imagined that breaking in and mail bombing was the best way to fight spam. So that might have had something to do wit the Web site being unreachable.

I then used whois and got the mail address, phone and email contact for AGIS. I phoned the AGIS director of security. He told me that they have been helping us folks fight spam by identifying guilty Internet host computers and giving out this information to any ISP that asked for it so they could block spam at the routers.

 Newbie note: Routers are like Internet traffic cops. They direct traffic and can block spam—if it knows the Internet address of the computer that is sending spam.

Some hackers have claimed that their breaking into AGIS computers and mail bombing them are what forced AGIS to give the boot to several spammer customers. But according to AGIS, they canceled those accounts—despite a lawsuit— because they had evidence that some of those customers used mail forging to not only send out spam, but also to attack their critics.

What next? We have the option of also complaining at higher levels in the traceroute. We've ruled out complaining to AOL because, even though the management fights spam, it is overloaded fighting it. But maybe we can complain to another backbone provider on this route, as well.

This can be surprisingly effective. In September 1997, several backbone providers gave the UUNET backbone the "Internet sentence of death" by cutting off any communications that had passed through UUNET at any point in its travels. The reason? UUNET had become notorious for making it too easy for spammers to use it. Remember, the Internet is voluntary. It is possible to cut spammers off at any point in the Internet, if we can convince the owners of that part of the Internet to do so.

Playing with traceroute, I find a second Internet backbone provider: ANS.net. Although a whois query turns up empty, dig gives me:

```
bash$ dig ans.net
; <> DiG 2.1 <> ans.net
;; res options: init recurs defnam dnsrch
;; got answer:
;; ->HEADER<- opcode: QUERY, status: NOERROR, id: 6
;; flags: qr aa rd ra; Ques: 1, Ans: 1, Auth: 3, Addit: 3
;; QUESTIONS:
;;      ans.net, type = A, class = IN
;; ANSWERS:
ans.net.         900     A       147.225.5.5
;; AUTHORITY RECORDS:
ans.net.         900     NS      nis.ans.net.
ans.net.         900     NS      ns.ans.net.
ans.net.         900     NS      knock.aa.ans.net.

;; ADDITIONAL RECORDS:
nis.ans.net.     900     A       147.225.1.2
ns.ans.net.      900     A       192.103.63.100
knock.aa.ans.net.    900     A       999.83.21.10

;; Total query time: 192 msec
;; FROM: mack to SERVER: default—999.59.162.1
;; WHEN: Sun Sep 28 21:09:30 1997
;; MSG SIZE  sent: 25  rcvd: 147
```

Aha, now we have the names of a bunch more ANS.net computers! First we check to see whether there is a Web site associated with the domain name ANS.net. At http://www.ans.net we discover it is part of America Online. Shoot! We're back to trying to either get email through to tosspam@aol.com or else phoning customer support. I call customer support because this is a big problem AOL is going to have to deal with.

Sorry, there is no free lunch. I love AOL, but it charges too little money to be able to hire the legion of spam fighters it needs. Let's be good guys and make it easier for them by emailing tosspam@aol.com and giving them this analysis. Maybe AGIS will cut off this spam customer, too, especially if AOL also asks AGIS.

Also, is it possible to also directly bug ANS? They say the squeaky wheel gets the grease.

Here's a fast way to find out how to email ANS:

```
bash$ telnet knock.aa.ans.net 25
Trying 999.83.21.10...
Connected to knock.aa.ans.net.
Escape character is '^]'.
220 knock.aa.ans.net ESMTP Sendmail 8.8.5/8.7.1; Sun, 28 Sep
1997 23:15:44 -0400
```

Because knock.aa.ans.net is running sendmail, we know it is a Unix computer. Therefore email to root@knock.aa.ans.net should get through, because normally that address will go to the sysadmin of that computer. Just to be safe, also try postmaster@knock.aa.ans.net and abuse@knock.aa.ans.net.

Remember, no hippo jpegs! What will work best is to send the spam with the complete header, and any analysis you have been able to complete. Remember, ANS doesn't want to pay to carry all that spam, and neither does AOL. They are on our side.

But, back to that spam porno site. We still haven't tried out our trusty helper telnet. So I simply telnet to that web IP address:

```
Trying 209.14.999.210...
Connected to 209.14.999.210.
Escape character is '^]'.

Red Hat Linux release 4.2 (Biltmore)
Kernel 2.0.27 on an i586
login:
```

Aha! Red Hat Linux runs on PCs. Chances are this is some guy with a computer in his bedroom who bought some spam software and hooked up with some spammer-only ISP through AGIS. I'll bet he scanned some old Hustler magazines to provide his porn content. I'd sure like to send this d00d a message. A quick way to find out if I can mail him is to telnet into his mail server:

```
bash$ telnet 209.14.999.210 25
Trying 209.14.999.210...
```

```
telnet: Unable to connect to remote host: Connection refused
```

Afraid of mail bombs, is he? But note that we have gotten the version of Red Hat he's using. A bad guy hacker would use that info plus a port scanner to break into the spammer's computer.

> **You can go to jail warning: It would be illegal to break into this computer. Besides, we have better ways to deal with that guy's ilk.**

We have another possibility for finding a way to complain to the spammer. It may be possible to forward email to this guy. The way we do this is to try to telnet into port 25 of each of the computers above him in the traceroute.

On ANS we had discovered that knock.aa.ans.net accepts email. So we then try addressing a message to root%209.14.999.210@knock.aa.ans.net. The "%" tells the my mail system to first send it to knock.aa.ans.net and ask it to forward the message to our spammer on the Red Hat box. (Note: your ISP may not be able to handle "%" forwarding of mail you send.) However, I get back:

```
Date: Mon, 29 Sep 1997 10:20:50 -0400
From: Mail Delivery Subsystem AILER-DAEMON@noc.ans.net
To: cpm@fubar.com
Subject: Returned mail: Host unknown (Name server:
209.14.999.210: host not found)
        (snip)
```

If I want to get persistent, I would try to find a chain of several Internet hosts through which I would forward this message, hoping that the last one would be authorized to deliver email to the culprit. Boy, would that surprise him, he, he. But this can take a long time to figure out. Unless my plan was to mail bomb the culprit—naughty, naughty!—this isn't worth the effort.

We learn from this exercise that the Red Hat spammer appears to be hidden behind a chain of guardians. In this case, unless you want to take the illegal route, your best recourses are to complain to AGIS and ANS.

What Sysadmins Can Do to Fight Spam

If you are the systems administrator of a computer whose users are getting lots of spam, what can you do to fight it? You can, of course, block all packets with headers indicating they have originated at known spam sites. In this case, you would want to block, for example, 205.137.51.999. Another trick is to block packets revealing obviously forged IP addresses, for example with numbers above 255 in them. (That is how I am fubaring IP addresses in this book.)

You should set your mail servers so they do not forward mail. Be especially sure to disable that trick of specifying a mail forwarding route using "%". These two precautions will also keep your system from being abused by mail bombers.

Of course you do run ident and log shell account and email activity?

Another thing you can do is watch out for ads requesting that you sell extra bandwidth on your T1 or T3 connections. Your new customer may well be a spammer.

In October 1997, Candy Cremona learned this the hard way. She runs the New Millennium Cafe. She told the press she believed Cyberpomo when the company arranged with her to buy her extra T1 capacity. She said Cyberpromo told her it was for a Web server. Instead, she found out the hard way that they were holding her in reserve for when their other spam pipelines got cut off.

When spam began to pour through her server, computer vigilantes went on the attack. According to Jerry Trowbridge, posting to the news group news.admin.net-abuse.email, the primary—and innocent—victim ended up being the owner of the company from which she was leasing her T1: "Nick Nolter, at PGNC Leasing, a high bandwidth provider in South Florida." According to Trowbridge, "Nolter's third-party relationship with Cyberpromo has cost him several thousand dollars. This weekend, cyber-attackers took out his DNS servers, and one of his backbone providers cut him off for thirty hours . . ."

Why do you suppose his Internet backbone provider cut him off? Because spam watchdogs alerted the backbone provider to the flood of Cyberpromo spam.

Even online giant America Online has come under serious attack by a spammer. For a while this spammer was forging return addresses of real ISPs on its mail, using lists that were crammed with bad addresses. When the bad addresses bounced, they created so much mail daemon notices to the forged addresses that this crashed the mail servers of several ISPs. They, in turn, complained to AOL.

Some sysadmins at AOL retaliated against the spammer. First they figured out where he was mailing this spam from. Then they saved up many gigabytes of bad address—and dumped them back to the sender all on one huge batch. AOL has big pipes! This, of course, crashed the spammer's ISP. Then AOL got a court order to force spammers to quit that dirty tactic.

In the meantime, once-gutsy ISPs have since backed down on that tactic of sending all those bad addresses to the real sender, as spammers have gone to court to fight the practice.

How ISP Owners Can Fight Spam

October 20, 1997, AOL filed a law suit against Prime Data Worldnet Systems Inc., which hosts domains such as "getrichfast.com" and "lotsofmoney.com." Prime Data also sells spam mail software and "Stealth Mailer," which it advertised as being able to defeat AOL's mail controls that should allow a user to block spam. This followed an Oct. 2, 1997 suit against a Las Vegas-based company called Over the Air Equipment Inc. for sending bulk E-mails to AOL users advertising pornographic Web sites (probably the company behind our d00d with the Red Hat Linux box full of recycled porno pix).

"We will pursue all legal remedies to protect our members and uphold the integrity of the AOL system," said AOL General Counsel George Vradenburg in a statement to the press.

What if you are too small an ISP to sue huge spam empires? AOL, several ISPs and the Electronic Frontier Foundation are, as of this writing, putting together a consortium to battle spam. To check on how this group may be able to assist you, check out the Electronic Frontier Foundation at *http://eff.org*.

As AGIS's Addison has pointed out above, that Internet backbone provider will work with small ISPs to identify IP addresses associated with spammers so you can block it at your routers.

However, we recommend against the practice of some ISPs of automatically filtering and discarding email with key words and phrases often found in spam. Netcom used to do this, but stopped because customers complained about losing legitimate email this way. It turned out that the management of Netcom wasn't even aware this was being done. Over-zealous sysadmins had taken the spam problem into their own hands.

Fight Spam the Hacker Way—Illegally

Yes, there are plenty of illegal ways to fight spam. We're talking hacker justice, and hacker war here. We are also talking about hitting innocent victims as often as you get the guys you want to lynch. Remember, a favorite spammer tactic is to trick illegal hackers into attacking the people who are fighting spam! Don't do it!

There have been media reports that Cyber Promotions has been targeted by a wide range of hacker attacks, of which the Candy Cremona case is only one. Those attacks were totally unnecessary. Getting cut off by their Internet backbone provider, which is totally legal, was all that was needed to ensure the problem got fixed fast.

Other news stories claim Cyberpromo's president, Sanford Wallace, is making up these stories to win sympathy from the public. As of this writing, no arrests have been made of his alleged attackers. This has led some reporters to assume Wallace is lying.

He isn't. By now you realize how easy it would be to take out the spam servers, and all those little Linux boxes out there pumping spam into those spam empires. You know it would be miraculous if Cyberpromo had never been hit.

In fact, if my friends who have been known to stray to the wrong side of the law are telling the truth, there is all-out illegal hacker war going on between spam hackers and anti-spam hackers. The director of security at AGIS also confirms that they have been attacked in retaliation for formerly hosting Cyberpromo, Nancynet and Quantcom, all major spammers.

These attacks, according to AGIS, have included death threats, mail bombing, and breaking into computers.

For example. June 4, 1997 the following message, titled "I am the AGIS hacker," was posted from a hacked root account on an AGIS computer to news.admin.net-abuse.misc. "Today I wiped AGISGATE and all of AGIS's name servers. I will only stop until [sic] AGIS changes their policies and enacts an acceptable use policy. This means drastic changes. This means getting rid of all of their spammers—most importantly Cyber Promotions." This attack took down the entire AGIS backbone, probably the most destructive denial of service attack in Internet history after the Morris Worm.

You may go to jail warning: Although law enforcement officials have so far been reluctant to spend large amounts of taxpayers' money trying to protect spammers, attacking an Internet backbone provider is guaranteed to mobilize a lot of law enforcement firepower. By the time you read this, the AGIS cracker may well be behind bars.

At times I am tempted to feel that those who break the law while fighting spammers are underground heroes. But then I remember: those guys are often tricked into hitting innocent victims, or even into attacking other spam-fighters. Worst of all, those who use criminal tactics can—and often do—use the same tools to violate our freedom of speech. But that is a topic of a later chapter: hacker wars!

Section 3, Chapter 3
Email Bombs

There's a new name for evil on the Internet—the Unamailer. The hacker wannabe appears to have begun his vandalism campaign . . . after learning how to cobble together a script that automatically subscribes a victim to hundreds of mailing lists. Then he stepped up his efforts, targeting the e-mail accounts of more than a dozen journalists and media folks, as well as the likes of Bill Clinton, Bill Gates and Church of Scientology counsel Helena Kobrin.—"Unamailer wreaks havoc on the Internet," by Chris Stamper, Netly News, http://www.now.com.

'johnny xchaotic,' also known as the 'Unamailer,' is back, and twenty-one individuals—many of whom are deeply involved in the Internet—journalists, the heads of computer companies such as Microsoft, politicians, and religious figures—received a . . . Christmas present they wished they didn't have. johnny, and possible friends of johnny, effectively halted these individuals' ability to send and receive E-mail, a denial of service attack which may take days to restore.—Lew Koch, writing in CyberWire Dispatch, http://cyberwerks.com.

"The net is chaos, we are on the net, therefore we must be chaotic . . . why our actions . . . ? too many people on the net do not belong."—johnny xchaotic, AKA the Unamailer, in a manifesto explaining his attacks.

Email bombs! They may sound faintly humorous. Some hackers think mail bombs are no big deal, and use them casually to harass people that they dislike.

But try telling that to the owner of Southwest Cyberport. Try waking up at 5 AM Christmas morning, 1996, to the sound of the beeper that alerted him to a mail-bombing which had crashed the mail server of one of the largest ISPs in New Mexico.

Try telling that to people such as the Basque rebels who are being hounded off the Web by email bomb attacks against whoever hosts their site.

Email bombs are now the number one tool of today's crypto-fascists who are trying to deny freedom of speech to those whom they oppose.

In this chapter you will learn:
- what is an email bomb
- why email bombers do their thing
- several types of email bombs
- the kinds of damage email bombs can cause
- how to fight mail bombings
- how to keep mail bombers from using your computer system to launch attacks against others

What Is an Email Bomb?

Email bombs are attacks in which a large amount of email is sent in a short period of time to the target address or ISP. A thousand emails in one day may make it almost impossible to find your real mail in that sea of junk.

Some mail bombings can even send the victim gigabytes of email per day. This can do much more than keep one user from being able to read email. It can fill up the mail server of an entire ISP, making it impossible for any user to receive email. The worst mail bombing attacks have shut down an ISP's email server for days on end.

Email bombs are a kind of spam, forgeries used to send email to those who don't want it. But while most spam is an act of greed, mail bombing is usually an act of anger that may intend to deny the victim access to email, extort ISPs to totally deny the victims access to the entire Internet, or even as warfare to shut down entire ISPs.

A hostile nation or terrorist group could even use mail bombs crash the entire Internet. Because of this frightening power, email bombs can land the sender in jail.

You can go to jail warning: In the US a mail bomber can get up to five years in prison and a $250,000 fine.

Yet email bombs are easy to launch and terrible in their temptation. If you've read the chapters on forging email, you have probably already figured out at least one way to commit a mail bombing, and may even have realized how to guarantee you won't get caught.

Email bombing is not rocket science. With the right software in hand, it's something even little children can do. For awhile, there was even a web site where all you had to do was type in your insult and how many of these insults you wanted to send, click the button, and off went another wave of destruction.

So I won't insult your intelligence or tempt you to crime by spelling out ten or twenty different ways to commit the perfect mail bombing crime. In fact, with just a few simple instructions, anyone can turn a certain popular email program for Windows 95 into a deadly and stealthy mail bomber.

Let me make one thing perfectly clear. I'm totally opposed to mail bombing. Sure, as you could see in the previous chapter, sometimes I'm tempted. It's easy to be seduced by that much power and by the knowledge of how easy it could be used to get away with the crime.

But mail bombing is an attack on the fundamental freedoms of the Internet. The freedom of the Internet to even exist. The freedom to say what you want to say without self-styled digital cops blasting your email service to smithereens.

Why Email Bombers Do their Thing

But mail bombs are such a powerful, easy weapon! Why not use them to fight the bad guys?

You don't need to mail bomb in order to win the battle against Internet bad guys. We can fight even the mail bombers themselves without ever using these widespread weapons of mass digital destruction. We'll see some of these ways in this chapter.

Back in 1996, the media made a big deal about two mail bombings committed by a character the press called johnny xchaotic. This guy bombed dozens of people on Christmas Eve 1996. According to Janet Kornblum, writing for CNET News at *http://www.news.com*, "johnny's victims ranged from prominent right-wing politicians such as Pat Buchanan and David Duke to the Ku Klux Klan and companies that he accused of censorship, such as MTV. He has also targeted journalists, including Carolyn Meinel, who runs a hacker mailing list."

As xchaotic argued in a manifesto he later emailed to many journalists, "Your happy hacker mail list is demented. You are trying to get those people busted, aren't you? You give them enough rope for them to hang themselves with, and then try to preach about not using the information. Give up."

Why do mail bombers do their thing? xchaotic says he email bombed because he was trying to be heard. Putting up a Web site, posting to news groups and mail lists just weren't enough for his ego.

Others may bomb to shut down spam or mail bomb sites. I have been tempted to do that myself. But then I would become no better than the spammers, abusing email to punish others who abuse it. However, many other people have bombed the ISPs that have hosted mail bomber program download sites, lowering themselves to the level of these criminals.

But there are legal, nondestructive ways to get those bomber download sites off the Internet. Usually all it takes is just one email or phone call to the ISP that hosts the offending Web site to get it taken down. In the US, the threat of lawsuits has gotten several recalcitrant ISPs to remove bomber download sites.

Another motivation for mail bombing is revenge against the ISPs that these programs use for the mail servers that must pump out this spam. "I am not threatening anyone, but a correctly placed default setting in my future (email bombing) programs could definitely cost some net pigs a hell of a lot of money," pointed out Acid Angel, the author of the Up Yours series of mail bomber programs. This probably has been the most popular and powerful (ugh!) ever written.

Others email bomb because they want to force ISPs to shut down Web sites that carry opposing political views. In the following chapter on hacker wars we will read much about how mail bombing has been a staple in the arsenal used to drive off—or try to drive controversial groups off the Internet.

You can keep your right to speak freely on the Internet, if you use the techniques for fighting mail bombs that us scarred veterans have discovered.

What Kinds of Email Bombs Are there?

But first we must understand what kind of email bombs there are. Alas, there are so many ways to bomb that this chapter will miss several. But here's a try at describing most of them.

1) The hardest to fight, and one of the most powerful, is known as the "flamer." It is a program that goes to one domain name after another, discovers all the mail lists being run from that domain, and subscribes the victim to them all. In a few hours a flamer program can subscribe the victim to thousands of mail lists. Each of these lists probably sends out ten or more emails per day. This is enough mail volume that just one flamer attack can crash an ISP's mail server.

A more common mail bomb sets up an endless loop in a program that sends the same email over and over again.

Sometimes a hapless sysadmin will crash a mail server by misconfiguring the mail server software. For example, mail could get sent in an endless loop through a LAN. A really skilled mail bomber may misconfigure a mail server on purpose to flood the victim with emails bearing error messages.

Or, "Spammy" could send just a hundred or so emails— but attach a huge file to each.

Autoresponders and the "vacation" program, which send out a message to every incoming email, are hazards for both intentional and accidental mail bombs. A good sysadmin will not allow ordinary users to activate these programs because if user A has a program that sends a copy of all incoming mail to user B, while B sends all his email to A, it's mail server meltdown time.

A poorly configured email list can also be hit this way. People have been known to set up an autoresponder on purpose to crash a mail list. Or a program might automatically forward posts from one mail list to another and vice versa, creating an exponentially growing stream of mail that will crash the server of all affected mail lists. However, there are many mail list programs that can be set up to prevent these problems.

Because email bombing is so popular with people who are too clueless to figure out how to do it themselves, quite a few bomber programs are available for download on the Web. The download sites I have seen for them make out like you can use them without getting caught. This is absolutely false!

For example, one site claimed "The only two programs I have listed below that can not be tracked back, by normal means, is the . . . Up Yours or Avalanche line of programs." Another Web site listed these programs under the heading "anonymous mailers."

Here's the real story. The default settings in these programs make it ridiculously easy for you to get caught. In fact, as Acid Angel has pointed out, release of mail bomber programs with default settings for the mail server on which the attacks are forged can turn into an expensive denial of service attack against the mail bomb server. Also, if lots of mail bombings are going through the same computer, the police will take notice.

The important thing to remember about these mail bomber programs is that they are not anonymous. Why should someone so filled with hate that he wants to encourage total strangers to f*** up the entire Internet and violate people's freedom of speech care one bit about whether you, a total stranger, go to jail?

What Kinds of Damage Can Email Bombs Do?

I said above that email bombing could conceivably crash the entire Internet. This is not an exaggeration.

An email bomb can do much more than just keep one person from receiving email. As mentioned above, enough email, whether from spammers or mail bombings, can overwhelm the mail server for an entire ISP.

As mail bombing continues to grow in popularity, it can also eat up communications bandwidth the same way commercial spam does.

So picture a terrorist group or a nation at war unleashing bots that churn out spam focused on key gateways on the Internet. Spam with huge attached files. Hacked domain name servers sending this stuff bouncing back and forth from one backbone to the other a half dozen times before each message gets bounced out of the loop. There goes the bandwidth. Disk drives fill up. CPU use soars. See the Internet crash.

Even if no one ever uses mail bombing to crash the Internet, it is still scary because it is often an assault on freedom of speech. Repeat mail bombings are used to extort ISPs into kicking bombing victims off their accounts in the hope that the criminals who launched the attacks will go elsewhere. Will the Internet keep on being the place where anyone can set up a Web site, share ideas on Usenet, and send and receive email? Or will the mail bombers set up a rule of thugs?

How to Beat Bomber Attacks against Yourself

Since lots of computer criminals don't like the work I have been doing to reveal hacker secrets to the world, I have lots of experience fighting mail bombs. Here are some of my favorite defenses.

Number one defense: get your own domain name. Register it yourself and it only costs $100 for the first two years. Get yours at *http://internic.net*. When the bad guys extort your ISP into dropping you, simply move your email and Web site addresses to an ISP that has the courage and technical competence to stand up to the net fascists.

But, when you are under heavy attack, you'll need a backup. My first line of defense is to use several on-line services. That way, whenever one account is getting hacked, bombed, etc., you can just email all your correspondents and tell them where to reach you.

But that's the coward's way to handle email bombing. There are several ways that either your ISP or you can defeat these attacks head on. The simplest defense is to block attacks at the router by banning the domain from which the attack originated.

But what if the attack comes from many places on the Internet? So many places that your ISP would have to cut itself off from most of the Internet? That how johnny xchaotic's Christmas Eve attacks worked.

I was able to fix my problem within a few minutes of discovery. Johnny had subscribed all these lists to only one of my addresses, cmeinel@swfooport.com. But

I use my private domain, techbroker.com, to receive email. Then I pipe all this from my domain name host to whatever account I find useful at the time. So all I had to do was configure things to pipe email to another account.

You can reroute email by creating a file in your shell account named .forward. This file directs your email to another email account of your choice. But because the .forward file can be used to crash mail servers, your ISP may have (should have!) disabled it. But you can ask your sysadmin to set it up for you.

Even if you don't own your own domain name, you can easily find an ISP that will allow you to create new user names for yourself. For example, America Online (http://aol.com) will let you have up to four user names at any one time in addition to your primary email address. You also can set any of your accounts to reject email from any or even all sources. You can also delete your subsidiary user names and replace them with new ones without limit.

For bombings using email lists, one approach is to run a program that sorts through the initial flood of the email bomb for those "Welcome to the Tomato Twaddler List!" messages which tell how to unsubscribe. These programs then automatically compose unsubscribe messages and send them out.

However, people who have used them tell me these programs are computationally intensive. If you get subscribed to more than 200 or so mail lists, these programs will bog down, eating up CPU time and taking hours or days to finish. But if the attack you must fight isn't too big, perhaps the best of these programs is one first written by Kim Holburn of the University of Canberra in 1996. Email him at kim@canberra.edu.au to get a copy.

Another way to deal with flamer attacks is to simply forward all email to a nonexistent email address. (Warning: make absolutely certain you forward to a nonexistent address, or you will be mail bombing someone else!) Then two weeks later stop the forwarding. You will discover almost all those mailing lists have unsubscribed you. The remaining ones can be dealt with by hand.

If you get your email from a Unix shell, you can also filter out mail bombs using a free program called Procmail. One place to get it is at *ftp://ftp.informatik.rwth-aachen.de/pub/packages/procmail/*. However, the problem with procmail is that it doesn't bounce unwanted email back with a bad address message. In the case of a flamer attack, that means your ISP will continue to be subjected to that flood of mail list posts. Be kind to your ISP and make sure you clean up those flamer attacks.

Warning: this technique—every technique we cover here—will still cause you to lose some legitimate email. But I figure, why get obsessive over it? According to a study by a major paging company, a significant percentage of email simply disappears. No mail daemon warning that the message failed, nothing. It just goes into a black hole. So if you are counting on getting every piece of email that people send you, dream on.

But this switching around of email addresses and blocking incoming email doesn't solve the problem your ISP faces. He still has to deal with the bandwidth problem of bouncing all that crud flooding in. And it's a lot of crud. One of the sysadmins at Southwest Fooport, which is a medium-sized regional ISP, told me that almost every day some luser email bombs one of their customers. In fact, it's amazing that johnny xchaotic got as much publicity as he did, considering how commonplace email bombing is. So essentially every ISP somehow has to handle the email bomb problem.

How to Keep Mail Bombers from Using your Internet Host for Mail Bombings

The only way we will ever remove the threat of mail bombings on a massive scale is for enough systems administrators to make it impossible to bomb. Fortunately, if you are a sysadmin, there are things you can do to make it much harder for people to email bomb on your system.

- Run an ident daemon. This is a program which automatically identifies who is on your computer (unless the bad guy is spoofing his IP address).
- Log all use of your mailer daemon and keep the logs for at least a week in case the good guys need to track down some Spammy type who used your system as the pivot to take down someone else's mail server.
- If you have a Unix system, run qmail. It is really easy to configure so outsiders can't exploit it.
- If you absolutely must run a different mail daemon, disable mail forwarding from those outside your domain. Make the big Internet backbone providers do all the mail mover work.
- If people run mail lists on your system, make sure they require confirmation from all who subscribe. This simple step will make the flamer bombers obsolete.
- Don't let users on your system set up their own autoresponders and mail forwarders. Do it for them.

So, are you ready to save the Internet? Alas, even these techniques won't entirely halt mail bombings. But these safeguards will at least force the bad guys to work harder and longer to do their damage.

Section 3, Chapter 4
Hacker Wars

It appeared to start, as so many hacker wars do, in the aftermath of a Def Con hacker convention. Want to go to one? It's a great way to get people madder than heck at you, even if it seems at the time as if everyone liked you.

If they can keep on suckering hotels into hosting these cons (for Def Con V they had to tell the Las Vegas Aladdin it was the "DC Communications Conference"), you will find out about the next one at *http://defcon.org*.

In this Chapter you will learn:
- are hacker wars elite?
- what are some tactics of hacker wars?—Web page hacking—denial of service—sniffing—social engineering—ISP hostage taking
- the damage hacker warriors may do to bystanders
- why you may get hit someday
- how to get into a hacker war (some people want to!)
- defense techniques that don't break the law

Only eight days after the 1997 Def Con, Bronc Buster emailed me, "I'm getting out of this scene totally. It's making me sick." In a phone conversation he told me he was repelled by the hatred, the childishness his associates displayed at the con.

But getting out of the gang he was in, Global kOS, was painful. According to Bronc, harsh words, then threats, passed back and forth. Shadrack[1] emailed me about

---

1 Some of the names in this chapter have been changed to protect the innocent (or guilty, as the case may be). Logic may suggest to you that some of the people we quote in this book are guilty, guilty, guilty of whatever. But just because some people take delight in attacks on others, or are involved in amazing coincidences, or say they speak on behalf of the attackers, may not mean anything at all. Nosirree. Seriously, anyone who is a fan of murder mysteries knows that the obvious culprit may be a red herring. It would be really, really lame to retaliate against someone you assume has hacked you, or Bronc, or whomever, and end up in prison for attacking the wrong

Bronc: "I dislike him as a person, think he isn't qualified to be called 'hacker' by any definition."

Then on Oct. 4, 1997, at 4:10 AM Mountain Standard Time, Shadrack emailed me, "Looks like one of your pet hicks went and p***ed someone off. finger bbuster@succeed.net"

Why was Shadrack up and about at 4:10 AM Mountain daylight time? Says Shadrack, "My normal hours have me sleep from 8 - 10am, until 2 - 4pm. That puts me up all night." Perhaps it was just coincidence that Sat., 4 Oct 1997, 3:41 AM Pacific Daylight time—apparently half an hour after he emailed me, someone sent the following post from Bronc's account to the HH-Chat list:

```
From: Ball Buster of NAMBLA <bbuster        @main.succeed.net>
 (snip)
People please look at my web site and tell me if they think it looks
really studly! http://main.succeed.net/~bbuster.  Also, look at the
public statement I'm making, finger me (ooh!) finger -l bbuster@suc-
ceed.net
```

You guessed it, the Web site and finger info were obscene, making out like Bronc was a self-confessed pedophile.

Bronc's account, running on a BSD2 box, had been hacked. According to Bronc, a team of two working together under a spoofed IP address managed to break into the root account. The culprits turned off logging, deleted log files, and installed back doors before turning to their main task: defacing Bronc's accounts, and sending a seemingly self-incriminating post to at least one hacker chat list.

 Evil Genius tip: BSD2! Why wasn't the box Bronc used running BSD3, the latest version? Why didn't Bronc upgrade to BSD3 as soon as the first intrusion was detected? Sometimes ISPs will keep a insecure box on their network as a sacrificial server that does nothing except detect computer criminals at work. The fact that all other Succeed.net computers were running BSD3 should have tipped off the attackers.

According to Shadrack, "Culprit . . . single . . . You are using Bronc's GUESS."

What was the motivation? The immediate objective might have been to incite self-styled anti-kiddie porn vigilantes to attack. Because spammers often trick antispammer vigilantes into attacking innocent people, I though it wise to contact _RSnake_ , the leader of Ethical Hackers Against Pedophilia. He assured me that his group is cautious about whom they target and how, and could easily tell this was merely a crude hack. (See *http://www.hackers.com/ehap* for information on this group.)

---

person. As you saw in the chapter on how to fight spam, a favorite tactic of spam purveyors is to trick the people who oppose spam into attacking each other. Don't let me, or anyone, trick you into attacking someone.

The obscene finger information stayed up for over two days. Why didn't Bronc delete it right away? "I left that .plan there on purpose," insisted Bronc.

Remember, too, that Bronc has a job and school, and Robert Lavelock (the owner of succeed.net) has a business to run, so they couldn't simply drop everything and work around the clock. So they were at a disadvantage to the attacking team. They had to focus on their most serious task. But the attackers, judging from their behavior, must have assumed the .plan was staying up because Lavelock and Bronc didn't have the skills to quickly fix the hack.

According to Shadrack, however, "The attackER, works 70 hours a week at his job. To qualify my statement, I know who did the original attack (to a degree. I was on irc with the person who was doing it)."

So far, this was typical hacker war. Nasty words, threats of violence, a lame hack. According to Shadrack, Bronc uploaded dirty joke files to Shadrack's ftp server. Something about a gerbil. Bronc, however, insists he sent nothing of the sort. He says the files he uploaded said things like "You preach freedom of speech, but you censor people who don't agree with you."

Meanwhile, whoever was after Bronc struck back over and over, deleting Bronc's accounts as fast as he could create them. The attacks also became more ingenious.

```
From: Shadrack@dimensional.com
Date: Wed, 8 Oct 1997 20:06:04 -0600 (MDT)
To: Meeshach <Meeshach@erols.com>
cc: "Carolyn P. Meinel" <cmeinel@techbroker.com>
Subject: Re: facelift

>Did Bronc put his .plan back up because I fingered
>bbuster@succeed.net and it was back up again?  Weird!!!

Checking further shows that erik@ has the same plan, and two
interesting forwards. I wouldn't suggest sending mail to that address
lest you find yourself on some interesting mail lists.
```

Soon Robert Lavelock and Bronc were dealing with a team of attackers who continued probing and breaking in—24 hours a day, day after day. The attackers appeared to have no lives, being willing to devote all their waking hours to the task of harassing Bronc.

Shadrack, however disputes the the attacker(s) mounted a nonstop barrage. "The attacker spent less than two hours every three days. If they thought that was a serious attack, they should learn more about computers. The cry of 24/7 attacks is ludicrous."

I asked Bronc why he was important enough to inspire them to spend so much time and take such serious risks. Bronc had no idea.

The problem with these round the clock attacks is that the Succeed.net team was installing new security features and sniffers. But, for a few days there, every time they were on the verge of installing something new, the attackers deleted the files.

To get a breather from the attacks, Lavelock sent a surrender message to whom he assumed were his attackers. Shadrack forwarded a copy to me.

```
From: Shadrack@dimensional.com
Date: Fri, 17 Oct 1997 17:49:45 -0600 (MDT)
```

```
To: Colorado People <col@sekurity.org>
Subject: BBuster has been deleted (fwd)


Victory!@#$!@$#!

———Forwarded message———
Date: Sat, 18 Oct 1997 00:25:47 -0700
From: Robert Lavelock <lavelock@succeed.net>
To: "'Meeshach@erols.com'" <Meeshach@erols.com>
Cc: "'Shadrack@dimensional.com'"<Shadrack@dimensional.com>
Subject: BBuster has been deleted

Due to too much trouble, Bronc Buster user at
Succeed.Net has been deleted.
If you still have trouble from him, it will no longer be from
Succeed.Net.
He was trying to help us catch the culprits, but I have decided that
he no longer needs to be involved with any system functions.
```

According to Shadrack, "You are taking things completely out of context. This letter was in response to me complaining to Robert about Bronc slandering me. This was not in response to 'attackers' hitting their machines. Unlike Bronc, I can provide mail from both sides showing the entire email thread."

The surrender note didn't work, perhaps because the attackers realized it was a trick to buy time. They increased the ferocity of their attacks. But they apparently never asked themselves, why were Lavelock and Bronc trying to buy time?

Shadrack objects, "That attackER knew this was a trick right away. Since I was not in touch with the person at that time, it took Meeshach and I (sic) two days to determine this using finger, monitoring web hits to certain sites, and then Bronc ULing more s*** files to sekurity.org . . . that was a nice give away that he was still using the account despite what Lavelock told me."

The evening of Oct. 21, Bronc and I were on the phone discussing how, on the evening of the 20th, the criminals had taken out the succeed.net mail server. This had blocked all users of Succeed.net from sending or receiving email.

Shadrack adds, "This was not done by the person who rm'd Bronc's account and originally messed with the server as far as I know."

The sophistication of their attacks were increasing. The learning curve looked suspiciously steep. Had the attackers brought in reinforcements?

Then four painfully naive attackers joined the team. Two telneted in without spoofing their IP addresses. They telneted in from their dial-in accounts. As Bronc explains it, "We got logs saying 'Failed login attempt from: dial-12.dumbfoo-bar.psi.com' and such. I'm not sure how many times exactly, but it was a *lot*." The four got into users' accounts using stolen passwords that the sophisticated attackers apparently had given to them from sniffed login sessions. (Lavelock and Bronc had found cached cleartext user names and passwords hidden in a file on a Succeed.net computer.)

You can go to jail warning: Don't use stolen passwords! Seasoned computer criminals will trick newbie hackers into breaking in by giving them passwords.

Then, if the law officers don't know any better, they bust the newbies, leaving the serious criminals free to raid again.

Bronc was looking up something for me in his shell account when he muttered "What?" I heard furious key clicks. "My account's gone. How'd they do that? They had to search through . . . Oh . . ." I heard more clicking sounds. "They rmed . . . Carolyn, got to go!"

The attackers had disabled all logins to the server except from the console, destroying Bronc's traps that he almost had working.

The attackers then left the system alone long enough for Lavelock and Bronc to finish their final set of traps. So when the intruders returned on the 22nd, they discovered they no longer could edit or delete files.

Lavelock and Bronc had implemented TCP Wrappers and used the "chflgs" command to set the files to "append only." This way files couldn't be deleted, but the log files that would record vital evidence could be added to. In addition, they set it up so all logs were being piped to a computer owned by one of the überest of überhackers—Fatal Error.

> **You can go to jail warning: Lots of hackers will tell you that hackers don't try to get computer criminals busted. Sure, if they see people committing crimes that are mostly harmless, like getting inside a stranger's computer but just looking around, hackers don't tell on hackers. But when a computer breakin turns ugly, the best hackers on the planet will join forces to catch the bad guys. Trust me, the Succeed.net attackers are toast.**

Little did the attackers know that this was the least of their troubles. They had never, apparently, questioned why Bronc's accounts, where they had first broken in, as Bronc surmised, through sendmail, were on a relatively insecure BSD2 box.

Shadrack disputes Bronc's version of how they broke in. "Sendmail?! Give up. The fact is, the original break-in was done using a '0day' bug that has never crossed Bugtraq or any other list. It went unnoticed in BSD 2.x, and ended up in BSD 3.x as well. That is the only bug the original attacker used to repeatedly get in. And one other thing . . . that bug works with or without TCP Wrappers."

Can you say "bait"? The attackers had industriously been deleting and editing log files, blind to the fact that their every move had been instantly piped to a secure computer that they never dreamed existed. They had done all this under the watchful eyes of the FBI and a security expert from the AGIS Internet backbone provider—a fellow with the handle Fatal Error.

The attackers were in trouble. Big trouble.

As the attackers began to dimly realize they had messed up, they panicked. They panicked in the worst possible way. Under the blinding light of surveillance, trying to cover up their crime, they put the system into single-user mode, and used ftp to bring in a new operating system. They compiled a new kernel (the heart of an operating system), rebooted the computer, and used it to reformat the hard disk on the main system computer for Succeed.net.

This time the entire ISP was down for 17 hours, ensuring that this had become enough of a crime to trigger a serious attempt to jail the attackers.

You can go to jail warning: It is illegal to break into computer without the permission of the owners. But you might get away with it if you do no harm. Take down an entire ISP, however, and the fools who did it are on a countdown to becoming road kill, yes! on the Information Superhighway.

When it came back up, Succeed.net was now one of the most secure ISPs around. It also was about the least fun for any hacker to use. The owner had disabled nearly all services, including telnet and ftp. Only dialup and Web page access is now allowed. TCP Wrappers is in place.

But the attackers, terrified now that they knew they had blundered into a trap, never came back to see the new defenses.

As of this writing, a reliable source says that one of the attackers had already been picked up and had agreed to work as an informant to gather evidence on the others in exchange for his freedom. Apparently the team had been on a major crime spree, with Bronc being only one of many targets. So you may never see a headline saying the Succeed.net attackers were arrested. But you will someday read of hackers arrested for a rampage in which they wiped out the hard disks of computers.

Meanwhile, the defenses Succeed.net is now using are the price the rest of us pay for the acts of malicious hackers. If the bad guys keep this up long enough, today's deliciously fun ISPs with their shell accounts and lots of ports running lots of services for us to play with will go the way of the dodo birds, which were all clubbed to death by visiting sailors.

Are Hacker Wars Elite?

What do honorable hackers think of hacker war? One of the most famous and respected of us, Silicon Toad, writes, "I consider them taboo and a waste of energy . . ."

So please don't assume that many of us start or approve of these ugly conflicts. I don't. No hacker I respect launches hacker wars.

But unfortunately, there are haxors who like to start these wars. So we need to know how defend ourselves— legally.

What Exactly Are Hacker Wars?

Hacker wars are attempts to damage people or organizations using cyberspace. There are several types of hacker war tactics.

Web Page Hacking

Lots of people ask me, "How do I hack a Web page?" Alas, gentle reader, the first step in this process ought to be physiologically impossible and unsuitable for description in a family publication.

The typical Web page hack begins with getting write permission to the hypertext markup files on the Web server that has been targeted. Amazingly, many Web sites already offer write permission to the general public! If so, all the hacker warrior need do is create a bogus Web page, give it the same name as the desired page on the Web site to be hit, and then transfer it via ftp.

Otherwise it is usually necessary to first break into the Web server computer and gain root or administrative control.

A recent example was a reported attack on the web server raptor.netfubaring.com, which sources say was part of a war between the "sin" (who bring you the Haxor Brothers) and the "confidence remains high" gangs. The attacker allegedly talked a friend who worked for Netfubaring.com into giving him a password so he could deface a few hacker pages on the server. But then the attacker, perhaps afraid that he might get caught if he were on the system too long, decided to just log on briefly and turn loose a program that automatically found every file named "index.html" on the server and replaced it with another file of the same name. This bogus file consisted of, um, blush, certain male anatomy.

Newbie note: On a Web site, the first page is usually named either index.html or index.htm. So if you surf over to http://techbroker.com the first thing you will read will be the file I named "index.htm."

This is typical. Hacked web pages usually consist of dirty pictures and bad language. I have hunted down many hacked Web sites. Wise political analysis, witty repartee and trenchant satire have been absent from every one I have ever seen—with the single exception of one in Indonesia by the East Timor freedom fighter group. Perhaps because they risked their lives to have their say, they made their hack count.

But maybe my standards are too high. Judge for yourself. Parental discretion and anti-nausea medicine advised. Collections of hacked Web pages may be found at *http://www.skeeve.net/* or *http://www.2600.com/hacked_pages*.

However, even if your cause is good and your commentary trenchant, messing up Web sites is a pitiful way to get across a message. They are quickly fixed. You have to hack a really famous Web site to get your hack recorded in an archive.

If you are serious about making a political statement on the Web, the legal and effective way is to get a domain name that is so similar to the site you oppose that lots of people will go there by accident. For example, http://clinton96.org was hilarious, clean, effective, and legal. http://dole96.org was also taken by parody makers. They are both down now. But they were widely reported. Many political sites linked to them!

To get your web spoof domain name, go to http://internic.net. You will save a lot of money by purchasing it directly from them instead of through an intermediary. In fact, all you need to do is promise to buy a domain name. If you get tired of your parody Web site before you pay for it, people have told me they have just given the name back to Internic and no one demanded payment.

You can get punched in the nose warning: If you get a parody domain name so you can put up a Web site that makes fun of big corporation, even though you are not breaking the law, you may get sued. Even if you win the lawsuit, you could spend a lot of money in self defense. But you may be able to get lots of good publicity by alerting reporters to your plight before taking down your Web site. So in the

end, especially if you get sued, you may make your views known to even more people than if you had hacked their Web site.

Here's how to use a legal spoofed Web site in a hacker war. Let's say the guys who are going after you have the Web site *http://evil_haxor_dudes.org*. You can get the domain name *http://evil_haxor_d00dz.org* (substituting zeros for the letter o's), put hilarious stuff there, and then advertise it to hacker mailing lists.

You can get sued warning: A web site parody was put up which included a photo of the girlfriend of the hacker they were making fun of, with a phony solicitation for sexual services. This was libel. If your victim can afford to sue you, you could have to pay out lots of money. For guidelines on how to make fun of people on your Web site in such a way that you are unlikely to get clobbered by lawyers, get *The Associated Press Stylebook and Libel Manual*, **Norm Goldstein, Editor, Addison-Wesley.**

DOS Attacks

A second form of hacker war is denial of service (DOS) attacks. Because they harm many people other than the direct targets, DOS may well be the most serious type of hacker war. Hans Husman has written an excellent tutorial on denial of service attacks, which may be found at *http://www.student.tdb.uu.se/~t95hhu/c-war.html*.

Spammers are a favorite target of DOS warriors. Spammers also, if my sources are telling the truth, fight back. The weapon of choice on both sides is the mail bomb. Spammers also sue anti-spammers.

Recently (June 4, 1997 and Sept.-Oct. 1997), hackers fought a massive war against spammer kingdom Cyber Promotions, Inc., with the AGIS Internet backbone provider caught in the middle. Cyberpromo went to court to force AGIS to give it Internet access (AGIS eventually won and kicked off Cyberpromo). But in the meantime it was seriously hurt by a barrage of computer vandalism.

While those who attacked AGIS probably think they have a better cause than the usual one of offending people, they have been doing more damage than any hacker war in history, and harming a lot of innocent people and companies in the process.

According one source who wrote to me on the AGIS attacks, "The person who really did it 'owned' all of their machines, their routers, and everything else in-between." So, although the attacks on AGIS apparently consisted of computer break-ins, the use of the break-ins was to deny service to users of AGIS.

 Newbie note: An Internet backbone is a super high capacity communications network. It may include fiber optics and satellites and new protocols such as Asynchronous Transfer Mode. An outage in a backbone provider may affect millions of Internet users.

You can go to jail warning: Attacking an Internet backbone provider is an especially easy way to get a long, long stay in a prison.

Other DOS attacks include the ICMP (Internet Control Message Protocol) attacks so familiar to IRC warriors; and an amazing range of attacks on Windows NT systems. *http://www.ntbugtraq.com* has exploit programs for these NT DOS vulnerabilities, while Bronc Buster's *http://showdown.org* is great for Unix DOS attacks. Please note: we are pointing these out so you can study them and test your own computer or computers that you have permission to test.

You can go to jail, get fired and/or get punched in the nose warning: DOS attacks in general are pathetically easy to launch but in some cases hard to defend against. So not only can one get into all sorts of trouble for DOS attacks—people will also laugh at those who do them. "Code kiddie! Lamer!"

Sniffing

Sniffing is observing the activity of one's victim on a network (usually the Internet). This can include grabbing passwords, reading email, and observing telnet sessions.

Sniffer programs can only be installed if one is root on that computer. But your email—and maybe passwords in the clear—may go through 20 or more computers on their way to a final destination. That's a lot of places where a sniffer might be installed. If you really, seriously don't want some hacker vandal who has slipped a sniffer into an Internet backbone computer watching everything you do online, there are several solutions.

The Eudora Pro program will allow you to use the APOP protocol to protect the password you use when you download email. However, this will not protect the email itself from snoopers.

If you have a shell account, Secure Shell (ssh) from Datafellows will encrypt everything that passes between your home and shell account computers. You can also set up an encrypted tunnel from one computer on which you have a shell account to a second shell account on another computer—if both are running Secure Shell. Warning: I have found that when using ssh to go to one shell and then ssh to telnet into yet another shell account, things can get really slow.

Important note: To keep your login password from being sniffed you must use the RSA login option, not the "password" login option.

You may download a free ssh server program for Unix at ftp://sunsite.unc.edu/pub/packages/security/ssh, or check out http://www.cs.hut.fi/ssh.

If you are a sysadmin or owner of an ISP, you can keep sniffers in the dark by running kerberos on your LAN.

For a client version of ssh that will run on your Windows, Mac or any version of Unix computer, see the DataFellows site at http://www.datafellows.com/. But remember, your shell account must be running the ssh server program in order for your Windows ssh client to work.

To get on the ssh discussion list, email majordomo@clinet.fi with message "subscribe ssh."

But ssh, like APOP, will not protect your email. The solution? Encryption. PGP is popular and can be purchased at http://pgp.com. But PGP offers two algorithms,

RSA and Diffie-Hellman. But the RSA encryption algorithm is the more secure of the two.

Newbie note: Encryption is scrambling up a message so that it is very hard for anyone to unscramble it unless they have the right key, in which case it becomes easy to unscramble.

Evil genius tip: While the RSA algorithm is the best one known, an encryption program may implement it in an insecure manner. Worst of all, RSA depends upon the unproveable mathematical hypothesis that there is no polynomial time bounded algorithm for factoring numbers. That's a good reason to keep up on math news!

The key plot element of the movie *Sneakers* was a fictional discovery of a fast algorithm to factor numbers. Way to go, *Sneakers* writer/producer Larry Lasker!

You can go to jail warning: In some countries there are legal restrictions on encryption. In the US, the International Traffic in Arms Regulations forbids export of any encryption software good enough to be worth using.

Social Engineering

In the alleged "sin" vs. "confidence remains high" gang war, a key exploit supposedly was to talk a sysadmin at Netfubaring.com into giving out a password. This is "social engineering."

Social engineering usually consists of telling lies that are poorly thought through. But a skilled social engineer can convince you that he or she is doing you a big favor while getting you to give away the store. A really skilled social engineer can get almost any information out of you without even telling a lie.

According to the book *Corporate Espionage* by Ira Winkler, one hacker posted his home phone number on the bulletin board of a large company, telling the employees to call him for technical support. He provided great tech support. In exchange, he got lots of passwords. If he had been smart, he would have gotten a real tech support job. But then I can never figure out some of these haxor types.

ISP Hostage Taking

A favorite ploy of the aggressor in a hacker war is to attack the victim's Internet account. Then they trumpet around how this proves the victim is a lamer.

But none of us is responsible for managing the security at the ISPs we use. Of course, one could get a domain name, set up a computer with lots of security and hook it directly to an Internet backbone provider with a 24 hr phone connection. It would cost one heck of a lot of money, but then we could take responsibility for our own Internet host. But as we learned from the AGIS attacks, even Internet backbones can get taken down. So we are always held hostage to the security of whatever company connects us to the Internet.

But those of us without money to burn would rather make do with an account with an ISP (Internet service provider).

If you point this out, that you are not the guy running security on the ISP you use, bad guy hackers will insult you by claiming that if you really knew something, you would get a "secure" ISP. Yeah, right. Here's why it is always easy to break into your account on an ISP, and almost impossible for your ISP to keep hackers out.

While it is hard to break into almost any computer system from the outside, there are vastly more exploits that will get you superuser (root) control from inside a shell account. So all your attacker needs to do is buy an account, or even use the limited time guest account many ISPs offer, and this bad guy is ready to run rampant.

You can increase your security by using an ISP that only offers PPP (point to point) accounts. This is one reason that it is getting difficult to get a shell account. Thanks, Super Duper Haxor d00dz, for ruining the Internet for the rest of us.

But even an ISP that just offers PPP accounts is more vulnerable than the typical computer system you will find in a large corporation. This is because your ISP must be easy to use.

Because it is easy to break into almost any ISP, haxor d00d types think it is kewl to take an ISP hostage by repeatedly breaking in and vandalizing it until the owner surrenders by kicking off the victim of the attacks.

Why Should I Give a Darn?—Ways Bystanders Get Hurt

To most people, hacker wars are Legion of Doom vs. Masters of Destruction stuff. Interesting, but like reading science fiction. What does it have to do with your life? You may figure that if you never do anything that gets some haxor mad, you won't have a problem.

Yet chances are that you may already have been brushed by hacker war. Have you ever tried to login to your online provider and couldn't make a connection? Did you call tech support and they told you they were "down for maintenance"? Tried to send email and gotten a message "cannot send mail now. Please try again later"? Sent email that disappeared into cyberspace without a trace? Gotten email back with a "User unknown" or worse yet, "host unknown" message, but you knew that address was good? Been unable to surf to your favorite Web site?

It could have been technical error (cough, cough). But it may have been more. A cardinal rule of almost all online services is to never, ever admit in public to being hacked. Only if a reporter "outs" them first will they reluctantly admit to the attack.

It is common for hacker wars that start as a private disagreement to spill over and affect thousands or even millions of bystanders. For example, in Sept. 1996, syn flood attackers shut down the Panix ISP for several days. As noted above, in Oct. 1997, the ISP Succeed.net was shut down several times by a team of hackers. Many other ISPs have suffered shutdowns from hacker wars, often because the attackers objected to political views expressed on their Web pages.

Tomorrow these skirmishes could pit nation against nation and spread throughout the infrastructure that is controlled by computers: power grids that serve hundreds of millions failing in the dead of winter; air traffic control systems going awry with planes crashing; hundreds of billions, trillions of dollars in banking systems disappearing without a trace. Pearl Harbor. Digital Pearl Harbor. Famine. It could be years before we could climb out of an economic collapse as bad as the Great Depression.

Winn Schwartau has been warning the world of this since June of 1991. Someone must be listening, because in September 1997 an industry group formed in the wake of hearings by the US Senate's Permanent Subcommittee on Investigations appointed Schwartau leader of the Manhattan Cyber Project Information Warfare/Electronic Civil Defense team. For more information, see *http://www. warroomresearch.com* and *http://www.infowar.com.* Or read Schwartau's book *Information Warfare*, published by Thunder's Mouth Press.

Those of us who have been on the front lines of cyberwar have seen these attacks first hand. We know what it does to us, and we know what it does to bystanders.

Why You May Wind Up in the Bullseye

Hacker war targets other people, right? Spammers get hacked. Hacker gangs pick fights with each other. But if you behave politely around other hackers, you are safe, right?

Wrong. Dead wrong.

Let's look at an example of a hacker war, one that doesn't seem to have any motivation at all. We're talking the Internet Chess Club. Not exactly controversial. In mid Sept. 1996 it was shut down for many days by a syn flood attack.

Many hacker wars are instigated by gangs that want to suppress other people's freedom of speech.

Jamie McCarthy is director of operations for the Nizkor Project (http://www.nizkor.org/). This Web site is about the Holocaust, including attempts by historical revisionists to deny that it happened. McCarthy reports that they are frequently targeted by mail bombings seeking to shut them down.

In July 1997, the nonprofit Institute for Global Communications came under cyber attack for hosting a Basque independence Web site. The protest was launched against the Basque terrorist group ETA's kidnapping and killing of a Spanish politician that month.

Attacks included, according to spokeswoman Maureen Mason, "thousands of anonymous hits to our mail servers from hundreds of different mail relays, with bogus return addresses," "spamming our staff accounts (apparently scoured off our own Web page) and IGC member accounts (Usenet postings from Spain have encouraged people to do AltaVista searches for "@igc.org" addresses); clogging our orders Web page with bogus credit card orders; and threats to employ the same tactics against organizations using IGC services."

You guessed it, the Happy Hacker list and yours truly have also been targeted by one battle after another. For example, on Dec. 6, 1996, someone had written to the dc-stuff list saying:

```
I think they (or maybe 'we') will survive, Carolyn's book.
```

Rogue Agent replied:

```
I'm just doing my part to make sure that it doesn't happen.  Ask not
what the network can do for you, ask what you can do for the network.
We shall fight them in the routers, we shall fight them in the fiber,
we shall fight them in the vaxen... I'm an activist, and I won't
stop my activism just because I know others will take it too far.
     —Rogue Agent, posting to the dc-stuff email list.
```

Two weeks later, on Dec 20, Rogue Agent wrote to me:

```
Ask Netta Gilboa; her magazine's in shambles and her boyfriend's in
prison, while she lives in fear. Ask Josh Quittner (coauthor of
Masters of Deception); for a while there, he had to change his
(unlisted) phone number literally every two weeks because of the
nightly anonymous calls he was getting. Somehow they always got the
new number.  Ask John Markoff (coauthor of the hacker best-seller
Takedown); he can't even let people know what his email account is
or he gets spammed the next day.

This is not a threat... All I'm doing is telling you what's coming...
you're playing with fire. There is a darker element in my culture,
and you're going to meet it if you keep going.
```

Five days later, while it was still dark on Christmas morning, the owner of the Southwest Cyberport ISP (where I had an account) was awakened by an alarm. His mail server was down. A massive mailbombing by someone styling himself johnny xchaotic had been sent to me—and took out everyone else's mail with it. Shadrack surfaced as the public spokesman for the attacker, claiming intimate knowledge of johnny xchaotic's techniques and motivations.

Three days later, the evening of Dec. 28, someone cracked the dedicated box that Cibola Communications had been providing at no cost to run the Happy Hacker majordomo. The intruder erased the system files and sent email to the owners threatening worse mayhem if they didn't cave in and boot us off. The attackers also wiped the system files from a computer at the University of Texas at El Paso that I was using for research, and sent threats to all email addresses on that box.

This was but the first of many hacker barrages against us. Damaged computers, threats, extortion, blackmail. But after awhile it gets kind of boring, yawn—just kidding.

 Newbie note: In case you are wondering whether you can get killed in one of these battles, I have found no reports, not even rumors, of any hacker war deaths. If someone should threaten to kill you, you should, however, report it and any associated hacker attacks. Despite what you may hear, those of us hackers who are not computer criminals cooperate enthusiastically with law enforcement.

How to Get into a Hacker War

"I want to fight in a hacker war. How do I get in?"

I get email like this all the time. Many newbie hackers long for my frequent experiences of being attacked by talented gangs of computer criminals. The excitement! The opportunity to go mano a mano with bad dudes and prove you are better than them!

There is some truth to this view. To be honest, I get a thrill fighting those criminals—using legal tactics, of course. While I have never turned in someone who was merely doing harmless but illegal experimentation, yes, I do help the Feds catch criminals!

But then I also enjoy taming wild horses, and those critters can kill you. So don't be too eager to get into a situation where you must stand up to the worst that the criminals can throw at you.

I've survived. I'm still active on the Internet. And, shoot, I'm just an old lady. So if you, too, want to attract a hacker war, be my guest.

So just how do you get into a hacker war? As you might guess from the Succeed.net story, the easiest way is to attend a hacker convention. There are all sorts of twisted people at these things, kind of like the bar scene in Star Wars. "He said, he doesn't like the way you look."

Another good way is to write articles or books about hackers, as Gilboa, Markoff, Quittner, and I have all learned.

Or you could get into a war the easy way by teasing some hacker who lacks a sense of humor.

Another way to get into a hacker war is to find one aready raging and jump in. Every time a major war gets to raging about me, chivalrous hacker gentlemen offer to commit crimes against the culprits.

This is no good! My attackers are not worth risking a long vacation in jail. You also may harm the innocent while dishing out vigilante justice. Don't expect me to pat you on the back for breaking the law on my behalf.

How to Keep from Getting Caught

So you want to be the attacker in a hacker war? So you think you can keep from getting caught? Guess what. No one is talented enough to teach you how to keep from getting caught. I'll tell you exactly why, too.

At that infamous Def Con V panel I hosted, Shadrack boasted to the audience that "When I break in, I close the doors behind me." He makes a big deal about how hackers can keep from getting busted by deleting or modifying log files.

Let me tell you the *real* story about what happens when hackers think they are covering their tracks. Sure, an ordinary sysadmin can't restore a deleted file on a Unix system. But there are people out there with the technology to restore deleted files—even files that have been overwritten hundred of times. There are people out there who can extract everything that has ever been on a hard disk for the last several months—or years.

An example of a law firm that specializes in extracting data from hacked hard disks is Computer forensics, *http://www.forensics.com*.

Or there could be some 31337 haxor sitting at his box raising hell and "closing doors after him." What he doesn't know is that thanks to a court order inspired by his boasts, someone is sitting in a van a hundred yards away—picking up every keystroke. It's Van Eck radiation, luser.[2] Or maybe the authorities are picking up the signals that run down the power cord of your computer. Ever heard of Tempest? The US National Security Agency has spent many years figuring out how to eavesdrop on electronic communications.

Even if the cybercrime detective doesn't have all this high-tech hardware on hand, the history of hacker crime shows that criminals will talk in exchange for lenient sentencing or even getting away free. Commit one easy-to-prove federal felony, let's say posting someone's stolen email on one's public ftp server, and the Feds have lots of bargaining power against that dummy. Soon his friends will amazingly enough start getting arrested.

So even if I wanted to help people become uncatchable übercriminals, I can't. Not because I don't know how. Because there is no way. The 31337 d00dz who tell you otherwise are seriously ignorant.

I predict that the Succeed.net attackers, whoever they may be, will wind up in jail. Soon. Perhaps not for that particular crime. But their days of freedom are numbered. It is only a matter of picking which of their many crimes will hold up best in court, and who will give evidence against whom. Time for the criminals to study game theory—"prisoners' dilemma."

"But, but," I can hear Super Duper computer criminals sputtering. "My buddies and I break the law all the time and we've never been busted. Okay, okay, my other buddy got busted, but he was layme."

It's just a matter of time. Go straight before your number is up. Or make the decision to obtain your "get out of jail free" card by informing on your friends before they trade info on you first for their freedom.

Hacker War Techniques that Don't Break the Law

What, getting caught up in a hacker war doesn't sound immensely entertaining? You don't want to be the innocent bystander caught in the crossfire of an rm * or fdisk command? Here are a few techniques that can help you. But remember, these are only the most basic of protections.

If you are a sysadmin, there are plenty of resources out there. For starters, tighten up the security holes in your system by studying the Bugtraq and NT Bugtraq archives. Another great resource may be your Internet backbone provider. For example, MCI has released the free "Denial of Service Tracker" at *http://www.se-*

---

2 See "Electromagnetic Radiation from Video Display Units: An Eavesdropping Risk?" by Wim Van Eck, *Computers & Security*, 1985, Vol. 4.

curity.mci.net. This program works against SYN, ICMP flood, bandwidth saturation, and concentrated source attacks.

Of course, law enforcement people can help you deal with chronically destructive attackers. No one wants to deal with d00dz who have nothing better to do with their lives than attempt to destroy computer systems 24 hours a day, seven days a week. D00dz who are this far gone definitely need an extended vacation, at government expense—in jail.

But you need to be patient with law enforcement, and find ways to help. Remember, there is lots of computer crime, yet few law enforcement people have learned how to fight it.

It is essential to start by showing the authorities that you are dealing with a serious crime. If it is just some kid harmlessly looking around, forget it. Give the kid a break.

You also should be prepared to help gather forensic evidence. Make sure your logs get piped immediately off the system to a secure box. As with Succeed.net, detectives welcome us good guy hackers when we can help them by setting traps to catch computer criminals in the act.

Here's an important tip for how to make sure your syslog files accurately show who is getting onto your computer. Most versions of syslog take the IP address (a numerical address) of your visitor and automatically look up the domain name and log that instead of the IP. But the Domain Name Server syslog uses almost certainly uses cached information, which can easily be out of date. A solution is to specify that it use a root DNS server for lookups. Of course, this doesn't work if you are dealing with a spoofed IP address.

Remember that a good investigation moves slowly. The computer crime detectives want to make sure the right guys get arrested, that the charges will stick, and they will get a long, government-paid vacation as the girlfriends of cell mate Spike.

What if you are a just a user with shell and POP accounts to defend? Here are some easy ways to make hacker wars easier to survive.

Top Ten Defenses in Hacker Wars

10) Backup, backup, backup.

9) Assume anything is being sniffed, unless protected by strong encryption.

8) Assume your phone is tapped.

7) Never, never, ever telnet into your shell account unless you are on a direct dialup connection to your ISP. Use Secure Shell instead.

6) Pick a good password. It should be long, not a name or a word from a dictionary, and should include numbers and/or characters such as !@#$%^&*(. If you use a computer where others have physical access to it, don't write your password down.)

5) Assume your attacker will get root or administrative control anyhow, so your password won't do you any good.

4) Don't keep sensitive files or email addresses in your shell account. Your saved mail files are a good place for the bad guy to find email addresses.

3) Regularly patrol your Web site. You never know when it may sprout rude body parts.

2) Maintain your sense of humor. If they rattle you, they have won.
And, the number one defense:

1) Pray

"Wait, wait," you say. "I don't want to play pure defense. I want to fight back—legally!" Okay, here are some ways to deal severely with your attackers. But don't come crying to me if these tactics lead to the biggest hacker war in history!

10) Report the attackers to every ISP they use in their assault. Be sure to provide evidence rather than merely saying "Those guys are dorks." People who start hacker wars are usually not terribly welcome. Chances are you can get them kicked off their accounts.

9) Be friends with the sysadmins at your ISP. When those haxor d00dz attempt to break in, your sysadmin friends may invite you to sit at the console with them and help them mess with the bad guys' heads. This can be insanely funny, especially in a case like the Succeed.net hack where the attackers thought they were being sooo elite.

8) Put up an insultingly funny Web site with a similar URL to their Evil Haxor web site, and advertise it widely.

7) Send out email that makes fun of their user names and flame style. For example, one of the gangs that has attacked me signs its destructive work "G.A.L.F." They often work out of escape.com. So I got the email address galfina@escape.com to tease them from.

6) Port surf any computers on which you know they are root and leave humorous messages in the syslog file. Better yet, run SATAN against them every hour.

5) Figure out how to break into their computers and then don't. Instead, explain to them their security flaws and tell how to fix them. There shall be much gnashing of teeth!

4) If you see them at a hacker con, be super friendly. Wave at them across a room and shout a cheerful greeting that all may hear. Offer to buy them dinner.

3) If they work for an ISP, get an account there. Leave torturous shell log files that will keep them puzzling until late every night.

2) If you run into them on IRC, pretend to be a woman.

And the number one way to get back at your attackers:

1) Tell them you are actually Carolyn Meinel.

Section 4, Chapter 1
The History of Hacking

Here it is, the history of hacking like it has never been told before. Who are we? Where did we come from? Where are we going now?

Where shall we start? How about 17 years before this book was written, and the World Science Fiction Convention in Boston, Massachusetts. Back then, in 1980, the World Cons were the closest thing we had to hacker conventions. We're talking about a time when personal computers numbered in the thousands. Ted Nelson is running around World Con with his Xanadu guys: his top sidekick, Roger Gregory; H. Keith Henson, now waging war against the Scientologists; and K. Eric Drexler, later to build the Foresight Institute. They dream of creating what is to become the World Wide Web.

Nowadays guys at hacker cons might dress like vampires or have all sorts of body parts pierced. In 1980 they wear identical black baseball caps with silver wings and the slogan: "Xanadu: wings of the mind." The hotel staff has to close the swimming pool in order to halt the sex orgies. We're insanely excited over the CP/M operating system and Apple and those new 300 baud modems.

Oh, but this is hardly the dawn of hacking. Let's look again at the Boston area, but yet another seventeen years further back, the early 60s. At the Massachusetts Institute of Technology (MIT) students are warring for control of the school's mainframe computers. They use machine language programs that each strive to delete all other programs and seize control of the central processing unit. Back then there are no personal computers.

In 1962 Paul Baran of the Rand Corp. think tank, yes, the place that cooks up strategies for fighting nuclear war and defeating the Viet Cong, publishes a paper, *On Distributed Communications Networks*. This is the birth of what becomes "packet switched network" technology. Little does the outside world realize the earth-shaking events that will follow. But computer scientists at MIT and the University of California at Los Angels (UCLA) see the future and join in on developing this new communications technology.

In 1965, Ted Nelson, later to become leader of that silver wing-headed Xanadu gang, first coins the word "hypertext" to describe what will someday become the World Wide Web. Nelson later spreads the gospel in his book *Literacy Online*. The back cover shows a Superman-type figure flying and the slogan "You can and must learn to use computers now."

But in 1965 the computer is widely feared as a source of Orwellian powers. Yes, as in George Orwell's ominous novel, *1984*, that predicted a future in which technology would squash all human freedom. Few are listening to Nelson. Few see the wave of free-spirited anarchy the hacker culture is already unleashing. Technology is our enemy, right? Tune in, turn on, drop out, right? But LSD guru Timothy Leary's daughter Susan begins to study computer programming.

Around 1966, Robert Morris Sr., the future NSA chief scientist, decides to mutate these early hacker wars into the first "safe hacking" environment. He and two friends code a game they call "Darwin." Later "Darwin" becomes "Core War," a free-form computer game played to this day by some of the uberest of uberhackers.

Let's jump to 1968 and the scent of tear gas. Wow, look at those rocks hurling through the windows of the computer science building at the University of Illinois at Urbana- Champaign! Outside are 60s antiwar protesters. Their enemy, they believe, is the campus' Advanced Research Projects Agency computer system: Plato. Inside are nerdz high on caffeine and nitrous oxide. Under the direction of Roger Johnson, they gang together four CDC 6400s and link them to 1024 dumb vector graphics terminals. Plato becomes the first realization of cyberspace. Plato terrifies the shaggy-haired protesters—is it *1984* on the march?

Also in 1968 Great Britain's National Physical Laboratory sets up the first test network to try out packet switching.

In fact, 1968 turns out to be the most portent-filled year yet for hacking.

Around Labor Day that year, the US Defense Department's Advanced Research Projects Agency funds a second project to hook together four mainframe computers so researchers can share their resources. Based at UCLA, this system doesn't boast the vector graphics of the Plato system. Its terminals just show ASCII characters: letters and numbers. Boring, huh?

But this new network, which becomes known as ARPAnet, is eminently hackable. Within a year, its users hack together a new way to ship text files around. They call their unauthorized, unplanned invention "email." ARPAnet has developed a life independent of its creators. It's a story that will later repeat itself in many forms. No one can control cyberspace. They can't even control it when it is just four computers big.

Little do the people who first link those four ARPAnet computers know that they have launched the network that would grow forever.

In 1969 John Goltz teams up with a money man to found Compuserve using the new packet switched technology being pioneered by ARPAnet.

1969 also is the year of a remarkable birth at Bell Labs as Ken Thompson invents a new operating system: Unix. It is to become the gold standard of hacking and the Internet, the operating system with the power to perform miracles of computer legerdemain.

Steve Crocker writes the first RFC (request for comments).

In 1971, Abbie Hoffman and the Yippies found the first hacker/phreaker magazine, YIP/TAP (Youth International Party—Technical Assistance Program). YIP/TAP essentially invents phreaking—the sport of playing with phone systems in ways the owners never intended. They are motivated by the Bell Telephone monopoly with its high long distance rates, and a hefty tax that Hoffman and many others refuse to pay as their protest against the Vietnam War. What better way to pay no phone taxes than to pay no phone bill at all?

Blue boxes burst onto the scene. Their oscillators automate the whistling sounds that had already enabled people like Captain Crunch (John Draper) to become the pirate captains of the Bell Telephone megamonopoly. Suddenly phreakers are able to actually make money at their hobby. Hans and Gribble peddle blue boxes on the Stanford University campus.

1972 the InterNetworking Working Group (INWG) is created to agree upon ARPAnet protocols. Chairman is Vinton Cerf, later to become acclaimed for this and later work as the "father of the Internet."

In June 1972, the radical left magazine *Ramparts*, in the article "Regulating the Phone Company In Your Home" publishes the schematics for a variant on the blue box known as the "mute box." This article violates Californian State Penal Code section 502.7, which outlaws the selling of "plans or instructions for any instrument, apparatus, or device intended to avoid telephone toll charges." California police, aided by Pacific Bell officials, seize copies of the magazine from newsstands and the magazine's offices. The financial stress drives them bankrupt.

As the Vietnam War winds down, the first flight simulator program in history unfolds on the Plato network. Computer graphics, almost unheard of in that day, are displayed by touch-sensitive vector graphics terminals. Cyberpilots all over the US pick out their crafts: Phantoms, MIGs, F-104s, the X-15, Sopwith Camels. Virtual pilots fly out of digital airports and try to shoot each other down and bomb each others' airports. While flying a Phantom, a player sees a chat message on the bottom of her screen. "I'm about to shoot you down." Oh, no, a MIG on my tail. She dives and turns hoping to get her tormentor into her sights. The screen goes black. Her terminal displays the message "You just pulled 37 Gs. You now look more like a pizza than a human being as you slowly flutter to Earth."

One day the Starship Enterprise barges in on our simulator, shoots everyone down and vanishes back into cyberspace. Plato has been hacked! Even in 1973 multiuser game players have to worry about getting "smurfed"! (When a hacker breaks into a multiuser game on the Internet and kills players with techniques that are not rules of the game, this is called "smurfing.")

1975. Oh blessed year! Under an Air Force contract, in the city of Albuquerque, New Mexico, the Altair is born. Altair. The first microcomputer. Bill Gates provides the operating system. Then Bill's mom persuades him to move to Redmond, WA where she has some money men who want to see what this operating system business is all about. The seed that will grow into Microsoft has been planted.

Also in 1975, the US Defense Department, which still owns ARPAnet, puts out the welcome mat. Private computer networks begin to link up with it. The world of computer networks is still friendly, a global village where everyone knows everyone else and trust reigns.

Remember Hans and Gribble? They join Silicon Valley's Home Brew Computer club and choose Motorola microprocessors to build their own. They begin selling their computers, which they brand name the Apple, under their real names of Steve Wozniak and Steve Jobs. A computer religion is born.

The great Apple/Microsoft battle is joined. Us hackers suddenly have boxes that beat the heck out of Tektronix terminals.

1975 is also the year that Raphael Finkel first releases the *Jargon File*, which is the dictionary used by hackers and other computer obsessives of all sorts.

In 1978, Ward Christenson and Randy Suess write the first personal computer bulletin board software. Soon, linked by nothing more than the long distance telephone network and these bulletin board nodes, hackers create a new, private cyberspace. Phreaking becomes more important than ever to connect to distant BBSs without running up impossibly high phone bills.

Also in 1978, The Source and Compuserve computer networks are now catering to recreational users. Even though the interface is pure text, little more than email, chat, news groups and file transfer protocol, users quickly discover the possibilities. "Naked Lady" runs rampant on Compuserve chat groups (actually quite staid in real life) and naughty image files are traded across the wires. The first cybercafe, Planet Earth, opens in Washington, DC. X.25 communications protocol networks reign supreme.

1979 is the year that Usenet comes to life, founded by Tom Truscott and Steve Bellovin. It begins as a group of people sharing ideas and figuring out problems with Unix. But soon Usenet news groups proliferate to discuss physics, aeronautics, sex, obnoxious jokes, pets, and on and on.

In 1980, the "414 Gang" is raided. Phreaking is more hazardous than ever.

In 1980 ARPAnet begins planning for a mutation. This is completed on Jan. 1, 1983, when it catapults from Network Control Protocol, which had limited its reach to 256 computers, to Transmission Control Protocol/Internet Protocol (TCP/IP). Now ARPAnet can span tens of millions of hosts! Thus in 1980-83 the Internet is conceived within the womb of the DoD's ARPAnet. The framework that would someday unite hackers around the world is now in place. Plato fades, forever limited to four mainframes and 1024 terminals.

Famed science fiction author Jerry Pournelle discovers ARPAnet. Soon his fans are swarming to find excuses—or whatever—to get onto ARPAnet. ARPAnet's administrators are surprisingly easygoing about granting accounts, especially to people in the academic world.

ARPAnet is a pain in the rear to use, and doesn't transmit visuals of fighter planes mixing it up. But unlike the glitzy Plato, unlike the chatty Compuserve and Source, ARPAnet is really hackable and now has what it takes to grow. Unlike the network of hacker bulletin boards, people don't need to choose between expensive long distance phone calls or phreaking to make their connections. It's all local and it's all free.

In the early 80s hackers already love to pull pranks. Joe College sits down at his dumb terminal to his university's DEC 10 and decides to poke around the campus network. Here's Star Trek! Here's Adventure! Zork! Hmm, what's this program called Sex? He runs it. A message pops up: "Warning: playing with sex is hazardous. Are you sure you want to play? Y/N"

Who can resist? With that "Y" the screen bursts into a display of ASCII characters, then up comes the message: "Proceeding to delete all files in this account." Joe is weeping, cursing, jumping up and down. He gives the list files command. Nothing!

Zilch! Nada! He runs to the sysadmin. They log back into his account but his files are all still there. A prank.

1981 the IBM Personal Computer swaggers onto the stage powered by Bill Gates and his Microsoft MS-DOS operating system. The empire of the CP/M operating system falls. Hard. Within the next two years, essentially all microcomputer operating systems except MS-DOS and those offered by Apple will be dead, and a thousand Silicon Valley fortunes shipwrecked. The Amiga hangs on by a thread. Prices plunge, and soon all self-respecting hackers own their own computers. Sneaking around college labs at night in hopes of making magic with terminals fades from the scene.

In 1983 hackers are still almost all harmless pranksters and geeky guys who eat, sleep and breathe computers, folks who for the most part keep their distance from the guys who break the law. MIT's *Jargon File* defines hacker as merely "a person who enjoys learning about computer systems and how to stretch their capabilities; a person who programs enthusiastically and enjoys dedicating a great deal of time to computers."

In 1983 a piece of ARPAnet buds off to form the US Department of Defense's MILNET. Military funding of ARPAnet innovations wane. But the freedom and reach of the network of networks that centers around ARPAnet is so wonderful that ARPAnet lives on. Some say that this is the year that the Internet was born.

1984 the US National Science Foundation's Office of Advanced Scientific Computing gets into the act. Building on ARPAnet, it creates NSFnet, a civilian branch of ARPAnet. Then the US National Aeronautics and Space Administration, National Institutes of Health and Department of Energy join the party, laying more connections, linking more computers. Outside the US, other networks also continue to grow and link. There are now so many networks connected through ARPAnet and Transmission Control Protocol/Internet Protocol that we are calling this spontaneous creation the Internet.

In 1984 Emmanuel Goldstein launches *2600: The Hacker Quarterly*. The Legion of Doom hacker gang forms. Congress passes the Comprehensive Crime Control Act giving the US Secret Service jurisdiction over computer fraud. Fred Cohen, at Carnegie Mellon University, writes his PhD thesis on the brand new thing called computer viruses.

1984. It was to be the year, thought millions of Orwell fans, that the government would finally get its hands on enough high technology to become Big Brother. We would all be crushed into a faceless sea of identical automata, meekly working and shopping and void of dreams.

Instead, science fiction author William Gibson, writing *Neuromancer* on a manual typewriter, coins the term and paints the first picture of "cyberspace." "Case was the best . . . who ever ran in Earth's computer matrix. Then he doublecrossed the wrong people . . ."

In 1984 the first US police "sting" bulletin board systems appear. The Internet now links 1,000 computers.

1985 is the birth of the hacker ezine *Phrack*, which continues to this day to provide excellent, although inflammatorily worded information on "topics of interest to the international computer underground."

The 80s are the war dialer era. Despite ARPAnet and the X.25 networks, the vast majority of computers can only be accessed by discovering their individual phone lines. Thus one of the most treasured prizes of the 80s hacker is a phone number to some mystery computer.

Computers of this era might be running any of dozens of arcane operating systems and using many communications protocols. Manuals for these systems are often secret. The hacker scene operates on the mentor principle. Unless you can find someone who will induct you into the inner circle of a hacker gang that has accumulated documents salvaged from dumpsters or stolen in burglaries, you are way behind the pack. Kevin Poulson makes a name for himself through daring burglaries of Pacific Bell.

1986 NSFnet gets a 56Kbps backbone. This is the speed that we can get today with a cheap modem over an ordinary phone line, but back then it was remarkable. That 56Kbps backbone was all that held together most US Internet users.

1987. The Internet now spans 10,000 computers.

Despite the barriers to knowledge faced by hackers, despite the rarity of networked computers, by 1988 hacking has entered the big time. According to a list of hacker groups compiled by the editors of *Phrack* magazine on August 8, 1988, the US alone hosts hundreds of them.

The US Secret Service, recently charged with the task of fighting computer crime, covertly videotapes the 1988 SummerCon hackers' convention.

1988. Jarkko Oikarinen writes the first IRC (Internet Relay Chat) program. Now hackers who have Internet access have a place to gather.

In 1988 Robert Tappan Morris, son of NSA chief scientist Robert Morris Sr., yes, son of the man who co-invented the Core War game, yes, son of the man who co-invented safe hacking, writes an exploit that will forever be known as the Morris Worm. It uses a combination of finger and sendmail exploits to break into a computer, copy itself and then send copy after copy on to other computers. Morris, with little comprehension of the power of this exponential replication, releases it onto the Internet.

Soon 10% of the 60,000 Internet hosts of that day are filled with worms and are clogging communications links as they send copies of these worms in hunt of other vulnerable computers. Operators shut down the young Internet as they scramble to diagnose the worm and devise remedies. Morris is arrested, but gets off with probation.

1989 the NSFNET backbone is speeded up to a T1 (1.544Mbps).

In 1990 ARPAnet formally dies. But it is only the death of a name. Its users barely notice the change, for the network that ARPAnet had become is now the Internet. It is the network that will never die. It now spans 100,000 computers, ten times as many as it held only two years before, 100 times what it linked in 1984.

1990 is the next pivotal year for the Internet, almost as significant as 1980 and the launch of TCP/IP. Inspired by Nelson's Xanadu and work at the Xerox Palo Alto Research Center, Tim Berners-Lee of the European Laboratory for Particle Physics (CERN) conceives of a new way to implement hypertext. He calls it the World Wide Web. In 1991 he quietly unleashes it on the world. Cyberspace will never be the same. Nelson's Xanadu, like Plato, like CP/M, is too little, too late and fades. But the spirit Nelson unleashed with his concept of hypertext is soon to revolutionize cyberspace.

1990 is also a year of unprecedented hacker raids and arrests. The US Secret Service and New York State Police raid Phiber Optik, Acid Phreak, and Scorpion in New York City, and arrest Terminus, Prophet, Leftist, and Urvile. The Chicago Task Force arrests Knight Lightning and raids Robert Izenberg, Mentor, and Erik Bloodaxe. It raids both Richard Andrews' home and business. The US Secret Service and Arizona Organized Crime and Racketeering Bureau conduct Operation Sundevil raids in Cincinnatti, Detroit, Los Angeles, Miami, Newark, Phoenix, Pittsburgh, Richmond, Tucson, San Diego, San Jose, and San Francisco. A famous unreasonable raid that year was the Chicago Task Force invasion of Steve Jackson Games, Inc.

In June 1990 Mitch Kapor and John Perry Barlow react to the excesses of these raids to found the Electronic Frontier Foundation. Its initial purpose is to protect hackers. They succeed in getting law enforcement to back off from the hacker community. Later the EFF will fight those who would censor the Internet or violate the privacy of its users.

1991 the business world first invades the Internet.

In 1992 US Vice Presidential candidate Al Gore tells voters that if elected, he and Bill Clinton will build a "National Information Superhighway." The NSFNET backbone upgrades to a T3 (44.736Mbps).

1993 over one million computers link together through the Internet..

In 1993, Marc Andreesson and Eric Bina of the National Center for Supercomputing Applications release Mosaic, the first WWW browser that can show graphics. Finally, for the first time after the fade out of Plato, we have decent cyberspace graphics! This time, however, graphics are here to stay.

Mosaic takes the Internet by storm, driving a 341,634% annual growth rate in Web traffic that year. Soon the Web becomes the number one way that hackers boast and spread the codes for their exploits. Bulletin boards, with their tightly held secrets, fade from the scene. Andreesson goes on to co-found Netscape.

In 1993, the first Def Con invades Las Vegas, courtesy of Jeff Moss. The era of hacker cons moves into full swing with the Beyond Hope series, HoHocon and more.

1994 two Arizona lawyers, Laurence Canter and Martha Siegel, mail their offer to sell legal help to foreign nationals to obtain green card work permits in the United States . . . to over 6000 newsgroups! They have just invented spam. With the threat of the Internet being drowned in junk email at stake, the shadow war between hackers and spammers has begun.

Also in 1994, Stanford University offers a free Usenet search service. Email your question, and their software emails you back with relevant Usenet posts. It is the birth of the Yahoo search service. By the end of 1994 there are several competing programs that crawl automatically across the Web indexing sites on behalf of searchers.

April 1995 the US National Science Foundation, which had been running the Internet, turns it over into private hands. Advertising, which had been forbidden under NSF rules (despite Canter and Siegal's flaunting of the rule), is now officially unleashed. Privately-owned Internet Service Providers (ISPs) quickly overtake academic institutions and the US military as the primary way people can get on the Internet. Even the old gray lady of cyberspace, Compuserve, has gotten her act together and linked to the Internet. Across the planet, one online service after another links to the Internet.

1996 Aleph One takes over the Bugtraq email list and turns it into the first public "full disclosure" computer security list. Yes, for the first time in history, security flaws that can be used to break into computers are being discussed openly and the complete exploit codes are shared.

In August 1996 I start mailing out Guides to (mostly) Harmless Hacking in which I share newbie hacking instructions. A number of hackers come forward to help run what becomes the Happy Hacker Digest. Much of the information we share in that ezine ends up in this book.

1996 is also the year when documentation for routers, operating systems, TCP/IP protocols and much, much more begins to proliferate on the Web. The era of daring burglaries of technical manuals fades.

In early 1997 the readers of Bugtraq begin to discover huge numbers of flaws in the Windows NT operating system. A new mail list, NT Bugtraq, is launched just to handle the high volume of NT security problems discovered by its readers. Self-proclaimed hackers Mudge and Weld of The L0pht, in a tour de force of research, write and release a password cracker for WinNT that rocks the Internet.

Many in the computer security community have come far enough along by now to realize that Mudge and Weld are doing the owners of NT networks a great service as they provide all details, including the password cracking program, to the public.

Thanks to the willingness of hackers to share their knowledge on the Web, and mail lists such as Bugtraq, NT Bugtraq and Happy Hacker, the days of people having to beg to be inducted into hacker gangs in order to learn hacking secrets are now fading. The public reputation of hackers, which hit bottom in the massive raids and arrests of 1990, is improving as people realize most hackers would rather fix problems than cause them.

But 1997 is also the year that attacks on ISPs aimed at driving those with controversial views off the Internet become widespread. Tactics include reformatting hard disks of Internet host computers and mail bombing large numbers of customers of ISPs to extort the owners of these ISPs into refusing service to those with the "wrong" political views. Fallout from these attacks may soon turn all hackers into pariahs, the innocent and guilty alike.

Where next will the hacker world evolve? If you choose to be a hacker, you hold the answer to that in your hands.

Section 4, Chapter 2
How to Meet Other Hackers

You're on IRC and some kewl d00d who tYp3z 11K3 Th1s offers to be your mentor. To take you step by step through the mysteries of hacking. To give you programs you can run to generate valid credit card numbers so you can make international phone calls for free.

You ignore him, of course. You know he's bad news. But let's face it, it's much easier to learn about computers if you have friends to help you get over hurdles.

I hope this book has helped you get over lots of hurdles to learning. By now you probably can do as much as the average hacker (sorry, that's not saying much), and probably more. Maybe you have already pursued those Evil Genius tips and discovered exciting things way beyond what this book explains. Because you know you can hack without breaking the law, you are probably headed for a career in computers, or at least a satisfying, lifelong hobby, instead of a long visit with cell mate Spike.

But you know in your gut that friendship with fellow hackers, ones you can trust and admire, will both speed your progress and enrich your life.

So how do you meet and befriend hackers you can trust? People who won't get you into trouble? People who actually know what they are talking about?

Many newbies first search for friends on IRC channels with names such as #hack. But lo and behold, they discover these channels are sorry pits of flamers, porno traders, red boxers, credit card fraud artists—and worse. Unmoderated email chat lists are rarely any better.

As for hacker conventions, yes, they can be great meeting places. But you take the risk of accidentally angering those d00dz with twisted minds who flock to the cons.

Also, most of the people you meet at cons are newbies. Yes, these cons are mostly great swirling masses of newbies trying to worship the occasional real hacker they discover. For example, at the 1997 Def Con, Daniel Gilkerson (High School Computers technical editor of this book) conducted an informal poll. He asked attendees "what is the 'cat' command?" Less than half had even heard of it. So if you seek a mentor at a hacker con, you'll be competing with a crowd of wannabes.

 Newbie note: To learn what the cat command can do, in your Unix shell account, give the command "man cat." Next, read up on pipes. Then play with this wonderful toy.

Don't let this discourage you. Real hackers are rarely the oddly dressed, ignorant, hostile characters you see so often on IRC and at hacker cons. More often, we are quiet folks who lead ordinary lives.

Top Ten Ways to Make Hacker Friends

10) Who are your friends today? Do they want to hack, too? So what if none of you are überhackers? Start working together. You'll be surprised at how fast you will progress.

9) If you are in school, make friends with the people who work in computer lab. That consultant who chuckles as he rereads the *Bastard Operator from Hell* files (next chapter)—want to bet he's a hacker? Your teacher who likes tweaking the school computers—is he another closet hacker?

8) Be nice to tech support people at your ISP. If the only time they hear from you is when something goes wrong, you've blown it. When they announce upgrades, block spam, install ssl or APOP or anything else cool, tell them they are great. When they help you solve a problem, thank them. Offer to take them out for pizza. At least one tech support person at every ISP is almost certainly a hacker. Heck, the owners of your ISP probably used to run a hacker bulletin board back in the 80s.

7) Go to college and major in computer science or electrical engineering. Many of your classmates will be hackers.

6) Use your computer science or electrical engineering degree to get a job in computer security or systems administration. The right employer will pay you to learn from you boss and coworkers how to hack circles around everyone else.

5) Get an advanced degree in computer science and find a job with a company that produces operating systems. Ask to be assigned to the department that codes new releases of operating systems so that they fix security flaws. Again, they will pay you to learn from them how to become an überhacker. The average programmer in a company such as Sun or BSDI can walk all over any 31337 haxor you would ever meet on IRC.

4) Get an advanced degree in mathematics and go to work for the National Security Agency's cryptography research group. Your fellow workers will teach you math you didn't dream existed. For example, the NSA knew of a fast solution to Diffie-Hellman public key encryption years before an outside mathematician, Leonard M. Adleman, discovered it.

3) Or use your advanced math degree to get work at a place such as RSA, Inc. That's the company Adleman, along with fellow mathematicians Ronald L. Rivest and Adi Shamir, founded to commercialize their RSA

(Rivest/Shamir/Adleman) public key encryption, one of the strongest known today.

2) Get a Ph.D. in physics or electrical engineering and go to work for the National Security Agency on Tempest technology. You will discover how impossible it is for computer criminals to get away with anything if the harm they cause is enough to justify the time and cost of using that cool equipment you'll get to play with.

And, my favorite, easiest way to make friends with hackers . . .

1) Make friends with any people you may meet who reveal that extra something—a hunger for adventure and love of technology. That's how I've found hacker mentors such as Terry McIntyre, who befriended me on a Christian libertarian email list. Thank you, thank you, Terry, for suggesting that I telnet to port 25 and give the "help" command!

Section 4, Chapter 3
Hacker Humor

Folks, this is it. Time to find out whether you have learned enough to be a real hacker. Here's the test: laugh, and you are one of us!

Unix Wars

A long time ago, at an installation far, far away . . .

It is a time of intra-system war, as forces of the User Alliance struggle to break the iron grip of the evil Admin Empire. Now, striking from a hidden directory, they win their first victory.

During the battle, User spies manage to snarf source of the Empire's ultimate weapon, the dreaded 'rm-star', a privileged root program with the power to destroy an entire file system at a keystroke.

Now, hotly pursued by the Empire's sinister audit trail, Princess LA36 races aboard her shellscript—custodian of the stolen listings that can save her people and restore freedom and games to the network . . .

==

As we enter the scene, an Admin multiplexer is trying to kill a User ship. Many of their signals have gotten through, and RS232 knows that a core dump is imminent. They have scant microseconds to fork off a new process and put megabytes of virtual space between themselves and their implacable foes. His companion, 3CPU, follows him only because he seems to know where he's going . . .

"Oh, I just *know* I'm going to regret this!" cried 3CPU as he followed RS232 through the access pipe. Quickly RS232 closed the read end and execl'd, and their new craft detached itself from the burning shell of the ship.

The Admin commander was feeling quite pleased with the progress of the attack when his XO called out.

"Another process just forked, sir. Instructions?"

"Hold your fire—that last power failure must have caused a trap through zero. It's not using any cpu time, so don't waste a signal on it."

A short while later the infamous Lord Vadic himself strode through the still-smoldering wreckage of the User ship, followed closely by a nervous commander.

"We can't seem to find that data file anywhere, Lord Vadic. Perhaps it was deallocated when . . ."

"What about that forked process?" Vadic growled. "It could have been pausing, holding a channel open. If any links are left I want them removed or made inaccessible. Search the entire system at nice -20 until it is found!"

Meanwhile, the two droids' tiny process dove headlong towards the only nearby disk.

"Are you *sure* you can ptrace this thing without aborting it?" queried 3CPU. "Its relocation bits were almost all stripped during the attack, and I never was any good at patching binaries . . ."

As RS232 was about to reply their process reached its endpoint and terminated abruptly, dumping them in the midst of a large unallocated region on the unknown volume.

Many random seeks later they trudged up to the looming wreckage of a deallocated i-node.

"Shelter!" croaked 3CPU, but RS232 had barely begun to emit a NACK when a horde of dwarfish code fragments warmed out of it to overwhelm them. They had been captured by Glitchas.

Enter Luke Vaxhacker, bartering with the Glitchas for replacement parts for his uncle. They tried to sell him 3CPU, but the 'droid didn't know protocol for an 11/40 under RSTS, so Luke would need some kind of conversion hardware.

"How about this little RS232 unit?" said 3CPU "I've interfaced with him many times before and he's excellent at keeping his bits straight."

Luke was pressed for time, so he took 3CPU's advice. The Glitchas wanted to barter some more, but the three left before getting swapped out.

RS232, however, wasn't the type to stay put without retaining screws. He promptly scurried off into the empty disk space.

"Oh, great!" said Luke "He'll probably map himself into a bad block somewhere. I guess we'd better go after him."

Hours later the two traced him to the home of old PDP-1 Kenobi, who was busily running a diagnostic on the little RS unit.

"Is this droid yours? His status registers are stuttering and someone's done some odd things to his interrupt lines. Leaving something like this on-line is just asking for downtime—but I think I may have him fixed for now."

Later that evening, during a futile attempt to interface RS232 to Kenobi's Asteroids cartridge, Luke accidentally crossed the small droid's CXR lead with his Initiate Remote Test. A projector crackled to life, casting a hologram of a young lady with her hair done up like twin Danish pastries imploring help from some General OS/1 Kenobi.

"Darn," mumbled Luke "I'll never get this Asteroids game worked out."

"Why, that's the Princess!" 3CPU said.

Luke peered at the image critically. "No, that's a modified Steinburg dither with anti-aliasing. Nice sculpted surfaces . . ."

Kenobi interrupted Luke with a frown. "Luke, this message changes things. Listen . . ."

Kenobi seemed to think there was a possible threat to Luke's $HOME. If the Admin troops were indeed tracing this 'droid, it was likely they would more than just charge for cpu time.

They sped off to warn Luke's kin (taking a relative path) only to find a vacant directory.

"Take your father's bytesaber, Luke." Kenobi said. "You will need to learn the ways of the Source now."

"The . . .Source?" Luke queried, wide-eyed.

"The Source—the cosmic template of the System, within which all knowledge and power can be had. But you must always beware of the Dark Side . . ."

Later, after a short skim across the surface in Luke's flying read-write head, PDP-1 had them stop at the edge of the cylinder containing /usr/spool/uucp.

"Unix-to-Unix Copy Program" said PDP-1. "You may never see a more wretched hive of bugs and flamers. We must be cautious."

As our heroes' process entered /usr/spool/news it was met by a newsgroup of Admin protection bits.

"State your UID!" commanded a burly syscall.

"We're running under /usr/guest" said Luke. "This is our first time on the system."

"Let's see some temporary privilege bits, please."

"Uh . . ."

"This isn't the process you are looking for," Kenobi said softly. "We can go about our business." Several bits momentarily pulled low.

"You're free to go about your business. MOV along now!"

PDP-1, Luke and the droids made their way through a long and tortuous nodelist (cwruecmp!decvax!ucbvax!harpo!ihnss!ihnsc!ihnsc!ihps3!stolaf) to a dangerous netnode frequented by hackers and only seldom polled by the minions of Admin. As Luke stepped up to the crossbar, PDP-1 went in search of a suitable server.

Luke had never seen such a collection of device drivers. Long ones, short ones, ones with stacks; EBCDIC converters, local-net handlers, CRT drivers, routines for archaic printers. A CAT interface twitched pointed ears at him.

"#@{&*^%^$$#@ ":?," transmitted a particularly unstructured piece of code.

"He doesn't like you," decoded his coroutine.

"Er . . . sorry . . ." replied Luke, beginning to backup his partitions.

"I don't like you either. I am queued for deletion on 12 systems."

"I'll be careful," Luke said nervously.

"You'll be deallocated!" snarled the coroutine.

"This little routine isn't worth the overhead . . ." murmured PDP-1 Kenobi, overlaying into Luke's address space.

"This little routine isn't worth the overhead," repeated the coroutine dazedly.

"^%#%#@$&^%&*&*&^%^#$$%%^^&%^#@#@$%^(*&^^###%^^!!!" encoded his companion as it attempted to overload Kenobi's segment protection. With a stroke of his bytesaber Kenobi dyked out the offending code. The coroutine retreated hurriedly. Kenobi turned to Luke.

"I think I've found an I/O handler that might suit us."

"The name's Con Sole0" said the routine next to PDP-1. "I hear you're looking for some relocation."

"Yes indeed." said PDP-1 "if you've got fast enough hardware. We must get off this device."

"Fast hardware? The Milliamp Falcon has made the ARPAgate run in less than twelve netnodes! Why, I've even outrun canceled messages. It's fast enough for you, old version."

"Fast hardware?" said Luke unbelievingly. "That thing is a paper-tape reader!!" He might have grown up in an out-of-the-way terminal cluster where the natives only spoke BASIC, but he knew an ASR-33 when he saw one.

"It needs an FIA conversion at least," sniffed 3CPU, who (as usual) was trying to do several things at once. Lights flashed in Con Sole0's eyes as he whirled to face the parallel processor.

"I've switched a few jumpers. The Milliamp Falcon can run current loops around any of Admin's TTY fighters. She's fast enough."

"Who's your copilot?" inquired Luke, eyeing the hairy hulk that had just shambled out of the Falcon to join the group.

"Oh. Meet Sixpacca, my Bookie."

The creature emitted an enormous belch and gesticulated wildly with a wad of tip sheets clenched in one fist. Luke eyed the beercan in the other dubiously.

"Er, isn't he dr-" Suddenly RS232 emitted an ear-splitting beep and began to chitter wildly. They turned to see an Admin command group riding the local bus directly at them.

"That's a shutdown sequence if I ever saw one!" shouted Con, sprinting into the ship with the others close behind. "Crank up the sysclock, Brewie!"

"Okay, Con," Luke said grimly. "You said this crate was fast enough. Get us out of here."

"Shut up, kid, you bother me. Initialize this heap, Brewie—I'll try to keep their buffers full."

As his Bookie computed the vectors into low core, spurious characters flashed around the Milliamp Falcon.

"They're firing at us!" shouted Luke. "Can't you do anything?"

"Making the jump to system space takes time, kid," Con growled. "One missed cycle and you could come down right in the middle of a pack of stack frames!"

Bright chunks of position-independent code flashed by as the ship jumped through the kernel page tables. The group emitted a sigh of relief as they indirected into free space.

===

Meanwhile, on a distant page in user space . . .

Two Admin troopers ushered Princess LA36 into a conference room behind Lord Vadic.

"Moff Tarchive" she spat. "I should have expected to find you hanging on Vadic's aux cable. I recognized your unique pattern when I was first brought aboard." She eyed the 0177545 tattoed on his header coldly.

"Charming to the last." Tarchive observed smoothly. "Vadic, have you retrieved any information?"

"Her resistance to the logic probe is considerable," Vadic rasped. "Perhaps if we boosted the supply voltage . . ."

"You've had your chance. Now I would like the Princess to witness the test that will certify this module fully operational. Today we enable the -r beam option, and we've chosen the Princess's $HOME of /usr/alderaan as the primary target.

"No! You can't! /usr/alderaan is an unprotected public directory. We have no backup tapes! You can't . . ."

"Then name the rebel i-node!" Tarchive snapped. A voice announced from a hidden speaker that they'd arrived in /usr.

"2317" she whispered. "They're on /dev/rm5, i-node 2317. /mnt/dantooine." She turned away.

Tarchive sighed with satisfaction. "There, you see, Lord Vadic? She can be reasonable. Proceed with the operation."

It took several clock ticks for the words to penetrate. "What?" the Princess gasped.

"/dev/rm5 is not a currently mounted file system." explained Tarchive "We require a more visible target to demonstrate the power of the rm-star. We will, of course, mount an attack on /mnt/dantooine as soon as possible.

As she watched in horror Tarchive typed 'ls -la' on a nearby terminal. The screen showed: no such directory.

Abruptly the Princess double-spaced and went offline.

===

Meanwhile, the Milliamp Falcon hurtled through free space . . .

Con Sole0 finished checking the control and status registers, finally satisfying himself that they'd lost the Admin bus signals as they'd passed the terminator. An irritable belch from Sixpacca disturbed him not at all; he knew the Bookie got grouchy when losing at chess, and RS232 had just caught him in the Fischer set with a seven-ply search.

Across the room Luke was too busy practicing bit-slice technique to notice the commotion.

"On a word boundary, Luke," said PDP-1 "Don't just hack at it. Remember, the bytesaber is the ceremonial weapon of the Red-Eye Knight. It is used to trim offensive lines of code. Handwaving won't get you anywhere. Attune yourself with the Source."

Luke turned back towards the drone humming in the air beside him. This time his attack complemented its actions perfectly.

Con Sole0 was not impressed. "Forget this bit-slicing stuff. Give me a good old PROM blaster any day!"

"Glork!" said PDP-1 indistinctly. He looked momentarily vacant.

"What's wrong?" asked Luke.

"Strange. I thought I felt a disturbance in the /src. It's gone now."

"We're coming up on user space!" called Sole0 from the CSR. They slipped safely through stack frames and emerged in the new context, only to find themselves bombarded by floating freeblocks.

"What the . . ." gasped Sole0. The Bookie belched unhappily. The screen showed /usr/alderaan: not found.

"This is the right i-node, but it's been cleared! Brewie, where's the nearest file?"

The Bookie was beginning to belch a reply when he was interrupted by a bright flash off to the left.

"Admin TTY fighters!" Con shouted "A whole DZ of them. Where are they coming from?"

"The host system can't be far," said PDP-1 "They've all got direct EIA connections."

As Sole0 began evasive action the ship lurched suddenly. Luke noticed that the link count was 3 and climbing rapidly.

"This is no ordinary file . . ." murmured Kenobi "Look at that ODS directory structure ahead! They seem to have us in a tractor feed."

"There's no way we can unlink in time," said Sole0 "We're going in."

The Milliamp Falcon was swiftly pulled down to the open collector of the Admin module. Lord Vadic surveyed the battered ship as Admin Storm-Flunkies searched for passengers.

"The ls scan shows no one on board, sir" was the report. Vadic was unconvinced.

"Send a fully equipped ncheck squad aboard. I want every location in that thing searched." He stalked away.

Aboard the Falcon .Luke was puzzled. "They just walked in, looked around, and walked out . . .why didn't they see us?"

.Con smiled. "Old munchkin trick. See that period in front of your name?"

.Luke spun around in time to glimpse the decimal point. "Huh? Where'd that come from?"

"Spare part from the last time I tinkered with the floating-point accelerator" said .Con. "Handy for smuggling blocks across file system boundaries, but I never thought I'd have to use them on myself. They aren't going to stay fooled for long, though. We'd better figure a way out of here."

"I can sneak us into their private space during the next maintenance period" said PDP-1 "We'll have to find out how to unlink the Falcon before we can escape."

Some time later our heroes catfooted their way through an empty section of the structure.

"Find us a terminal," whispered PDP-1. Con nodded and poked his PROM-blaster around a corner.

You are in the Hall of the Mountain King, with passages off in all directions. A large green fierce snake bars the way!

"Oops! Wrong turn." Con muttered. They took the opposite direction. Suddenly marching feet sounded at the other end of the corridor. They ducked through the nearest door.

The lone StormFlunky in the room barely had time to register surprise before Con's blaster de-rezzed him.

"That's funny . . ." Luke said "I wonder why he was carrying an axe? . . ."

"Look! We're in luck!" said 3CPU. "He was logged in!."

"Don't just stand there, Kenobi, su it! said Con eagerly. The old Red-Eye stepped up to the keyboard. They watched as he began to infiltrate the Admin software. Some minutes later . . .

You have new mail

"Is that an error?" Con said.

"%SYS-W-NORMAL . . .I don't think so. Someone here must know me—but I can't stop to investigate that now. I've found the i-node they've tied the Milliamp

Falcon to. I'll have to slip in and patch the reference count, alone." He disappeared through a nearby exit().

Meanwhile, RS232 had found a serial port and gone on-line. He began to chitter furiously.

"He keeps saying 'She's here, she's here!'" explained 3CPU "I do believe he means Princess LA36. She's being held on one of the privileged levels."

Luke remembered sculpted curves. "We've got to rescue her!"

RS232 flashed a complete structure chart of the Admin module on the terminal screen. Four heads bent intently over the diagram.

"I think I see a promising access method" said Luke " . . . through here. Con, you and I and Sixpacca will knock out a couple of Admin Storm-Flunkies and use their uniforms. We'll keep a channel open to these 'droids . . ."

" . . . and get terminated as soon as their security catches wise," broke in Sole0. "Oh well—I guess I don't have much of a choice."

RS232 twittered reproachfully at him. A planning phase or two later they slipped into the corridor again, with Luke clad in the ex-StormFlunky's uniform.

"So far, so good . . ." whispered Luke as the party came up on the last turn in their route, " . . .but 3CPU told us there'd be two guards posted around this corner."

"Sixpacca still doesn't have a uniform!" Con hissed.

"That's O.K—I've got an idea. Listen . . .'"

A minute later the two walked boldly around the corner towards the two guards, Sixpacca held between them and rumbling plaintively.

"Good day, eh?" said the first guard.

"How's it goin', eh?" said the second. "Like, what's that, eh?"

"Control transfer from block 1138, dev 10/9, one for the brig." said Con, voice muffled by the StormFlunky mask. "Caught him drunk and disorderly—commander said to bring him down here to cool off."

"Take off, it is not!" said the first guard. "Nobody told *us* about it, and we're not morons, eh?"

The Bookie suddenly emitted a gargantuan belch, surged out of the grip of his quondam captors and began hurling beercans in all directions.

"Look out, he's *loose*!" yelled Con. He and Luke started blasting ROMS left and right. The guards had no time to catch on before the beams hit them.

"Quickly, now," said Con "which buffer is she in? It won't take long for the Admins . . ." The intercom interrupted him, so he took out its firmware with a short blast " . . . to zero in on that commotion."

Minutes later Luke found the interface card he'd been looking for. The three followed the cables to a soundproof enclosure. He lifted the lid to peer inside.

"Aren't you a little slow for FCL?" printed Princess LA36.

"Wha? Oh, the Docksiders." He took off his shoes (for industry) and explained "I've come to relocate you. I'm Luke Vaxhacker."

Suddenly, forms began to burst all around them. "They've blocked the queue!" shouted Sole0. "There's only one way out of this stack!"

"OVER HERE!" said LA36, printing with overstrikes. "THROUGH THIS LOOPHOLE!" Luke and the Princess disappeared into a nearby feature.

"Belch!" said Sixpacca dubiously, obviously reluctant to trust an Admin over-sight.

"I don't care how crufty it is!" shouted Con pushing the Bookie toward the crock. "BLT yourself in there pronto!"

With a last blast that de-rezzed two StormFlunkies, Con joined them, only to wince in dismay. The "feature" had landed them in the middle of a garbage-collection area. Data chunks that hadn't been accessed in weeks floated in pools of decaying bits.

"Bletch!" was Con's first comment. "And foo and barf!" was his second. The Bookie looked as though he'd just paid off a 555-to-1 long shot. Luke was polling the garbage for useful items.

"What's this?" He dusted off a flat black box with a panel display on one side and "Don't Panic" in large friendly letters on the others.

"This can't possibly help us now," he said, and tossed it aside. The Bookie was about to lay odds on it when he disappeared.

He popped up across the pool, shouting "This is no feature, it's a bug!" and promptly vanished again.

Con and the Princess were close to panic when Luke reappeared. "What happened?" they queried concurrently.

"I don't know!" Luke gasped. "The bug just automagically dissolved, as far as I could tell. Maybe it hit a breakpoint."

"I don't think so," Con said. "Look how the pool is shrinking. I've got a bad feeling about this . . ."

The princess was the first to catch on. "They've implemented a new compaction algorithm!" she exclaimed.

Luke remembered their channel to the 'droids. "RS232—shut down that recursion, quick!"

Back in the control room RS232 searched the process table for a LISP interpreter. "Hurry!" said 3CPU. "Hurry, hurry!" added his other two processors. RS232 found the LISP, interrupted it, and altered the stack frame to allow a normal return.

"Scramble as many local control paths as you can from there and head back to the ship." Luke ordered. "We've got the Princess!"

===

Meanwhile, PDP-1 made his way deep into the core of the rm-star, using his ability to manipulate label_t to slip from context to context undetected. Finally he caused a random trap and (through no fault of his own) arrived at the central i-node table.

Activity there was always high, but the Spl6 sentries were too secure in their belief that no mere user could interrupt them to notice the bug that PDP-1 introduced. He twiddled the i-node and device numbers on a passing input, carefully maintaining parity, to free the Milliamp Falcon. They would be long gone before the corrupted i-node was diagnosed . . .

He began traversing module structures towards the subprocess where the Falcon had been grounded. During the context switch he felt his priority drop. "That's not nice!" he muttered, then recognized the dark shape before him.

"I have waited a long time for this event, PDP-1 Kenobi!" rasped Dec Vadic. "We meet again at last; the circuit is closed."

They looped several times, locking bytesabers. Mesmerized by the sight, the few StormFlunkies nearby failed to notice Luke, Con, Sixpacca, the Princess and the droids until they'd nearly gained the Falcon's input port. A brief firefight blazed as the six hurled themselves into the ship, but PDP-1 and Lord Vadic seemed too absorbed in their duel to notice. Luke paused at the port, his gaze riveted on the pair. He gasped; was that phase jitter he saw around the old version?

"If my blade finds its mark" Kenobi warned "you will be resolved to your component bits—but if you slice me down I will only gain computing power."

"Your documentation no longer confuses me, old version!" Vadic rasped. "My status is bus-master now!" With a sweeping stroke, his bytesaber sliced through Kenobi's declaration list. As PDP-1's main body shimmered away Vadic noticed his UID go negative. Odd, he thought, since UID's are unsigned . . .

Vadic whirled to face the Falcon just as the others dragged a protesting Luke into the ship.

"We will meet again . . . Luke!" he rasped softly to himself, as the ship blasted free.

As the Milliamp Falcon hurtled away from the rm-star, the droids were uncharacteristically silent, and Princess LA36 printed comforting messages for Luke. He was unconsolable, hung from the loss of his friend. But strangely, it seemed as though he heard PDP-1's voice in the distance, saying

May the Source be with you!

==

Unix Wars was written by Eric S. Raymond and posted widely on Usenet and the Web. It is now published here, with his permission for the first time in, yes, the world of Gutenberg. Raymond tells us it is "greatly expanded from the DEC Wars spoof by Alan Hastings, Steve Tarr, Dave Borman, and a few hangers on, first posted to Usenet in 1983."

Raymond also is the author of *The New Hackers Dictionary*, now in its 3rd edition, (MIT Press 1996, ISBN 0- 262-68092-0). You can view it online at *http://www.ccil.org/jargon*.

Bastard Operator from Hell #9

I'm driving to work and I'm stuck behind this old guy, the classic slow driver from hell, whose car red-lines at 20 mph and can't take corners at more than 5. I honk my horn but his hearing aid's probably turned way down to "whisper", so I'm stuck.

I make a mental note of his license plate. In fact, I did that 60 times a minute for 15 and a half minutes. Oh dear . . . oh dear . . . Looks like another call to the DMV Database to register a vehicle as stolen by out of town arms dealers . . .

I get to work, flick the excuse page over. "ELECTROMAGNETIC RADIATION FROM SATELLITE DEBRIS". Fair enough, it looks like it's going to be a good day.

I log into "F***YOU", (the help-desk inquiries username) and go into mail. There's 3 new messages, the first of which is 117 lines long, so it's obviously a storyteller. I hate that. Instead of saying "My account needs more disk space" they tell you about how they're doing this bit of research for a lecturer and how it's got to be in yesterday, and they almost had it but their second cousin twice removed had a perforated herpes scab and lost a lot of blood and had to be rushed into hospital . . . etc etc. I delete the message.

Second message I read, but it's one of those people who can't handle the mail interface and send a null message, so all you get is headers. I reply to the message saying "No worries, we can do that by next Tuesday". Hope it was important.

The last message I leave for tomorrow, because Saturday would be a dull day if I ever had to work then.

The phone rings. I thought I'd fixed that!

I put it on hands free so I can slop some pizza into the microwave.

"Yes" I call

"Something's wrong with my Boot disk, I can't login to the server"

"Have you got your disk with you?"

"Sure!"

I go get the disk and put it and the pizza in for 5 minutes on "ULTRA-NUKE". Six minutes later, he rings back.

"It still doesn't work, and now my disk makes a funny noise and smells."

"OH S***! It's that electromagnetic radiation from satellite debris again!"

"Really? I think I heard about that!" (What a tool!)

"Yep, I'm sorry, you'll have to buy another disk"

"Oh, that's okay, I don't mind, the old one was getting worn. Thanks"

"Sure, no worries. And be sure to run it through our virus checker FDISK when you get a lot of important data on it . . ."

"I will! Thanks!"

"That's okay—it's my job!"

Xcbzone is running really slow so I kill off a whole lot of database backends that seem to be hogging all the cpu and get back into my game. Much better.

(It isn't easy on the front-line, work work work . . .)

I go to the cafeteria for a quick 2 hour snack—they're so nice to me there. They always have been, ever since that computer glitch that registered their kitchen as an organ recipient—very messy. I grab a couple of cans of coke and some cheese things and cruise on back to the office via the first year computer fundamentals lab. I look in the window on the scene that unfolds itself to me—a lab full of first years with no demonstrator.

WELL, I'LL JUST HAVE TO HELP!

I walk on in.

"Right, I'm your temporary replacement demonstrator and today we're going to put our assignments aside for half an hour to learn about the REMARK function, or, as it's known to the computer literate world, rm . . ."

I should've been a teacher, you know—I've got this way with people . . .

===

The *Bastard Operator from Hell* series was written by Simon Travaglia, an analyst programmer, at the University of Waikato in New Zealand. This is the first time in print for this priceless hacker humor. You can read more from Travaglia at *http://mrjolly.cc.waikato.ac.nz/*.

The Green Computer

If I had a Green Computer
I'd go find my old companion
at his Unix box on Sprintnet.
Ha! Ha! Ha! Ha! Ha!
I'd run Probe at his manly ports,
inside, his Web server and three other services
sprawl naked
on the Unix box floor.

He'd come running out
to my box full of heroic haxor 'sploits
and jump screaming at the console
for he is the greatest hacker.

We'd pilgrimage to the highest firewall
of our earlier .mil domain visions
laughing in each other's arms,
delight surpassing the highest port numbers,

and after old agony, drunk with new years,
bounding toward the comsat links
blasting .mil ports with original 'sploits
hot rod in the .mil domain

we'd batter up the obscurest port numbers
where angels of anxiety
careen through the Internet
and scream from computers.

We'd burn all night on the jackpine peak
seen from traceroute in the electron dark,
forestlike unnatural radiance
illuminating the Internet:

childhood youth time age & eternity
would open like directories
on the disk of a hacked box
and dumbfound us with files,

for we can see together
the beauty of stolen files
hidden like diamonds
in the clock of the world,

like Chinese magicians can
confound the mortals
with our 31337ness
hidden in the packets,

from the Green Computer
which I have invented
imagined and envisioned
on the roads of the world

more real than the engine
on a track in the desert
purer than Greyhound and
swifter than physical jetplane.

Iway! Iway! we'll return
roaring across the City & County Building website
which catches the pure emerald flame
streaming in the wake of our 'puter.

This time we'll hack the entire city!
I cash a great check in my skull bank
to found a miraculous college of the Net
up on the console keyboard.

But first we'll hack the boxes of downtown,
sendmail netstat finger POP
webserver down ftp
to the darkest daemons of WinNT

paying respects to Internet's father
lost on WWMCCS
stupor of ARPAnet and UUCP
hallowing the slum of his decades,

salute him and his saintly suitcase
of outdated RFCs, telnet
and smash the sweet protocols
on PDPs in allegiance.

Then we go scanning drunk on routers
where DNS queries march and still parade
staggering under the invisible
banner of Internic—

hurtling through the fiber
in the 'puter of our fate
we share an archangelic Jolt
and tell each other's fortunes:

fames of supernatural illumination,
bleak lagged gaps of time,
great art learned of desolation
and we beat apart after cracking six boxes . . . .

and on a fiber crossroad,
deal with each other in princely
IRC once more, recalling
famous dead talks of other servers.

So this Green Computer:
I give you in flight
a present, a present
from my imagination.

We will go hacking
over the Iway,
we'll go on hacking
all night long until dawn,

Then back to your Web design business,
your Web server and three other services
and broken leg destiny
you'll write html

in the morning: and back
to my visions, my office
and writing a book about Real Hackers
I'll return to Cedar Crest.

> *Carolyn Meinel*
> *Cedar Crest, September 1997*
> *— This poem is a takeoff on Allen Ginzburg's "The Green Automobile."*

Happy Hacking! Should we meet, let's share an archangelic Jolt, and may The Source Code be with you always.

INDEX